Home Affairs

Rethinking Lesbian, Gay, Bisexual and Transgender Families in Contemporary South Africa

Edited by Carien Lubbe-De Beer & John Marnell

Published by Fanele (an imprint of Jacana Media) in association with Gay and Lesbian Memory in Action (GALA)

Published by Fanele, an imprint of Jacana Media (Pty) Ltd, in association with Gay and Lesbian Memory in Action (GALA) in 2013

10 Orange Street
Sunnyside
Auckland Park 2092
South Africa
+2711 628 3200
www.jacana.co.za

© Individual contributors, 2013

All rights reserved.

ISBN 978-1-920196-33-2
This publication was made possible through the generous financial support of the Open Society Foundation for South Africa.

The contents of this book were subjected to a stringent blind peer-review process, pre-print.

Cover design by publicide
Set in Ehrhardt 11.5/16 pt
Printed and bound by Ultra Litho (Pty) Ltd, Johannesburg
Job no. 001981

See a complete list of Jacana titles at www.jacana.co.za

Contents

Editors' Note
Carien Lubbe-De Beer & John Marnell ix

Acknowledgements xi

SECTION 1
SITUATING FAMILIES: DISCOURSES, DEBATES AND CONTEXTS

Outsider Discourse Surrounding Children's Experiences of Familial Identity in Same-Sex-Parented Families
Diana Breshears & Aliza le Roux. 1

Familiar Claims: Representations of Same-Gendered Families in South African Mainstream News Media
Tracy Morison & Vasu Reddy 21

'The Best Interests of the Child': Reflecting on the Family
and the Law as Sites of Oppressive Hetero-Socialisation
Nadia Sanger & Cherith Sanger 50

Erased, Elided and Made Invisible? A Critical Analysis of
Research on Bisexual Parenthood and Families
Ingrid Lynch 68

SECTION 2
PORTRAITS AND VOICES: REPRESENTING DIVERSITY

Home Affairs: A Photographic Essay Celebrating Family
Diversity
John Marnell 89

Home Affairs Interview Extracts 93

M/Other Families: Some Introductory Comments to the
Project
Natasha Distiller & Jean Brundrit 116

M/Other Families Interview Extracts 126

SECTION 3
NEGOTIATING PARENTHOOD: EXPECTATIONS, PROCESSES AND EXPERIENCES

'Two Women Can't Make a Baby': South African Lesbians'
Negotiation with Heteronormativity around Issues of
Reproduction
Natalie Donaldson & Lindy Wilbraham 135

Planned Lesbian Parenting in South Africa: Reflections on
the Process of Clinically Assisted Donor Insemination
Carien Lubbe-De Beer 159

Resistance and Re(Production): Becoming Lesbian Parents through Assisted Reproductive Technologies
Karl Swain & Kerry Frizelle 185

Am I That Name? Middle-Class Lesbian Motherhood in Post-Apartheid South Africa
Natasha Distiller 208

SECTION 4
RELATIONSHIPS UP CLOSE: REAL LIVES, REAL ISSUES

Breaking the Silence: A Discussion on Intimate Partner Violence in Gay-Male Relationships
Gabriel Khan & Yolan Moodley 237

Coming Out to Families: Adolescent Disclosure Practices in the Western Cape
Veronica Robertson & Charmaine Louw 259

List of Contributors 287

Notes 294

Editors' Note

The idea for a book on same-sex families in South Africa started a few years ago. It was inspired, in part, by the growing body of local scholarship in this field, but also by the ongoing silencing of lesbian, gay, bisexual and transgender (LGBT) experiences in this country. This publication seeks to be an antidote of sorts to the one-dimensional image of same-sex families and relationships that is so often portrayed in mainstream media and, by extension, ingrained in the popular imagination.

In many ways, the inclusion of 'rethinking' in the title encapsulates our motivation in putting together this publication while also providing an insight into how we, as editors, approached the selection process. Indeed, this book doesn't claim to capture what a 'same-sex family' *is* nor does it purport to show what a same-sex family *should be* – rather, it seeks to highlight the wide range of experiences and practices that exist in contemporary South Africa and to celebrate the richness that comes from diversity. But more than anything, we hope that *Home Affairs* inspires future research, lively discussions and dynamic new ways of approaching advocacy campaigns.

It was with this purpose in mind that we decided not only to collate recent research and new knowledge, but to also feature portraits and first-person accounts from two significant art-based projects: 'Home Affairs: Love, Families and Relationships' and 'M/Other Families'. We believe strongly that these personal testimonies complement and enhance the academic research included in this collection. Moreover, we as editors feel that it is vital that any publication of this kind provides accurate and affirming representations of LGBT people and their own families.

As you will see, this book approaches the concepts of family and relationships from multiple perspectives. Although a large number of the chapters focus on starting new families and/or the parenting process, many also look at family formations and related issues from surprising theoretical angles. The decision to broaden out what is understood by families and relationships was deliberate, and we hope that some of the more radical interpretations of the central theme will lead to vigorous debates about how all of us – as researchers, activists, community members and individuals – should approach and talk about love, relationships, family, marriage and many related issues.

We hope you enjoy the collection.

Prof. Carien Lubbe-De Beer (University of Pretoria) & John Marnell (GALA)

Acknowledgements

THIS PUBLICATION WOULD NOT HAVE BEEN possible without the gracious funding of the Open Society Foundation for South Africa – it was, in fact, only thorough the support and encouragement of OSF-SA that this book was able to become a reality. As editors, we would like to express our gratitude to OSF-SA and GALA for their unwavering commitment during the development of the publication. We are especially grateful for the exceptional patience shown by Kira-Leigh Kuhnert, Senior Project Officer at OSF-SA.

We would also like to thank each author for their willingness to contribute to this volume, for each one's enthusiasm and passion, and for the patience and understanding shown during the editing and peer-review process. No less importantly, we would like to acknowledge the referees who conducted blind reviews of the individual chapters: Katherine Allen (Virginia Tech, USA), Johan Beckmann (UP), Karien Botha (UP), Diana Breshears (UP), Allister Butler (Anglia Ruskin University, UK), Ashley Currier (University of Cincinnati,

USA), Catherine Donovan (University of Sunderland, UK), Alfred du Plessis (UP), Helen Dunbar-Krige (UJ), Aliza le Roux (UFS), Ruth Mampane (UP), Kesh Mohangi (UP), Venitha Pillay (UP), Jennifer Power (LaTrobe University, Australia), Margaret Robinson, (University of Toronto, Canada), Susanna D Walters (Northeastern University, USA). All of the authors expressed their sincerest gratitude for the invaluable comments and feedback provided during the review process. We are, as editors, indebted to the reviewers' selfless dedication to enhancing the quality of this book.

Finally, we would like to express our gratitude to the many people who have – over the years – shared their expertise and knowledge. Without the feedback and guidance of the following people, this book would never have been possible: Karen Martin and Anthony Manion, both of whom played a significant role in conceptualising this publication; and Russell Clarke, Barbara Klugman and Steve Letsiki, whose early input and suggestions were invaluable.

SECTION 1

Situating Families: Discourses, Debates and Contexts

Outsider Discourse Surrounding Children's Experiences of Familial Identity in Same-Sex-Parented Families

Diana Breshears and Aliza le Roux

THE ADOPTION OF SOUTH AFRICA's post-apartheid Constitution in 1996, along with the more recent legislative changes relating to same-sex marriage, gave rise to an increase in public recognition and acceptance of queer individuals and same-sex-parented families (Louw, 2005; Reid & Dirsuweit, 2002). Despite the growing visibility of this type of family and the rights and protections guaranteed under the Constitution, conservative cultural attitudes toward same-sex relationships, and same-sex-parented families in particular, persist across many sections of South African society (Knoesen, 2004; Singh, 1995). As in many other countries, stigma around homosexuality and same-sex families remains deeply rooted within many South African communities (Lubbe, 2007a; Stacey, 2011). Globally, heteronormative discourses continue to position identifiable blood ties as the only acceptable or 'real' definition of a family (Floyd, Mikkelson & Judd, 2006), thus leading to the social invisibility and exclusion of any family formations that fall outside of this 'biologically determined paradigm' (Gabb, 1999:12).

The purpose of this chapter is to examine discourses relating to family identity that have been encountered by children of same-sex parents outside of their immediate family environment. We use the term 'outsider discourse' to refer to dominant understandings, values or positionings that originate beyond the nuclear family unit. International (Breshears, 2010, 2011b; Clay, 1990; West & Turner, 1995) and South African (Distiller, 2011) research has indicated that lesbian/gay parents are acutely aware of the complex implications their 'different' family identity may have on their children. These parents also believe that the negative discourses with which their children struggle most often come from outside the family unit and that these can impact upon the development and maintenance of a healthy familial identity (Breshears, 2010). Despite this, there have been very few studies examining the experiences of children within same-sex-parented families. Indeed, there is, in general, still a dearth of information on same-sex families in South Africa (Goldberg, 2010; Lubbe, 2007a).

Most extant research on same-sex families originates from the United States (for instance, Stacey, 2011). As South African social and political views on family structures are quite different from those in the US, it is likely that experiences, including exposures to dominant discourses and understandings, will differ substantially for individuals within these different contexts. Indeed, South Africans may, for a number of reasons, experience unique discourses relating to their same-sex family structure. In this chapter, we focus specifically on discourses that emerge within the contexts of society, school, peers and the extended family, and examine how such discourses can impact on children's understandings and self-identification. Given that most research in this field originates outside of Africa, we highlight congruence between international and local studies throughout our analysis, while emphasising the need for research and policy specific to the South African context.

FORMATIVE ROLE OF COMMUNICATION ON FAMILIAL IDENTITY

Like all relationships, the family relationship exists between people and relies on the interaction/discourse of family members to come into being (Galvin, 2006). Similarly, individual identities must be considered socially constructed through discursive and interactive life (Carbaugh, 1996). As Baxter (2004:3) explains, 'Persons and relationships are not analytically separable from communication; instead, communication constitutes these phenomena'.

Galvin (2006:3) claims that non-traditional families may be even more reliant on communication/discourse than traditional families in terms of constructing, negotiating and preserving their identity: 'Though all families engage in discourse-driven identity building, less traditionally formed families are more discourse dependent, engaging in discursive processes to manage and maintain identity'. When families are formed through differences, they are challenged because there are no prescribed roles, nor expectations of inclusion and support, as there are in more traditional family forms. Further, less traditionally formed families face unique concerns because they do not fit the societal norms and definitions of what constitutes a family. As Galvin (2006:4) notes, 'These definitional concerns surface as members face outsiders' challenges regarding the veracity of their claims of relatedness or as members experience a need to revisit their familial identity at different times'. Children regularly experience these challenging outsider discourses both within wider society and closer circles of family or friends.

DISCOURSES SURROUNDING CHILDREN'S EXPERIENCES OF FAMILIAL IDENTITY
Social Discourses

Although their familial rights are legally protected in South Africa, children in same-sex families are still subject to culturally ingrained stigmatisation relating to their family (and personal) identities. In contrast to developed countries, where homosexuality is viewed less negatively, few South Africans have a tolerant view of homosexuality: in a recent investigation conducted by the World Values Survey Association (2012), only 3 per cent of South African respondents consider homosexuality as 'always acceptable', compared to 28.7 per cent of respondents in developed nations. Interestingly, in the United States, homophobia is often bolstered by claims that legalising same-sex marriage would create a 'slippery slope' towards polygamy and bestiality. In South Africa, where diverse family structures (such as polygamous formations) are considered acceptable and same-sex marriage is legal, homophobia remains rife and in some instances socially condoned (Stacey, 2011). Writing on the origins and impacts of the Constitution's Equality Clause, Jacklyn Cock (2003:41) expounds on the disjuncture that persists between legislation and social attitudes: 'Despite the inclusion of the gay rights clause in the post-apartheid Constitution, homophobia is intense and widespread in post-apartheid South Africa. Gays and lesbians continue to be denied cultural recognition and are subject to shaming, harassment, discrimination, and violence.' Same-sex-parented families, specifically, must confront various social discourses challenging their right to become parents, many of which centre on the ill-effects such family formations may have on children and on traditional notions of family (Lubbe, 2007a).

Although only a small number of local and international studies have been undertaken on this topic, a clear picture has emerged of the societal discourses that lesbian/gay parents face. In particular, lesbian/gay parents often have to defend their right to have children, especially within social situations. Studies undertaken in both South Africa and the United States show that parents are frequently questioned over 'who is the "real" parent' (Distiller, 2011; Donaldson, 2000) and children may be asked where their father/mother is or where they came from (Breshears, 2011b). Through these demands for answers, the message is asserted to both parents and children that their family is different or abnormal.

The way in which their families are formed can also affect the support systems and burdens of same-sex-parented families. In her US-based study of 360 lesbian-parented families, Mary Ann van Dam (2004) found that lesbian stepfamilies have to contend with the dual stigma of being both a stepfamily and a lesbian-headed family. These families reported experiencing less familial support and more social stigma than families in which the partners established their lesbian relationship before having children together. With a general lack of positive family role models and an effective invisibility in wider societal discourses (Kumashiro, 2003; Wright, 2001), gay/lesbian parents are tasked with redefining 'family' – regardless of how theirs is formed – for themselves and their children (Dalton & Bielby, 2000). Recent studies in the United States also reveal that same-sex parents attempt to generate a positive sense of familial identity through the use of symbols, rituals, conversations with their children and by creating a healthy family environment (Breshears, 2011b; Suter, Daas & Bergen, 2008).

When discussing attitudes and opinions encountered by members of same-sex families, it is imperative to acknowledge the role of religious discourses in framing societal views of this type of family. It is often in religious arenas that homosexuality is openly condemned and people are taught that families with same-sex parents are unnatural and immoral. Furthermore, religious ideologies frequently motivate negative discourses in other contexts. A sample of 1749 lesbian and gay people in the United States ranked church as the least supportive and most hostile potential source of support (Bryant & Demian, 1994). In many instances, the lack of acceptance of homosexuality is attributed to religious beliefs (Breshears, 2011a; Rostosky, Riggle, Brodnicki & Olson, 2008). In South Africa specifically, researchers have noted the strong influence of religious beliefs on dominant social and cultural 'norms' (Richardson, 2004). Butler and Astbury (2005:5) also note the strong impact of conservative religious attitudes:

> Anti-gay sentiment is compounded in South Africa by a strong patriarchal Christian ethic that views same-sex sexual encounters as sinful and wrong. In this context, reaction[s] against homosexual rights are seen, for many, as upholding religious beliefs and therefore something to be proud of and actively encouraged.

The small body of extant child-focused research suggests that children in same-sex-parented families are highly vulnerable to these societal and religious discourses. Writing about the US context, Van Voorhis and McClain (1997:647) identify the enormous impact such discourses can have:

> As long as our society stigmatizes lesbians, children will feel sad about the loss of status that comes with not being part of the dominant family type... Losing privileges associated with being part of a heterosexual family include being shunned by family, neighbors, and friends; having your mother lose her job or be unable to obtain employment; having friends forbidden to associate with you; losing your home or not being able to live in a middle-income neighbourhood.

With all of these possible losses, it seems unlikely that children within same-sex families would not encounter negative messages about their family identity and their parent's sexuality. Indeed, adult offspring of lesbian/gay parents have reported encountering contradictory, often negative, messages about their family identity, and experiencing internal conflict about how open they should be about their family structures (Breshears, 2011a; Goldberg, 2007). Some social messages in South Africa, such as legal rights and positive media portrayals (Azuah, 2009), offer support and confirmation to children, while others may only offer support that is contingent upon secrecy (Butler

& Astbury, 2008). The struggles these children face are further magnified in the school environment.

School Discourses
Exposure to negative attitudes within an educational environment may impact powerfully on a child's formative processes, as school is usually the first context in which many children experience messages that contradict their personal understanding of their family form (Fedewa & Clark, 2009). South African schools have been accused of fostering and perpetuating homophobia and heterosexism (Bhana, 2012; Francis, 2012; Richardson, 2006). Teachers and administrators in school systems often assume that students come from identical heterosexual family structures, a practice that is troubling given the role of schools in socialising children's identities (Mercier & Harold, 2003). This common assumption also leads to curricula and class assignments that fail to leave space for diverse family structures, such as same-sex families, to be acknowledged and discussed (Fedewa & Clark, 2009; Lubbe, 2007b). Further, the majority of schools internationally, and all schools in South Africa, lack policies requiring affirmative representations and portrayals of diverse family formations (Kroeger, 2006; Richardson, 2006). The lack of positive images of same-sex families, combined with the abundance of negative stereotypes, communicates to children that these families are different, inferior and/or something to hide (Lubbe, 2007b; Ryan & Martin, 2000; Wright, 2001).

The role of teachers in creating a learning environment that is not supportive of lesbian, gay, bisexual, transgender or intersex (LGBTI) individuals or same-sex families has received much scholarly attention in recent years. Research shows that teachers are partly to blame for the perpetuation of homophobia and heterosexism in the South African classroom (Bhana, 2012; Butler & Astbury, 2008; Francis, 2012; Msibi, 2012). In many instances, teachers are hesitant to include LGBTI issues in their curricula, and in many cases instead disseminate prejudiced beliefs, due to tensions between these issues and their personal religious beliefs (Bhana, 2012; Francis, 2012; Msibi, 2012). Teachers' misinformation about LGBTI individuals also contributes to their lack of support (Msibi, 2012). While teachers rarely support physical bullying, verbal abuse is often condoned, either expressly or tacitly; children from same-sex families have reported that verbal abuse, from both teachers and students, is the most common form of discrimination they experience (Butler, Alpaslan, Strümpher & Astbury, 2003). The situation is further complicated by the fact that those teachers who are personally willing to address LGBTI-related topics in class often shy away from doing so because they are afraid of parental backlash and a lack of support from the school administration (Bhana, 2012; Francis, 2012). This combination of personal and institutional opposition and ignorance fosters negative attitudes and damaging discourses within the wider school system, in turn leading to the silencing of the needs of children in minority family types.

Peer Discourses
When parents come out to their children, one of the greatest fears children commonly experience is how their peers will react (Breshears, 2011a; Lynch & Murray, 2000). In Australia, Perlesz et al. (2006) found that almost all the children in their study had felt embarrassed about the make-up of their family, with these children coping with such anxieties by hiding their families from their peers. This is mirrored in several other studies, both in the United States and South Africa, in which children of same-sex parents reported a fear of being ostracised, physically attacked or verbally bullied by their peers (Baptiste, 1987; Breshears, 2011a; Butler et al., 2003; Lewis, 1980). It is likely that these fears stem from earlier exposure, either within their peer group or society generally, to negative discourses around homosexuality.

Though most of the literature in this field refers to anticipated discourses, a small number of studies have explored the negative attitudes and behaviours actually encountered by children with same-sex parents. In the United Stated, Gartrell et al. (2000) found that many of the children in their study had by the age of five already experienced some form of homophobia, usually from peers. Children are often confronted with negative comments from their peers about gay and lesbian people both directly and indirectly – whether being teased up front, or overhearing negative comments about gay and lesbian individuals in general (Breshears, 2011a, 2011b; Ray & Gregory, 2001). Even these indirect remarks may be interpreted by children as personal attacks and criticism of their parents.

As children get older, their fears and experiences of being teased and bullied lead them to be more secretive and guarded about how they describe their families (Ray & Gregory, 2001). One of the few studies of adult offspring of lesbian/gay parents was conducted by Goldberg in 2007. Writing in the US context, she found that children who were once proud to have lesbian/gay parents reported becoming ashamed when they reached school age and were exposed to negative reactions from peers, the parents of peers and teachers. These negative messages encouraged the children to hide their family identity from outsiders. Similarly, in Gianino, Goldberg, and Lewis' (2009) study, also undertaken in the United States, participants identified their middle-school years as the most difficult period in which to reveal their family identity, citing fear and a lack of language to explain their family structure as the primary reasons. Taken together, these studies demonstrate the need for intervention, both by parents and educational institutions, to find ways to foster positive familial identities in children with lesbian/gay parents.

EXTENDED FAMILY DISCOURSES

Most studies on communication between members of same-sex families and their extended families focus on the experiences of the parents themselves. As with the first disclosure regarding the decision to parent, the continuing conversations between lesbian/ gay parents and their families of origin can be alternately positive and negative in nature (Hequembourg & Farrell, 1999). Grandparents (Hequembourg, 2004) and other relatives (Gartrell et al., 1996) may refuse to acknowledge the children as part of their family, or question whether it is fair to the child to raise him/her in an alternative family (Rohrbaugh, 1989). Additionally, in the United States, Hequembourg (2004) found that many grandparents were worried about knowing how to introduce and explain their daughters' families. Whereas some same-sex couples and families eventually find acceptance within their families of origin (Van Zyl, 2011), the participants in Gartrell et al. (1996) revealed that familial homophobia was an ongoing source of sadness and hardship for them. As with societal discourses regarding their family identity, children of lesbians are also exposed to the opinions of their extended family regarding their family structure (Breshears, 2011a, 2011b).

Although lesbian/gay couples face challenges in disclosing their decisions to have children, in many instances they also receive support from their extended networks of friends and family (Breshears, 2011a). The couples in Gartrell et al. (1996) reported having biological relatives who welcomed the birth of their child. This study also found that many participants reported a strengthening of family ties with the arrival of a child into the family. Most of the women felt closer to their parents and reported that their parents were delighted to have a grandchild in their lives. Children raised in families with supportive extended family members are likely to experience positive discourses regarding their family identity (Breshears, 2011a).

Lewis (1980) raises an important point about the potential impact of the biological father's attitudes on children being raised in lesbian stepfamilies. She explains that the father's disapproval of the lesbian relationship might affect the children's efforts to accept the new partnership out of love for their mother. Some children in this study felt caught in the middle of their parents because of the negative discourses they were exposed to from their father. A similar conflict was evident in a recent study in which adult offspring of lesbian/gay parents reported tensions stemming from their biological parents' negative comments about their same-sex-parented stepfamilies (Breshears, 2011a). Notably, participants experienced negative as well as positive discourses within their extended families, but only negative discourses in wider society.

THE WAY FORWARD FOR SOUTH AFRICA

In South Africa, as elsewhere, societal acceptance of homosexuality and alternative family forms is slowly increasing, particularly among younger and more educated sectors of the population (Roberts & Reddy, 2008). A young democracy, South Africa is a country proud of its diversity, a sentiment powerfully symbolised by the country's moniker: 'the rainbow nation'. Despite the high value placed on diversity, same-sex people still face deeply entrenched prejudice. Members of same-sex families report an overwhelming sense that the opposition they encounter is couched in ignorance (Breshears, 2011a; Ochse, 2011). In the South African context, acceptance of LGBTI identities and families is significantly hampered by the commonly held notion that homosexuality is 'un-African' (Francis & Msibi, 2011; Stacey, 2011). South Africa's Constitution advocates for the rights of same-sex families, yet societal opposition to homosexuality is virtually identical to the rest of the continent (WVS, 2012). Interestingly, public discourses about families that fall outside of the 'nuclear' family form has been ignited by the government's recently released green paper on South African family life (The Presidency, 2012). Though the South African government acknowledges the diversity of family forms that characterise the country (only 23.3 per cent of families are headed by heterosexual married couples), it has committed itself to promoting the 'traditional' nuclear family. This has led to an ongoing public debate about the definition and diversity of South African families (De Vos, 2012; Joseph, 2012), a conversation that could lead to changes that will make a tangible difference to the lives of children in both traditional and non-traditional families.

The education system provides us with a significant opportunity not only to educate the younger generation on sexual diversity, but also to foster a supportive environment for children from same-sex-parented families. In contrast to the tide of negative messaging that dominates peer/school/social environments, some notable schools have produced positive discourses regarding same-sex-parented families (Bos, Gartrell, Peyser & Van Balen, 2008; Lubbe, 2007b). Bos et al. (2008) in the United States, and Lubbe (2007b) in South Africa, found that children who attended schools with LGBT curricula (such as lessons that discuss and/or include LGBT families and individuals) and/or had a general sense of openness were more protected against the negative influence of homophobic messages on their psychological adjustment. Such schools create an environment in which the children felt safe discussing their familial identity. Moreover, some educators teach children the meaning of stigmatisation, which has been shown to reduce the amount of bullying experienced by children with lesbian/gay parents. Constructive dialogue between schools and lesbian/gay parents also helps to foster a positive, consistent view of family identity in both environments (Casper, Schultz & Wickens, 1992).

Recent research in South Africa (Francis & Msibi, 2011; Harber & Serf, 2006; Richardson, 2004, 2008) and Australia (Jones & Hillier, 2012) demonstrates practical ways in which aspiring teachers can – and should – be empowered and challenged to create a safe environment. Strategies identified include showing appropriate films in class and encouraging themselves (and students) to examine their own preconceived notions about heteronormativity and discrimination. While this may be challenging, it is an ideal starting point from which to drive conversations on 'normality' and family, particularly in a country like South Africa that boasts a diverse range of family structures. This approach could circumvent a focus on sex and sexuality – a topic that is difficult for some educators, especially older teachers, to address (Francis, 2012). As LGBTI-friendly schools and curricula are far in the minority, we (along with others) strongly recommend a new focus in the compulsory Life Orientation classes to educate learners on diversity, tolerance, and inclusivity. To assist educators and students in this process, it is essential that new policies are implemented that address teacher training needs and that ensure adequate support structures are in place at schools and tertiary institutions (Francis, 2012; Jones & Hillier, 2012).

Despite opposition from most local cultural and religious groups to same-sex marriage, legally recognised unions have played a significant social function, including providing lesbian couples with an important sense of 'belonging' (Van Zyl, 2011). Yet we know very little about how South Africans in particular create this positive identity, and how they negotiate conversations with their children, given the many conflicting messages from outsiders. There is a distinct lack of research about the experiences of children in same-sex families in South Africa, and the ways in which these families create positive family identities through discourse. Our current knowledge of discourses is mostly based on Western societies, and could be significantly enhanced by research focused on and undertaken within this culturally, racially and religiously diverse country. How do same-sex families in South Africa negotiate contradictory outsider discourses? How do these familial and societal discourses interact to create meaning in these families' personal, relational and familial identities? How are family discourses affected by diversity within these family types themselves? Such information will be invaluable in fostering a society that can truly celebrate its unity in diversity.

REFERENCES

Azuah, U. (2009). Same-sex sexuality issues in some African popular media. *Canadian Journal of African Studies, 43*(1), 184–187.

Baptiste Jr, D. A. (1987). Psychotherapy with gay/lesbian couples and their children in 'stepfamilies': A challenge for marriage and family therapists. *Journal of Homosexuality, 14,* 223–238.

Baxter, L. (2004). Relationships as dialogues. *Personal Relationships, 11*(1), 1–22.

Bhana, D. (2012). Understanding and addressing homophobia in schools: A view from teachers. *South African Journal of Education, 32*(3), 307–318.

Bos, H. M. W., Gartrell, N. K., Peyser, H. & Van Balen, F. (2008). The USA national longitudinal lesbian family study (NLLFS): Homophobia, psychological adjustment, and protective factors. *Journal of Lesbian Studies, 12,* 455–471.

Breshears, D. (2010). Coming out with our children: Turning points facilitating lesbian parent discourse with their children about family identity. *Communication Reports, 23,* 79–90.

Breshears, D. (2011a). *A dialectical analysis of discourses surrounding children's experiences of parental disclosures of homosexuality.* Lincoln, NE: University of Nebraska-Lincoln.

Breshears, D. (2011b). Understanding communication between lesbian parents and their children regarding outsider discourse about family identity. *Journal of GLBT Family Studies, 7,* 264–284.

Bryant, A. S. & Demian. (1994). Relationship characteristics of American gay and lesbian couples: Findings from a national survey. *Journal of Gay and Lesbian Social Service, 1*(2), 101–117.

Butler, A. H., Alpaslan, A. H., Strümpher, J. & Astbury, G. (2003). Gay and lesbian youth experiences of homophobia in South African secondary education. *Journal of Gay & Lesbian Issues in Education, 1*(2), 3–28.

Butler, A. H. & Astbury, G. (2005). Over the rainbow: Recommendations for service provision as voiced by post-apartheid South African gay and lesbian youth. *Journal of Child and Youth Care Work, 19*, 126–136.

Butler, A. H. & Astbury, G. (2008). The use of defence mechanisms as precursors to coming out in post-apartheid South Africa: A gay and lesbian youth perspective. *Journal of Homosexuality, 55*(2), 223–244.

Carbaugh, D. (1996). *Situating selves: The communication of social identities in American scenes*. Albany, NY: State University of New York Press.

Casper, V., Schultz, S. & Wickens, E. (1992). Breaking the silences: Lesbian and gay parents and the schools. *Teachers College Record, 94*, 109–137.

Clay, J. W. (1990). Working with lesbian and gay parents and their children. *Young Children, 45*, 31–35.

Cock, J. (2003). Engendering gay and lesbian rights: The equality clause in the South African Constitution. *Women's Studies International Forum, 36*(1), 35–45.

Cock, J. (2005). Engendering gay and lesbian rights: The equality clause in the South African Constitution. In N. Hoad, K. Martin & G. Reid (Eds), *Sex and politics in South Africa* (pp. 188–209). Cape Town: Double Storey.

Dalton, S. E. & Bielby, D. D. (2000). 'That's our constellation': Lesbian mothers negotiate institutionalized understandings of gender within the family. *Gender and Society, 14*, 36–61.

De Vos, P. (2012). A marriage made in hell. Retrieved 15 September 2012, from http://constitutionallyspeaking.co.za/a-marriage-made-in-hell/

Distiller, N. (2011). Am I that name? Middle-class lesbian motherhood in post-apartheid South Africa. *Studies in the Maternal, 3*(1), 1–21.

Donaldson, C. (2000). Midlife lesbian parenting. *Journal of Gay & Lesbian Social Services, 11*, 119–138.

Fedewa, A. L. & Clark, T. P. (2009). Parent practices and home-schooling partnerships: A differential effect for children with same-sex coupled parents? *Journal of GLBT Family Studies, 5*, 312–339.

Floyd, K., Mikkelson, A. C. & Judd, J. (2006). Defining the family through relationships. In L. H. Turner & R. West (Eds), *The family communication sourcebook* (pp. 21–42). Thousand Oaks, CA: Sage.

Francis, D. (2012). Teacher positioning on the teaching of sexual diversity in South African schools. *Culture, Health & Sexuality: An International Journal for Research, Intervention and Care, 14*(6), 597–611.

Francis, D. & Msibi, T. (2011). Teaching about heterosexism: Challenging homophobia in South Africa. *Journal of LGBT Youth, 8*(2), 157–173.

Gabb, J. (1999). Imag(in)ing the queer lesbian family. *Journal of the Association for Research on Mothering, 1*(2), 9–20.

Galvin, K. M. (2006). Diversity's impact on defining the family: Discourse-dependence and identity. In L. H. Turner & R. West (Eds), *The family communication sourcebook* (pp. 3-20). Thousand Oaks, CA: Sage.

Gartrell, N., Banks, A., Reed, N., Hamilton, J., Rodas, C. & Deck, A. (2000). The national lesbian family study: 3. Interviews with mothers of five-year-olds. *American Journal of Orthopsychiatry, 70*, 542–548.

Gartrell, N., Hamilton, J., Banks, A., Mosbacher, D., Reed, N., Sparks, C. H., et al. (1996). The national lesbian family study: 1. Interviews with prospective mothers. *American Journal of Orthopsychiatry, 66*, 272–281.

Gianino, M., Goldberg, A. & Lewis, T. (2009). Family outings: Disclosure practices among adopted youth with gay and lesbian parents. *Adoption Quarterly, 12*, 205–228.

Goldberg, A. E. (2007). Talking about family: Disclosure practices of adults raised by lesbian, gay, and bisexual parents. *Journal of Family Issues, 28*, 100–131.

Goldberg, A. E. (2010). *Lesbian and gay parents and their children: Research on the family life cycle*. Washington, DC: American Psychological Association.

Harber, C. & Serf, J. (2006). Teacher education for a democratic society in England and South Africa. *Teaching and Teacher Education, 22*(8), 986–997.

Hequembourg, A. L. (2004). Unscripted motherhood: Lesbian mothers negotiating incompletely institutionalized family relationships. *Journal of Social and Personal Relationships, 21*, 739–62.

Hequembourg, A. L. & Farrell, M. P. (1999). Lesbian motherhood: Negotiating marginal-mainstream identities. *Gender and Society, 13*, 540–557.

Jones, T. M. & Hillier, L. (2012). Sexuality education school policy for Australian GLBTIQ students. *Sex Education: Sexuality, Society and Learning, 12*(4), 437–454.

Joseph, N. (2012). Zuma's new family plan sparks debate. *City Press*, from http://m.news24.com/citypress/Politics/News/Zumas-new-family-plan-sparks-debate-20120825

Knoesen, E. (2004). Queering the vote. *Mail & Guardian*, 3 March.

Kroeger, J. (2006). Stretching performances in education: The impact of gay parenting and activism on identity and school change. *Journal of Educational Change, 7*(4), 319–337.

Kumashiro, K. K. (2003). Queer ideals in education. *Journal of Homosexuality, 45*, 365–367.

Lewis, K. G. (1980). Children of lesbians: Their point of view. *Social Work, 25*, 198–203.

Louw, R. (2005). Advancing human rights through constitutional protection for gays and lesbians in South Africa. *Journal of Homosexuality, 48*(3), 141–162.

Lubbe, C. (2007a). Mothers, fathers, or parents: Same-gendered families in South Africa. *South African Journal of Psychology, 37*(2), 260–283.

Lubbe, C. (2007b). To tell or not to tell: How children of same-gender parents negotiate their lives at school. *Education as Change, 11*(2), 45–65.

Lynch, J. M. & Murray, K. (2000). For the love of the children: The coming out process for lesbian and gay parents and stepparents. *Journal of Homosexuality, 39*(1), 1–24.

Mercier, L. R. & Harold, R. D. (2003). At the interface: Lesbian-parent families and their children's schools. *Children & Schools, 25*, 35–47.

Msibi, T. (2012). 'I'm used to it now': Experiences of homophobia among queer youth in South African township schools. *Gender and Education, 24*(5), 515–533.

Ochse, A. (2011). 'Real Women' and 'Real Lesbians': Discourses of heteronormativity amongst a group of lesbians. *South African Review of Sociology, 42*(1), 3–20.

Perlesz, A., Brown, R., Lindsay, J., McNair, R., De Vaus, D. & Pitts, M. (2006). Family in transition: Parents, children and grandparents in lesbian families give meaning to 'doing family'. *Journal of Family Therapy, 28*, 175–199.

Presidency, The (2012). *Green paper on families: Promoting family life and strengthening families in South Africa.* Retrieved 15 September 2012, from http://www.thepresidency.gov.za.

Ray, V. & Gregory, R. (2001). School experiences of the children of lesbian and gay parents. *Family Matters, 59*, 28–34.

Reid, G. & Dirsuweit, T. (2002). Understanding systemic violence: Homophobic attacks in Johannesburg and its surrounds. *Urban Forum, 31*(3), 99–126.

Richardson, E. M. (2004). 'A ripple in the pond': Challenging homophobia in a teacher education course. *Education as Change, 8*(1), 146–163.

Richardson, E. M. (2006). Researching lesbian, gay and bisexual youth in post-apartheid South Africa. *Journal of Gay and Lesbian Issues in Education, 3,* 135–140.

Richardson, E. M. (2008). Using a film to challenge heteronormativity: South African teachers 'Get Real' in working with LGB youth. *Journal of LGBT Youth, 5*(2), 63–72.

Roberts, B. & Reddy, V. (2008). Pride and prejudice: Public attitudes toward homosexuality. *HSRC Review, 6,* from http://www.hsrc.ac.za/HSRC_Review_Article-121.phtml

Rohrbaugh, J. B. (1989). Choosing children: Psychological issues in lesbian parenting. *Women and Therapy, 8*(51–64).

Rostosky, S. S., Riggle, E. D. B., Brodnicki, C. & Olson, A. (2008). An exploration of lived religion in same-sex couples from Judeo-Christian traditions. *Family Process, 47,* 389–403.

Ryan, D. & Martin, A. (2000). Lesbian, gay, bisexual, and transgender parents in the school systems. *School Psychology Review, 29*(2), 207–216.

Singh, D. (1995). Discrimination against lesbians in family law. *South African Journal on Human Rights, 11*(4), 571–581.

Stacey, J. (2011). *Unhitched: Love, marriage, and family values from West Hollywood to Western China.* New York: New York University Press.

Suter, E. A., Daas, K. L. & Bergen, K. M. (2008). Negotiating lesbian family identity via symbols and rituals. *Journal of Family Issues, 29,* 26–47.

Van Dam, M. A. (2004). Mothers in two types of lesbian families: Stigma experiences, supports, and burdens. *Journal of Family Nursing, 10,* 450–84.

Van Voorhis, R. & McClain, L. (1997). Accepting a lesbian mother. *Families in Society: The Journal of Contemporary Human Services, 78,* 642–650.

Van Zyl, M. (2011). A step too far? Five Cape Town lesbian couples speak about being married. *Agenda, 25*(1), 53–64.

West, R. & Turner, L. H. (1995). Communication in lesbian and gay families: Building a descriptive base. In T. J. Socha & G. L. Stamp (Eds), *Parents, children and communication: Frontiers of theory and research* (pp. 147–169). Mahwah, NJ: Erlbaum.

Wright, J. M. (2001). Aside from one little, tiny detail, we are so incredibly normal: Perspectives of children in lesbian step families. In M. Bernstein & R. Reimann (Eds), *Queer families, queer politics* (pp. 272–290). New York: Columbia University Press.

World Values Survey Association (2012). World Values Survey: Online data analysis. Retrieved 12 September 2012, from http://www.wvsevsdb.com/wvs/WVSAnalizeQuestion.jsp

Familiar Claims: Representations of Same-Gendered Families in South African Mainstream News Media
Tracy Morison and Vasu Reddy

THERE HAS BEEN SIGNIFICANT REFORM of South African legislation pertaining to same-gendered families (Isaack, 2003; Reddy, 2006 & 2009).[1] The Constitution supports the rights of lesbian and gay individuals to establish life partnerships or, more recently, to enter into civil unions; to adopt children or to keep custody of their own children in divorce proceedings; and to undertake co-parenting of their created families (Lubbe, 2007). Despite – or maybe because of – these developments, public debate on these issues is as lively and vociferous as it has ever been (Roberts & Reddy, 2008). At the time of writing this chapter, for instance, a veteran journalist published a column in a national newspaper in which he denounced same gendered family 'arrangements' as 'neither the norm nor ultimately desirable' (Mulholland, 2013). Children in same-gendered families must be informed of this, he claimed. His argument was unsupported, save for unsubstantiated claims regarding the unnaturalness of same-gendered families, which he believes defy 'the natural order of things', and his vehement refusal to accept that 'same-sex matrimony is the same as that of heterosexuals' (Mulholland, 2013). Mulholland's column, which met with outrage by various activists and academics, demonstrates some of the ideas that circulate in public discussion of same-gendered families: concerns regarding the differences between homosexual and heterosexual families and the effects that these 'differences' might have on children living in 'alternative' families (Clarke & Kitzinger, 2005; Hicks, 2005; Landau, 2009; Riggs, 2004 & 2007).

In this chapter, we examine the public discussion, focusing on South African print media as a key site where debate has occurred. Recognising that public discussions of LGBTI issues – especially relating to coming out, rights, transgressions, stigma, discrimination and violence – have increased in visibility over recent years, this chapter concentrates on news stories in local print media centring on 'alternative' family arrangements that are in contrast to a traditional heterosexual nuclear family. Drawing on a selection of print media reportage, we examine the social and public discourses that underpin and resist normative meanings associated with 'the family' as a social unit and, specifically, how same-gendered families (often rendered invisible and pathologised) are constructed within this material.

THE RAINBOW NATION AND RAINBOW FAMILIES

Since the advent of democracy, South Africans have endeavoured to detach themselves from the systematic and hierarchical arrangement of difference that characterised the apartheid state (Distiller, 2011). Dubbed the 'rainbow nation',[2] South Africa was envisaged to be a state where diversity was celebrated and protected. Accordingly, the entitlement of homosexual people to various human and civil rights has been officially recognised (Lubbe, 2007 & 2008a; Reddy, 2009), as stated above. In reality, however, this group has, for the most part, attained 'theoretical citizenship'[3] (Distiller, 2011:13).

Lack of acceptance – ranging from intolerance and prejudice to outright punitive violence committed by fellow citizens – is commonplace in the lives of South African lesbian and gay individuals (Mkhize, Bennett, Reddy & Moletsane, 2010; Roberts & Reddy, 2008). These negative experiences are, of course, mediated by South Africa's particular race-class nexus that was entrenched during the apartheid era (Distiller, 2011). White middle-class homosexuals may experience more subtle forms of discrimination and 'mundane heterosexism' (Hicks, 2005) while poorer black lesbians and gays may encounter brutal violence (Mkhize et al., 2010). Nevertheless, it is fair to say that the general climate in South Africa is at best intolerant and at worst openly hostile toward same-gendered sexuality for reasons that highlight cultural taboos, morality and hetero-patriarchal sensitivities. Indeed, various political leaders have publically expressed negative views of homosexuality and fuelled claims that it is 'un-African': 'South Africa, like other parts [of] Africa, is currently knee-deep in state-sanctioned homophobia' (Distiller, 2011:4). For example, in 2009 President Zuma was reported as saying that same-gendered marriages are 'a disgrace to the nation and to God' and should not be tolerated in normal society ('Zuma rebukes king over gay remark', 2012). More recently, King Goodwill Zwelithini, the Zulu traditional leader, remarked on the unacceptability of homosexuality, calling homosexuals 'rotten' ('Zuma rebukes king over gay remark', 2012). It is against this backdrop of widespread and entrenched intolerance, homophobia and heterosexism that discussions and debates of same gendered families occur.

South African families are diverse in composition and traditional notions of *the family* are confronted with the increasing prevalence of diverse, unconventional family relationships brought about by a range of societal factors – such as HIV/AIDS, which leaves many households without adult caregivers, 'childfree' households, dual-earner families, divorce, adoption and, more recently, the same-gendered family (Lubbe, 2008b). Indeed, traditional nuclear families form only about a third of all family forms, as the table below presents (Holborn & Eddy, 2011).

Percentage of children (0–17 years) living with...

biological grandparents	8%
neither biological parent	23%
two biological parents	35%
father only	3%
mother only	40%

The absence of statistics on same-gendered families – as revealed in the table above – means there can be no clear picture of households in a changing South Africa. Moreover, official reporting of household statisics reveals a bias toward the nuclear family arrangements, shaped by the gender binary in hetero-patriarchal terms and pointing to the continuing myth of the 'normal' family.

Despite the large number of different family forms in South Africa, and their increasing visibility, the married two-parent heterosexual family continues to be viewed as the normative ideal (Lubbe, 2008a). This nuclear family model, shaped to a large extent by received notions of culture, represents the conjugal parental couple with biological children. The idea of a natural and healthy family arrangement, only made possible by reproduction, stands in marked contrast to family arrangements that deviate from this perceived standard. The popular US sitcom *Modern Family* (which centres on three interrelated families), for example, highlights issues of what constitutes an evolving 'modern' family that resists the traditional nuclear model. The myth of 'normal' is, therefore, a continuously debated source of meaning.

CHALLENGING THE MYTH OF THE 'NORMAL' FAMILY: REPRESENTATIONS OF SAME-GENDERED FAMILIES

Lubbe (2008a:49) argues that '[t]he scarcity of positive images and the abundance of negative stereotypes as well as the invisibility of same-gendered families in the institutions outside of the family combine to create a sense of difference, uniqueness and secrecy'. While the news media have increasingly reported on gay and lesbian issues in South Africa, these representations continue to be limited or restricted, with homosexual parents portrayed in problematic ways – that is, as 'heterosexual clones or exotic threats' (Landau, 2009:83).

Visibility and recognisability of homosexuality – and same-gendered families in particular – is critical for lesbian and gay politics and the development of identities. Media representations of homosexuality are important, as many communication scholars and media theorists assert, because the media, and especially the news media, play a significant role in constructing and challenging contemporary politics (Landau, 2009). Alwood (cited in Landau, 2009:81), writing in the North American context, argues: 'The news media have long been one of the public's few sources of information about homosexuals... [and] [f]or much of American society, what people see and hear in the news is what they accept as reality'. This assertion would be applicable beyond the Unites States.

Research on the ways that lesbian and gay individuals and issues are represented in mainstream media is therefore crucial, and a number of studies have been conducted. However, as Landau (2009) points out, there has been comparatively less scholarly attention directed toward representations of same-gendered families. Such research is scarce and Landau's own research is intended to address this gap. She examines representations of gay and lesbian families in United States print media, concentrating in particular on the ways that the verbal and visual work together to represent homosexuality. Landau concludes that although much of the reporting is overtly positive, it still maintains many heterosexist assumptions and ultimately does not further gay and lesbian politics. Likewise, Riggs (2007), who examined Australian mainstream media representations, concludes that supposedly positive representations of lesbian and gay parents are typically motivated by a desire to 'prove' the capability of gay and lesbian parents in relation to heterosexual parenting norms. Riggs' focus is on the ways in which constructions of race mediate the category of 'parent'.[4]

Another relevant study of media representations and debates about lesbian families was conducted by Clarke and Kitzinger (2005). The researchers studied the transcripts of 27 popular television talk shows and 11 documentaries about gay and lesbian families that were aired in the United Kingdom and New Zealand between 1997 and 2001. Adopting a discursive approach, they report on how traditional understandings of gender and sexual development are mobilised and sustained in discussions of the necessity of male role models for children growing up in lesbian families. No similar studies on representations of same-gendered families have been conducted in South Africa, where research on same-gendered families in general is limited (Distiller, 2011; Lubbe, 2008a).

THE DATA

The analysis that we present is based on an *ad hoc* collection of 41 newspaper articles that report on issues related to same-gendered parenting (for example, surrogacy, custody, adoption) between 1994 and January 2013. We have deliberately chosen this time period because it coincides with a number of significant legislative changes in relation to the civil and human rights of homosexuals – as a group – in South Africa (as discussed earlier). During this period of legislative reform, various landmark court cases occurred and were reported on in the media (for example, *Du Toit and Another* v *Minister of Welfare and Population Development and Others*; *J and B* v *Director of Home*

Affairs and Others; see also Isaack, 2003; Reddy, 2006).

The articles appeared in mainstream English (thrity-six) and Afrikaans (five) newspapers (print and online) and were located via the *SA Media* archive (hosted by the University of the Free State) and the *Independent Online* (*IOL*) search engines. The latter features news stories that have appeared in print media as well as original reports. The articles that were published in January 2013 were written by and in response to journalist Stephen Mulholland and appeared during the writing of this chapter, but did not emerge from the original search. We decided to include these particular articles due to the controversy that they created in South Africa and their relevance to our argument.

Afrikaans articles were analysed in the original and extracts that have been used in this chapter have been translated into English by the first author (using back translation to ascertain the veracity of the translation). We analyse the data within a constructionist framework, synthesising various discursive approaches, including discursive psychology and the narrative-discursive method (Morison & Macleod, 2013). Our objective in this chapter is to explore the constructions of same-gendered families in mainstream South African news discourse. Our analysis sought to answer the following questions:

(a) How are same-gendered families/lesbian and gay parents and their children rendered visible in contemporary print news?

(b) What understandings of same-gendered parenting, and sexualities more generally, are constructed in news reports?

ANALYSIS

Our analysis was informed by a combination of critical discursive perspectives and post-structural feminist theory. Below we discuss two overarching and interlinked concerns that were present in the data: (i) the issue of difference and sameness of homosexual families in relation to the heteronormative ideal of the nuclear family and (ii) concerns regarding the welfare of children who live in same-gendered families, specifically in terms of gay parents' ability to meet children's various needs, including the 'need' for gender role models.

Same, Different or Deficient?
A central feature in the discussion of same-gendered families is their unconventional or 'alternative' character. There are some commentators who equate difference from the heterosexual nuclear family with deficiency, limitation and loss and, as we discuss later, with potential disadvantage or damage to children. For example, in the recent controversial column discussed in the introduction, Mulholland (2013) states:

> There can be little argument against the desirability of a child being raised by two caring parents approved by the relevant authorities rather than in an orphanage, however well run it might be. But although same-sex couples have every right to their lifestyles and will have to pass scrutiny as desirable parents, some will argue in good faith that being brought up in a same-sex family is against the natural order of things. Certainly, mere observation and the biological methods devised by nature (or whatever) for the preservation of the species suggest that instructing children that same-sex matrimony is the same as that of heterosexuals flies in the face of reason... Thus, as same-sex relationships are increasingly, and appropriately, accepted in society, it is also fair to expect same-sex parents to be frank with their children that such arrangements are neither the norm, nor ultimately desirable – even if they are loving relationships.

In this excerpt, the invocation of the natural/unnatural binary renders the same-gendered family fundamentally and irrevocably different from heterosexual families. The scientific, almost Darwinian, language ('desirability', 'pass scrutiny', 'natural order of things', 'preservation of species') reinforces the author's appeal to 'reason' and common sense and to obvious differences given 'by nature'. Underwriting his argument is the authority and privileging of patriarchy (which we have progressively seen to valorise male power). This perspective confirms the view that reproduction of the species is interrupted by same-gendered parenting. The fact that homosexual couples cannot jointly produce a child without outside intervention is seen as setting same-gendered families apart, an inferior and ultimately undesirable poor cousin to the 'normal' heterosexual family. The same-gendered family, therefore, is viewed as a violation of the natural order and must be accounted for (Folgerø, 2008). As Walters (2001:211) points out, justification for discriminating against homosexuals has frequently been based on 'the assumption that gay "lifestyles" threaten the sanctity of the nuclear family by proposing and practicing a sexuality not centered on reproduction'.

Mulholland's argument rests on 'heterosexist and heteronormative ideologies that assume and privilege biological inception by intercourse between a male and female' (Landau, 2009:89). The 'logic' of this is so taken for granted and apparently self-evident, that he fails to even offer any substantiation of this point. This 'alternative' family form, the author suggests, may be tolerated simply due to the demand for good parents, but lesbian or gay parents had better account for their differences and, importantly, make their children aware of the inferiority. This family configuration therefore troubles essentialist and/or traditional understandings of kinship and parenthood (Folgerø, 2008).

Nevertheless, this denouncement of same-gendered families was exceptional in the corpus of data that we analysed. The majority of the articles, particularly those published in the last decade, emphasise homosexual couples' 'triumph' and have a somewhat celebratory or sympathetic tone. They tend to highlight the suitability and competence of homosexual parents by describing the stability of the relationship (most articles state the duration of a couple's relationship) and their couple's economic stability (the professional status of parents is almost always cited). In addition, the couples' desire for children and ability to care emotionally for children forms part of the narrative. Same-gendered parents are thus positioned as 'good parents' in these reports. Significantly, for the most part, the reports downplay or deny difference, arguing that lesbian and gay parents and families are just the same, or almost the same, as heterosexual ones, as seen in the following extracts:

> I try to encourage her [the daughter] to question these [stereotypes] by discussing different types of families... Like any other mother I feel I am trying to be the best parent I can be. (Henning, 1994)

> He [adoptive father] is also confident that whatever issues arise in their relationship, they will cope... His basic philosophy is: 'I'm a gay parent. I'm like every other parent just a little bit different'. (Beaver, 2000)

> Two children and their parents. A family. A happy family. Almost dead normal. Except that the two children are darker than their parents, are adopted children, and both of their parents are women. Quite a few things for a child to cope with... The De Vos-Du Toit family's story reads almost like a fairy tale with a horrible part and a (subsequent) happy part. Once upon a time there were two women who loved each other and wanted to have children. And there was a sister and her baby brother in an orphanage, and they would possibly spend their entire childhood there with thirty other children. Now these two are well-adjusted children who excel at school and will possibly attend university or technikon after school and realise their full potential, thanks to the love and attention of their two parents... Precisely because they are now a happy 'almost dead normal' family, Anna-Marie and Suzanne are prepared to bring an application to the

> high court… [to allow] them as a gay couple to both be recognised as the legal parents of the children. (Hudson, 2000)

These quotes demonstrate the way in which difference is minimised or denied, with parents positioning themselves as virtually the same as 'every other parent' – in other words, 'normal' heterosexual parents. The basis of this comparison is that they too love and want the best for their children. This is most apparent in the third extract where the claim about the children having a lot to 'cope with' owing to their different family form (trans-racial, same-gendered, adopted) is undercut by focusing on the parents' capability as being good caregivers.

In addition, the parents' desire to have children is rendered normal, familiar and understandable by utilising the recognisable fairytale storyline, thus drawing on a familiar script of romantic coupledom. This script rests on an array of positive socio-cultural norms about passion and romance (Fennell, 2006) and parenthood as a sign or overflow of a couple's love. This script is co-opted from the heteronormative storyline and thus functions to normalise the same-gendered family by using it to structure the family's story of origin. The description of this 'almost normal' family is therefore overwhelmingly positive.

Such positive renditions that seek to minimise difference, Riggs (2007) maintains, serve to establish that same-gendered mothers and fathers are capable and acceptable parents. These claims suggest a somewhat defensive position: to assert that same-gendered families are more similar than different from heterosexual families, that the differences are negligible and, importantly, do not render the families deficient (Hicks, 2005). In other words, they compare favourably with the heterosexual norm. Behind such claims, therefore 'rests a standard against which these are determined, and here this has to be a "heterosexual assumption"' (Hicks, 2005:163).

It is upon the basis of presumed difference that concerns and questions arise regarding the potential effects on children who grow up in same-gendered families. This features prominently in debates surrounding same-gendered families, which we turn to next. As we show, lesbian and gay parents are called to account for themselves and their parenting practices. Their family arrangements are open to scrutiny, and ultimately to regulation.

The Child's Best Interests
The wellbeing of children who live in same-gendered families is central to the public debate. The principle of 'the best interests of the child' is used by the courts to pronounce on matters related to lesbian and gay families, and is often the basis for public responses to same-gendered families. A large corpus of literature on the effects of homosexual parenting on children also exists (Landau, 2009; Lubbe, 2008b). This topic was a major preoccupation in media reports, with an overriding concern, as we have previously mentioned, being that of legitimating same-gendered parenting as 'just as good' as heterosexual parenting (Riggs, 2004).

'Needs Talk' in Discussions of Same-gendered Families
The notion of 'children's needs' is based upon the modern view of the sacralised child, a positioning in which children are seen as emotionally priceless, with their needs deemed to be paramount (Zelizer, 1985). This construction is based upon a particular contemporary construction of children as helpless, passive and wholly reliant on their parents (Woodhead, 1997). Talk of children's welfare or 'needs' comprises a significant and powerful discursive tool that acts as an unchallengeable discourse because the 'best interests of children' are given a moral priority (Andenæs, 2005). However, needs talk is not the transparent, apolitical talk it might represent itself as being. Rather, it is political and theory-laden talk that obscures the socio-political preoccupations underwriting its production through its claims to describe something inherent within a child's so-called

nature (Lawler, 1999). In this manner, 'needs' statements allow value judgements and normative relationships to appear to be timeless, universal facts and thus helps to lend them moral force (Meyer, 2007; Woodhead, 1997). Consequently, such talk is powerful and carries tremendous authority that compels others to act (Lawler, 1999).

Needs talk featured prominently in discussions about the ideal conditions for parenting. Implicit in these discussions are expert and often psychologised understandings of childhood and parenting (Woodhead, 1997). Indeed, expert commentators, most often psychologists (but also sociologists and similar), are cited in articles, thus lending further weight to whatever claims are being made about the effects of same-gendered parenting. Significantly, needs talk could be harnessed toward various discursive ends: explanatory, justificatory or regulatory, as well as a means of resistance.

On one hand, the rhetoric of children's needs provided a formidable defence of normative relationships. It was drawn upon to censure same-sex families and to legitimise the nuclear family form as the most appropriate context for childbearing. For instance, in a letter to the editor, which appeared with the headline 'Adoption by lesbians is not good for the child', the writer's status as a psychologist is stated in bold at the outset. She argues:

> The adopted child in a lesbian family can encounter many problems when he realises that he is adopted by two women and not by a mother and father like other adopted children. I do not by any means judge homosexuals, but I believe that it is unfair toward adopted children that have to be raised in such a home. A good self-image is the most valuable gift that any parent can give his child (Esterhuizen, 1994).

This denouncement is very much in line with Mulholland's column, discussed earlier, in which the author denies ill-feeling toward homosexuals, but instead mobilises children's welfare to condemn same-gendered families. Unlike Mulholland's piece, this letter attempts to substantiate the claim that same-gendered families are detrimental to children's wellbeing. As the extract shows, the author claims that psychological wellbeing (self-image) will be impaired due to the child's perception of being different from other adopted children. Another claim she makes in this letter, which we take up in more depth later, is that children's gender identity development will be impaired due to the absence of a father in the lesbian family.

This extract shows how the notion of children's needs may be harnessed to sanction childbearing under certain conditions and thereby proscribe parenthood for certain individuals, such as lesbian and gay persons. Needs talk masks and, in this case, preserves politically powerful and institutionalised beliefs about who should become a parent and, significantly, under what circumstances. These beliefs encourage parenthood in those who most closely resemble the ideal hetero-patriarchal family (that is, one that is white, heterosexual, able-bodied, middle-class and affluent), providing them with ever-expanding options and opportunities to become parents. In contrast, the desire to parent, and the actual parenting practices, of those who do not live up to the ideal are not similarly supported (Morell, 2000).

On the other hand, needs talk could also function to defend same-gendered parenting, such as in the following expert comment on a judgement in which a lesbian parent was granted custody:

> 'His [the judge's] decision to return the minor child to the custody of her mother is a signal to child care agencies, magistrates and courts to respect the Constitution and to act in the best interests of children... Removing a child from his or her parent's custody solely because of the parent's sexual orientation will further stigmatise and prejudice the parent as well as traumatise the child,' he said. Being lesbian or gay had nothing to do with the ability of parents to love and care for their children, he said. ('Lesbian mum gets custody of child', 1998)

In contrast to the preceding expert opinion, here we see that staying with a same-gendered parent is constructed as being in the best interests of children based on the potential trauma that separation could cause. The commentator refutes ideas of potential damage caused by the lesbian family by pointing out that lesbian parents are able to meet children's basic psychological/emotional and other needs by providing 'love and care'.

In addition to expert claims about children's welfare, the majority of the articles also quote parents on the issue, as in the following extract from an article about a lesbian family entitled 'An unusual, but happy family'. One of the parents is quoted as saying:

> We began doing research. We bought and read the book *Gay and Lesbian Parenting* by April Martin. We also read and kept every article on this issue in the *Unisa* [University of South Africa] library – we wanted to arm ourselves with scientific facts in order to convince a court that it would not necessarily be detrimental for children to be raised in a gay home... The findings also indicated that children who are raised in gay homes are exposed to more emotional challenges that make them more resilient. In homes where parents did not keep their sexuality a secret, children did not suffer any damage. We were convinced that it would be better for a child to be with us than in an orphanage, and that the child would be raised in a relatively normal way. (Hudson, 2000)

This quote functions to highlight the parents' consideration of what would be best for the child, rather than simply acting on their desire to be parents. This lengthy quotation also lists the research that the women undertook in order to ascertain whether and how a child might be affected growing up in their home, and how this impacted on their final decision to adopt. The mother cites expert evidence that highlights the benefits of lesbian families (for example, emotional resilience), although she implicitly concedes that their family is not entirely 'normal'. This concession inadvertently reiterates the structural and ideological underpinnings of the traditional heterosexual nuclear family and ultimately reinforces hetero-patriarchal norms.

Regardless of whether needs talk was used to denounce or support homosexual parenting, the construction of sacralised childhood and the belief in the intrinsic value of children remained central. This demonstrates both the ubiquity and power of this construction. Indeed, Landau (2009:85) argues that children are foregrounded in media discussions of same-gendered families, which frames same-sex parenting 'as if it is exclusively relevant for its impact on relationships with children. Children, then, become the yardstick by which gays, as parents, are evaluated'.

Emphasis was placed on one 'need' in particular in most of the articles: children's need for gender role models. As we discuss in the following section, this preoccupation stems from a concern regarding children's sexuality and 'proper' gender development (Clarke & Kitzinger, 2005; Folgerø, 2008; Hicks, 2005). We concentrate on how the articles address the idea that children of homosexual parents are 'at risk of experiencing "confusion" about their gender and sexuality, and, at worst, may themselves become lesbian or gay' (Clarke & Kitzinger, 2005:138). We focus especially on how parents' responses to this potential 'threat' are reported and the effects of their arguments.

Children's Gender Development and Compulsory Heterosexuality
Homosexual, especially lesbian, parents were frequently quoted talking about their children's gender identity and sexual orientation. This suggests that they may have been directly asked about this (by the journalist); that they themselves were familiar with and anticipated this particular charge; and/or that this was a personal concern. Some illustrative quotes appear below.

[A] 'Our child will be raised straight,' said Lucia. 'As soon as the child is old enough to understand what goes on in the world, we will explain to him: "she is your mom, and I am Lucia". Or "Aunty Lucia".' But children need male and female role models. What role model can two homosexual women be for a boy? Rouxnel answers that there will be more than enough uncles and grandfathers in his life. Lucia says that she will buy the boy a rugby ball and cheer from the side-lines of the rugby field. She reckons that she and Rouxnel will both be the father *and* the mother. 'If the child needs a hiding, then I will give it. But, if he has fallen and his knee is sore, then I have enough motherliness to also be a mother for him,' says Rouxnel. They want to raise the child with as much love in his life as possible. 'Rouxnel and I have so much to give.' (Van Rensberg, 1997)

[B] 'I don't have a problem with how I'm bringing up my daughter,' she says. Research has shown that most lesbians have heterosexual parents and most lesbian mothers produce heterosexual children. 'My daughter's dad is involved with a woman. Her grandparents are heterosexual. So she has a lot of influences other than me. I would never force anything upon her. Who knows, maybe I'm giving her something to rebel against!' (Henning, 1994)

[C] 'The scientific findings from the articles were dumbfounding. They indicated that exactly the same *percentage* of children that grew up in a gay household are gay or straight as those who grew up in straight homes. That the parents are gay has no influence on the children's sexual orientation. It was important for us to know that. We didn't want the children's choices to necessarily be influenced by our lifestyles.' ... Marié is 11, first in the standard 5 [grade 7] class, shines in various sports, is mad about horse-riding and is a leader in her class. She is conscientious and an achiever. Stephen is turning 8. He is in grade 2 and is mad about rugby and cricket. He takes part in wrestling, just so that he can have a bit of male bonding (Hudson, 2000).

[D] Michelle has been studying the findings of a Harvard University research project on lesbian and gay parenting. 'They found no evidence that lesbians and gays are unfit to be parents,' she says... 'There is also no evidence that suggests that the children of gay parents will themselves become gay' ... Michelle said that they were committed to allowing their child to develop in as normal an environment as possible. 'We do not intend to bring our child up in a solely gay and lesbian community. We want to raise our child within a mixed community and let him or her lead as normal and balanced a life as possible.' (Knowler & Donaldson, 2002)

In these extracts – all from reports about lesbian mothers – two main issues are emphasised. The first is the issue of children's appropriate gender development facilitated through gender 'role models', most explicitly raised in Extract A. As we see above, the mothers adopted one of two rhetorical strategies outlined by Clarke and Kitzinger (2005) to respond to arguments about the need for gender role models. First, they emphasised the presence of males in the children's lives, especially within the extended family. For instance, one mother (Extract A) claims that her child will have 'more than enough uncles and grandfathers' and another (Extract B) lists the various (heterosexual) family members who could act as role models. These women use extreme case formulations ('more than enough', 'a lot' and listing) to bolster their argument against disagreement. The second rhetorical strategy is the emphasis on influences beyond the same-gendered family and gay community. For instance, the mothers refer to their children having 'a lot of influences other than me' (Extract A) and the desire to raise the child in a 'normal and balanced' way 'within a mixed community' (Extract C) thus allaying possible fears that their children will be limited to all-female, or more precisely all-lesbian, environments without role models who can facilitate 'normal' development.

We also see how the gender presentations of children were

described in the articles. Many articles that focus on lesbian families include descriptions of children's gender-appropriate behaviour: for example, girls were 'mad about horse-riding' (Extract C) while boys are interested in rugby (Extracts A & C). These extracts engage with the common construction of gender 'as a fundamental and complementary difference between "man" and "woman"' (Folgerø, 2008:136) so that parents are able to make a unique contribution to meeting a child's needs, based on received notions of masculinity and femininity. Lesbian parents who were interviewed therefore engage with the belief that healthy or 'normal' child development depends on experiencing this fundamental difference within families (Folgerø, 2008). In Extract A, for instance, the parent claims that she and her partner 'will be the father *and* the mother' so that the child is able to receive both discipline and emotional care – roles stereotypically performed by men (fathers) and women (mothers) respectively.

This particular construal of gender is informed by a discourse of heterosexual gender complementarity. As Folgerø (2008:138) explains,

> The gender complementarity of heterosexual parents has in this perspective a universal and functional basis: to grow up with a 'mother' (female) and a 'father' (male) is an imperative prerequisite for a 'normal' development of personality, enabling boys to develop an identity as heterosexual men and girls to develop an identity as heterosexual women.

This thinking has been reinforced by psychological theories of gender development. The circulation of developmental psychological concepts and terms – such as that of a gender 'role model', 'identification' or 'socialisation' – in public debates regarding children's needs and best interests inform not only popular understandings of gender but also of (good) parenting (Folgerø, 2008), which in itself is a marker of preconceived value-laden beliefs that highlight a moral perspective in respect of perceived good parenting.

Discussions of role models were concerned specifically with *male* role models. In Extracts A and B the mothers discuss the male influences that their children will encounter and in Extract C the son is exposed to 'male bonding' through participation in a traditionally male sport. Folgerø (2008:136) reports that, in his study,

> the issue of 'role models' [was] a question of *father*hood, of the value of having a father participating in the care for the children. The informants clearly looked upon fathers as 'role models', while mothers simply were mothers. Mothers can certainly be good or bad, but the informants did not consider it necessary to argue that mothers are needed to ensure that children have 'female role models'. For this reason, there are plenty of discussions of fatherhood in the interviews while the gender specificity of being a mother was either absent or implicit in the interviews.

Likewise, in our data corpus, the unique attributes and skills of men *as men* – absent in lesbian families – were emphasised. As we have highlighted, the quotes above are unsurprisingly all from lesbian parents and reflect the general public concern with the lack of male role models in lesbian families (Clarke & Kitzinger, 2005).

Much of the attention that fathers receive in relation to children's welfare is focused on *absent* fathers. In both popular and academic fora, it is the father's physical presence/absence that is considered to be a determinant of how children – and boys in particular – turn out (Lawler, 1999). Likewise, in our study there was a relative lack of concern for children's need for a mother. This absence can be understood in relation to the unremarkable character of mothering for women. Such gender positioning is within the usual ambit of the female gender role – that is, women are traditionally children's caregivers.

As Clarke and Kitzinger (2005) point out, the reasons that male role models and fathers are necessary are not often spelled out. Hence, it appears that this idea is so much part of our cultural common sense that arguments for the necessity of male role models do not require much explanation or justification. Rather, 'it would seem that the mere presence of a man is what is important' (148–9). The lesbian parents' responses in these news interviews – highlighting the presence of men and other masculine 'influences' – effectively admit to the supposed necessity of male role models. Thus, as Clarke and Kitzinger (2005:137) maintain, such responses 'attend to and sustain traditional understandings of gender and sexual development'.

The second issue that is underscored by these extracts is the homophobic premise that same-gendered parents bring about homosexuality in their children. This premise rests on the dominant narrative of heterosexuality as the preferred and sanctioned mode of intimate relationships and family life (Lubbe, 2008b). The extracts above show lesbian parents responding to this concern. A common strategy is to cite research findings that 'prove' that this fear is unwarranted. The lesbian women therefore draw on expert knowledge to sanction their claim to motherhood. Several scholars point out the political and ideological problems with the research studies cited by the parents (Folgerø, 2008; Riggs, 2007). Such research may ostensibly appear to be 'homo-friendly' because the findings show that being raised by homosexual parents is not against children's best interests. Yet, the problem with this work becomes apparent if we envisage the potential implications if the findings had been the opposite. This research is based upon the heteronormative assumption that the heterosexual nuclear family is the ideal place to raise children (Folgerø, 2008). This rhetorical strategy effectively 'weights the negative implications of homosexuality and gay parenting... [and] reasserts heterosexuality as the ideal' (Landau, 2009:91).

DISCUSSION

Our examination of South African news articles about same-gendered families demonstrates that, as in the US media, representations of these families are for the most part positive and apparently progressive. It is possible to see that these representations do indeed present some challenge to traditional family forms, in that, as Lubbe (2008b:326) suggests, they raise 'uncomfortable questions such as: "What is a parent?"; "What is a family?"; "What is a father and what is a mother?"' These representations may potentially extend traditional notions of gender and sexuality. Nonetheless, like Landau (2009), we found that constructions of same-gendered families were rhetorically disciplined so that their potential challenge was minimised and hetero-patriarchy was re-stabilised.

Although at face value such claims to 'sameness' or 'normality' appear to be positive and may have positive effects, they may still operate to re-entrench heteronormativity (Clarke & Kitzinger, 2005; Hicks, 2005). Riggs (2007) lists a number of socio-political implications of claiming that gay parents are 'just like' straight parents: (1) the promotion of heterosexual parenting as the 'gold standard' against which all parenting is measured, (2) obscuring the radical differences that shape same-gendered parents' lives, (3) denial of the benefits of lesbian and gay parenting and (4) diverting attention from the ways in which institutionalised discrimination oppresses lesbian and gay parents.

Claims to sameness originate within a liberal equality discourse (Hicks, 2005) and are an outcome of mainstreaming politics that stresses common humanity and requires that sexuality be kept cloistered (Clarke & Kitzinger, 2005). Thus, while claims to sameness may serve to include same-gendered families in the mainstream, Clarke and Kitzinger (2005) maintain that they also structure resistance to heteronormativity in terms of the oppressor's discourse: the discourse of difference. This strategy is thus limited since it produces only virtual equality, one that asks 'only for tolerance within existing structures' (Hicks, 2005:164). The 'gold standard' of heterosexual parenting therefore goes unchallenged and the normative status of heterosexuality is reinforced.

As a result, same-gendered families are always compared against the normative benchmark of the heterosexual family (Hicks, 2005). The construction of 'the good parent' is judged by the standards of heterosexual parenting, and homosexual parents are required to prove their suitability in ways that straight parents do not. Thus, as Hicks (2005:163) argues, '"difference" is the effect of a range of discourses that locate, define and maintain the very idea of "the lesbian or gay family" as different, subordinate, and even subversive, not as a result of a set of essential characteristics'. This is illustrated in a satirical response to Mulholland's article entitled 'Heterosexuals: Should we let them raise children?' The author of this spoof article writes: 'Most critically of all, the exposure to the heterosexual influence of their parents may produce children who grow up to believe that heterosexual parenting is the only normal and desirable kind' (Davis, 2013).

As we have shown, gay parenting is condoned, or at best tolerated, on condition that heterosexuality is reproduced – that is, that straight children are produced. This, in our view, reconfirms a prevailing heteronormativity that shapes responses to gay parenting, fuelled by and underwritten through patriarchy. Engaging with concerns about proper gender and sexual development, especially in the psychologised terms of 'identification' and role modelling, legitimates heterosexist norms and reinforces traditional ideas about sexuality and gender (Landau, 2009). Attempts to refute claims that same-gendered family environments are lacking the necessary agents of gender socialisation – a *father* in particular – have limited efficacy. First, these defences amount to a concession to the hetero-patriarchal belief that children need fathers, or male role models at the very least, and that the absence of a father is bad for children. Second, using scientific evidence to counter these claims is not enough. Hicks (2005:165) maintains that

> we cannot and should not assess lesbian and gay parenting on the basis of 'research evidence' alone, since evidence is always open to a series of interpretations which ultimately relate to a moral and political stance... such homophobic discourses (as I see them) cannot be simply opposed by rational arguments that suggest an alternative 'truth' because there are no such truths about sexuality that can be based upon readings of 'the evidence'.

Instead, Hicks (2005:165) argues that 'gender and sexuality are not things acquired, but rather sets of ideas, or practices that are socially achieved'.

When parents themselves adopt the strategies we discussed in this chapter (emphasising their sameness; highlighting the presence of (male) role models in their children's lives; stressing their attempts to raise their children straight or in a 'balanced' way; and attempting to 'prove' that they will not impact on their child's sexuality) they position themselves as 'good gays' who are not a threat to the hetero-patriarchal order (Clarke & Kitzinger, 2005). Their children's (hetero)sexuality is used as evidence for good parenting (Landau, 2009).

Landau (2009:85) argues that the emphasis on children, and their needs and development, in news reporting means that "same-sex parenting is framed as if it is exclusively relevant for its impact on relationships with children". The rhetoric of children's needs is powerful and, as we have demonstrated, can be used to resist the normalisation of hetero-patriarchal arrangements like the nuclear family. However, this strategy may be limited. Andenæs (2005:214) argues that ideas about good parenting are often

> [i]nspired by the kind of developmental psychology that has constructed children as abstract individuals with universal needs, [so that] it is possible to turn one's gaze away from the actual conditions of those responsible for the children. It then becomes of minor

interest who these people are, whether they are men or women, and what their life circumstances are.

Consequently, children's needs may take precedence over those of the parents and, in turn, take priority over fairness and social justice in relation to family arrangements. This rhetoric could easily be re-appropriated and mobilised toward conservative ends insofar as the focus is on what is best for children and *not* on equity. Hicks (2005:163) argues that we would do better to instead highlight that concerns about children's welfare are rooted in ideas of difference and that 'this "difference" is the effect of a range of discourses that locate, define and maintain the very idea of "the lesbian or gay family" as different, subordinate and even subversive, not as a result of a set of essential characteristics'. Rather than engaging in debates regarding children's needs and wellbeing, and thus adopting a defensive and heteronormative stance, Hicks (2005:164–5) argues that we should be exposing the assumed heterosexual normality and homogeneity that underpin these concerns and the 'very system of sexual knowledge that organizes contemporary ideas about "sexuality"'.

The generally accepting tone in the articles we analysed is a provisional or 'paradoxical' acceptance. As Landau (2009:95) argues, 'gay families may be okay given that the children grow up to be "straight" – appropriately feminine or masculine and, of course, heterosexual'. Aside from their heteronormative basis, representations of same-gendered families as being no different to heterosexual families, and a space that can meet children's developmental 'needs' can be equally met, may well prove useful in the political debate and contribute toward transformation (Folgerø, 2008). However, the transformation is limited to the tolerance of 'alternative' families in hetero-patriarchal society. The dominance of the heterosexual nuclear family as an ideal, and the power of the father role within it, remains. True 'liberation for gay people is to define for ourselves how and with whom we live, instead of measuring our relationships by straight values' (Adam, 1995, cited in Landau, 2009:96). It is necessary then to represent same-gendered families on their own terms, not only in relation to heterosexuals and for reasons beyond just their homosexuality.

REFERENCES

Andenæs, A. (2005). Neutral claims – Gendered meanings: Parenthood and developmental psychology in a modern welfare state. *Feminism & Psychology, 15*(2), 209–226.

Beaver, T. (2000). She call him Daddy: Gay man adopts little girl after 3-year struggle. *The Tribune*, 27 August.

Clarke, V. & Kitzinger, C. (2005). 'We're not living on planet lesbian': Constructions of male role models in debates about lesbian families. *Sexualities, 8*(2), 137–152.

Davis, R. (2013). Heterosexuals: Should we let them raise children? *Daily Maverick*, 9 January. Available at http://www.dailymaverick.co.za/article/2013-01-09-heterosexuals-should-we-let-them-raise-children/

Distiller, N. (2011). Am I that name? Middle-class lesbian motherhood in post-apartheid South Africa. *Studies in the Maternal, 3*(1), from http://www.mamsie.bbk.ac.uk

Du Toit and Another v *Minister of Welfare and Population Development and Others*, CCT 40/01 2002 (10) BCLR 1006 (CC).

Esterhiuzen, A. (1994). Aanneming deur lesbiërs nie goed vir kind nie. *Die Burger*, 27 August.

Fennell, J. (2006). '*It happened one night': The sexual context of fertility decision-making*. Presented at the Population Association of America, 2006 Annual Meeting, Los Angeles, California, 30 March – 1 April 2006.

Folgerø, T. (2008). Queer nuclear families? Reproducing and transgressing heteronormativity. *Journal of Homosexuality, 54*(1), 124–149.

Henning, W. (1994). The story of a lesbian mother. *Sunday Times*, 7 August.

Hicks, S. (2005). Is gay parenting bad for kids? Responding to the 'very idea of difference' in research on lesbian and gay parents. *Sexualities, 8*(2), 153–168.

Holborn, L. & Eddy, G. (2011). *First steps to healing the South African family*. Johannesburg: South African Institute of Race Relations.

Hudson, M. (2000). 'n Vreemde en gelukkige gesin. *Insig*, 31 May.

Isaack, W. (2003). Equal in the word of law: The rights of lesbian and gay people in South Africa. *Human Rights, 30*(3), 19–25.

J. & B. v Director of Home Affairs, Minister of Home Affairs, & President of the Republic of South Africa, CCT 46/02.

Knowler, W. & Donaldson, H. (2002). Now the law can't hold us back anymore. *Independent Online*, 14 September. Available at http://www.iol.co.za/news/south-africa/now-the-law-can-t-hold-us-back-anymore-1.92812

Landau, J. (2009). Straightening out (the politics of) same-sex parenting: Representing gay families in US print news stories and photographs. *Critical Studies in Media Communication, 26*(1), 80–100.

Lawler, S. (1999). Children need but mothers only want: The power of 'needs talk' in the constitution of childhood. In J. Seymour & P. Bagguley (Eds), *Relating intimacies: Power and resistance* (pp. 64–88). Basingstoke, Hampshire: Macmillan.

Lesbian mum gets custody of child. (1998). *The Sowetan*, 22 April.

Lubbe, C. (2007). To tell or not to tell: How children of same-gender parents negotiate their lives at school. *Education as change, 11*(2), 45–65.

Lubbe, C. (2008a). Mothers, fathers or parents: Same-gendered families in South Africa. *Agenda, 22*(76), 43–55.

Lubbe, C. (2008b). The experiences of children growing up in lesbian-headed families in South Africa. *Journal of GLBT Family Studies, 4*(3), 325–360.

Meyer, A. (2007). The moral rhetoric of childhood. *Childhood, 14*(1), 85–104.

Mkhize, N., Bennett, J., Reddy, V. & Moletsane, R. (2010). *The country we want to live in: Hate crimes and homophobia in the lives of black lesbian South Africans.* Cape Town: HSRC Press.

Morell, C. (2000). Saying no: Women's experiences of reproductive refusal. *Feminism & Psychology, 10*(3), 313–322.

Morison, T. & Macleod, C. (2013). A performative-performance analytical approach: Infusing Butlerian theory into the narrative-discursive method qualitative inquiry. *Qualitative Inquiry, 19*(8). In press.

Mulholland, S. (2013). Same-sex parents have special duty to their children. *Sunday Times,* 6 January.

Reddy, V. (2006). Decriminalisation of homosexuality in post-apartheid South Africa: A brief legal case history review from sodomy to marriage. *Agenda, 20*(67), 146–157.

Reddy, V. (2009). Queer marriage: Sexualising citizenship and the development of freedoms in South Africa. In M. Steyn & M. Van Zyl (Eds), *The prize and the price: Shaping sexualities in South Africa* (pp. 341–363). Cape Town: HSRC Press.

Riggs, D. (2004). Resisting heterosexism in foster carer training: Valuing queer approaches to adult learning and relationality. *Canadian Online Journal of Queer Studies in Education, 1*(1). Available at http://jqstudies.oise.utoronto.ca/journal/view article.php?id=3&layout=html

Riggs, D. (2007). On being acceptable: State sanction, race privilege and lesbian and gay parents. *Reconstruction 7*(1).

Roberts, B. & Reddy, V. (2008). Pride and prejudice: Public attitudes toward homosexuality. *HSRC Review,* 6(4): 9–11.

Van Rensberg, G. (1997). Gay vroue oortree wet om kind te kry. *Beeld,* 14 July.

Walters, S. (2001). *All the rage: The story of gay visibility in America.* Chicago: University of Chicago Press.

Woodhead, M. (1997). Psychology and the cultural construction of children's needs. In A. James & A. Prout (Eds), *Constructing and reconstructing childhood: Contemporary issues in the sociological study of childhood* (pp. 63–84). London and New York: Routledge Falmer.

Zelizer, V. A. (1985). Pricing the priceless child: The changing value of children. Princeton, NJ: Princeton University Press.

Zuma rebukes king over gay remark. (2012). *Independent Online*, 23 January.

'The Best Interests of the Child': Reflecting on the Family and the Law as Sites of Oppressive Hetero-Socialisation

Nadia Sanger and Cherith Sanger

'THE BEST INTERESTS OF THE CHILD' is a refrain so commonly heard, particularly within legal contexts, that its contestable meaning often becomes obscured and its potential – as an implicitly value-infused judgement – for reinforcing and legitimising strict heteronormativity overlooked. The crucial need to identify and interrogate 'the constitutional and legal context in which sexuality issues are played out' (2011:29) has been correctly pointed out by Sylvia Tamale, who argues for a critical reinterpretation of the way in which African sexualities have historically been constructed and understood. The dominance of 'the best interests of the child' concept across multiple legal and social contexts, and the widespread acceptance of the legitimacy of such claims, marks the concept out as a key site for analysis, particularly in relation to notions of gender, sexuality, class and race. By looking closely at 'the best interests of the child' notion as it plays out within the contemporary South African context, this chapter aims to reflect on some of the ways in which hetero-socialisation operates within the family as an institution and within the law as an authority that lays claim to and delimits ideas of acceptable bodies and behaviours. Employing a multi-disciplinary approach, this chapter reflects on oppressive heteronormative values and how these often operate in opposition to the best interests of non-heterosexual children.

SEXUALITY, DISCRIMINATION AND RIGHTS IN SOUTH AFRICA

The institutionalised prejudice and discrimination of South Africa's apartheid period has nurtured a pervasive intolerance towards 'difference', be it in terms of race, gender, ethnicity, sexual orientation or myriad other grounds. Despite its much-lauded progressive constitution, South Africa's relatively new democracy continues to grapple with its past and struggles to find ways to better manage diversity and difference. Hate crimes targeting gender-nonconforming individuals (particularly masculine-presenting black lesbians) continue to plague the country, particularly in urban townships, with horrific sexual and physical assaults enacted as punishment for perceived sexual deviance and/or a disruption of traditional heteronormative gender roles. Despite growing media coverage of such cases, little effort has been made by the authorities to capture accurate statistical data relating to hate crimes perpetrated against lesbian, gay, bisexual or transgender (LGBT) persons. Although violent hate crimes are arguably the worst form of homophobia, this should not undermine the impact of other forms of discrimination faced daily by LGBT persons, including those not accompanied by direct or brutal violence. Hate crimes in all their manifestations expose the deeply entrenched homophobia present in South Africa. Identifying and unpacking social institutions that play a central role in enforcing heteronormative 'norms' (such as the family) are crucial for understanding how socialisation operates and its role in perpetuating homophobic attitudes and acts.

The South African nation-building project is built on multiple rights and principles that are intended both to 'correct' the injustices of the apartheid past and to protect individuals' democratic freedoms. However, neo-colonial discourses,[5] heterosexist masculinities and notions of culture continue to influence and shape how the national democratic project is exercised. Kopano Ratele (2006:59), in a discussion of ruling masculinities and sexuality, notes how 'the development of nations or cultures is imagined, arranged and regulated' and that within this 'regulating imagination... is the need to "protect" the nation or culture from "wrongdoers", "abnormalities" and "perversion"'. In the South African context, where dominant discourses continue to position same-sex desire as 'un-African',[6] LGBTI persons continue to be perceived as unacceptable and, by extension, as non-citizens.

Contemporary notions of citizenship[7] cannot be read outside of neo-colonial discourses on sexuality and the meanings ascribed within such discourses to bodies – and to black bodies in particular.[8] Citing Ifi Amadiume, Desiree Lewis (2011:215) articulates how

> many cultural meanings attached to gender, sexuality and material bodies – prior to colonialism – transcended the binaries, hierarchies and power relations that characterise the present. The explosion of transgressive representations of sexual identities and meanings today is therefore part of a long tradition, influenced by but neither determined nor initiated by Western modernity, of struggles for and over meanings associated with bodies and sexuality in Africa.

Similarly, Tamale (2011:16) locates the regulation of African sexualities not just within colonial history but also within global neo-colonial processes and systems. She notes that

> [t]he instrumentalisation of sexuality through the nib of statutory,

customary and religious law is closely related to women's oppression and gender constructions. Unfortunately, the colonial legacies of African sexualities linger today and we see them in contemporary accounts and theories.

The regulation of sexualities through entrenched colonial discourses should not be seen as an isolated site of oppression, but must also be understood as intimately linked to and reinforced by other systems of control. Patricia Hill-Collins (2005:88–9) speaks of the significance of a 'black liberatory politics' that 'includes a deep understanding of how heterosexism operates as a system of oppression, both independently and in conjunction with other such systems'. Such a politics would serve as an affirmation of black queer[9] sexualities by acknowledging and making visible'the roles sexuality and gender play in reinforcing the oppression rooted in many black communities' (2005:89). Hill-Collins' argument is especially significant for the South African context, where violence against black lesbians in their own communities reflects the ways in which race and (hetero) sexuality intersect as oppressive systems that are sustained through violence.

Scholarship and activism focused on gender and sexualities must account for the various ways in which heteronormativity operates and is policed, reproduced and contested within a variety of spaces. The family is a key site for hetero-socialisation and one that demands close academic scrutiny. There is currently limited local scholarship examining the intersection of LGBTI identities and families, and much less on the experiences of LGBTI children within heterosexual families. As such, this chapter aims to contribute to such scholarship by reflecting on laws relevant to children within the South African context.[10] Moreover, it exposes the potential for normative heterosexual families to reinforce forms of gender and sexual performance that are not in the best interests of a child.

THE CONSTITUTIONAL FRAMEWORK

The adoption of the post-apartheid Constitution in 1996 heralded a new era for South Africa, one in which the state committed to advancing human rights and dignity by formalising its obligation to 'respect, protect, promote and fulfil the rights' of all citizens.[11] The South African Constitution is explicit in its declaration that 'Everyone has inherent dignity and the right to have their dignity respected and protected'.[12] Human dignity goes to the core of who we are as human beings; it represents an acknowledgement of the intrinsic worth of all individuals. As with all the protections in the Constitution, the right to human dignity has a corresponding duty: in this case, the state must defend against violations of an individual's integrity, pride or self-worth (Sanger, Williams & Arnott, 2011).

The ground-breaking Equality Clause within the Bill of Rights theoretically ensures protection from discrimination based on sexual orientation and gender expression, and guarantees an individual's right to human dignity and privacy. In 1998, the Constitutional Court ruled that sexual orientation is

> defined by reference to erotic attraction: in the case of heterosexuals, to members of the opposite sex; in the case of gays and lesbians, to members of the same sex. Potentially a homosexual or gay or lesbian person can therefore be anyone who is erotically attracted to members of his or her own sex.[13]

Socially constructed and enforced gender norms – mediated through various other factors such as poverty and access to formal education – are root causes of gender inequality and often lead to discrimination on the grounds of actual or perceived sexual orientation and/or gender identity. The limited definition above may also be used to perpetuate discrimination against queer persons by failing to account for diverse gender identities or the complexities of human desire. Although this definition has been interpreted by some to extend to bisexual, transgendered or other persons,[14] it is clear that a revision of the legal understanding of sexual orientation is required. Such a limited legal definition is problematic in that it may prevent a non-heterosexual individual, particularly a child, from fully exercising his/her constitutional rights.

FAMILIES AS SITES OF HETERO-SOCIALISATION

Heteronormativity broadly refers to the normalisation of heterosexual desires and practices across institutions and social spaces. Judith Butler's (1990) much-quoted work on 'naturalised' heterosexuality is significant for any discussion on hetero-socialisation and the role of the family in regulating gender and sexuality. Arguing that 'the institution of a compulsory and naturalised heterosexuality requires and regulates gender as a binary relation in which the masculine term is differentiated from a feminine term' (1990:22–3), Butler contends that it is precisely this differentiation that is produced through heterosexual desire and practice, thus giving internal coherence to gender, desire and sex.

Gender norms are often written into the constitution of the family, reflecting hegemonic discourses around the ideal reproductive unit. Carien Lubbe (2007:271–2) articulately explains the central role played by families in naturalising heterosexuality:

> Because most families convey strong heterosexual messages, they provide many opportunities for their children to receive positive reinforcement, approval, and validation for their heterosexual orientation... myths of 'happy heterosexuality' abound at every stage of childhood development – from the playhouse of the nursery school to the dating games of senior primary and secondary schools and universities. Children come to understand that hetero/homosexuality is a natural dichotomy that 'proves' that heterosexuality is a normal and desirable end in itself. Heterosexual behaviour and language are

integrated and imposed to such a degree within the school culture that they have come to constitute a norm that reflects what is 'natural'.

The family environment – especially in terms of what parents or guardians condone as normal, healthy and acceptable behaviour – heavily influences a child's self-development, understanding of self, and physical and mental wellbeing. In the case of non-heterosexual young people, parental responses to gender identity and expression have an enormous impact on self-development. In their study *Out of the box: Queer youth in South Africa today*, Marian Nell and Janet Shapiro (2011:13) found that parental reactions strongly influenced how young queer persons 'went on to deal with their lives' and that rejection of a child based on his/her sexual orientation has in some cases led to depression, self-hurting, and alcohol and drug abuse.

Within heteronormative societies, the family operates as a performative space where gendered subjects recite various roles that help sustain and reproduce imaginary notions of an ideal family. As Lubbe (2007:274) explains, we '"do" the family through performing various acts in life, just as we "do" or perform gender. And just as gender is constructed, so also are families constructed'. Melissa Steyn and Mikki van Zyl (2009:4) also identify the family as one of the key social institutions through which sexuality is shaped. They define the family as

> sites of energetic social pressures, evoking equally energetic agencies on the part of individuals to conform, perform, enact, resist, undermine, revise or transform the constraining and enabling influences.

As such a significant site of socialisation, families – particularly their role in shaping and, by extension, limiting or repressing expressions of sexuality and/or gender – must be closely examined.

A South African-based study of matric balls provides an

interesting lens through which to consider how hetero-socialisation is enacted within a family context. Elaine Salo and Bianca Davids (2009) argue that matric balls in 'coloured'[15] urban communities can be read as a rite of initiation into successful heteronormativity. They note that mothers play a critical role in the preparations for the ball, thus ensuring that acceptable expressions of femininity are sustained across generations. Describing fathers as mostly passive onlookers, Salo and Davids note the active role of mothers in the lead up to the ball, particularly in terms of female participants' physical presentation, and the way in which this helps to produce successful feminine and feminised subjects. It must be noted, however, that through this process the mothers themselves are simultaneously positioned as subjects whose 'successful femininity to the local community cannot be underestimated' (Salo & Davids, 2009:49).

Butler's notion of gendered intelligibility is significant when considering both Salo and Davids' work and hetero-socialisation more generally. Butler (1991:17) argues that the coherent and intelligible gendered subject is one who can be deciphered in terms of the heteronormative script. Butler notes that 'persons only become intelligible through becoming gendered in conformity with recognisable standards of gender intelligibility'. In the context of the matric ball ritual, the successful feminine (and masculine) subjects signify intelligible gendered persons. In contrast, Caster Semenya, South Africa's 800m world champion, signifies an un-intelligible gendered and sexed subject whose body must be scrutinised and policed for some sign of intelligibility.[16] This is also similar to the treatment of Sara Baartman in the early 1900s: through colonialist logic, Baartman's body needed to be dissected and examined for intelligibility (in terms of race, sex and gender).

Families are not the only site of hetero-socialisation. Indeed, the enforcement of sexuality and gender norms through family structures should not be seen as operating in isolation, but rather as one part of a complex system of regulation. Thus, any discussion of hetero-socialisation must also take into account broader political and legal discourses. In the African context, a number of politicians continue to reinforce 'traditional' notions of gender and sexuality. In 2012, for instance, South African president Jacob Zuma revealed on national television his support of normative heterosexual values:

> I was also happy because I wouldn't want to stay with daughters who are not getting married, because that in itself is a problem in society. I know that people today think being single is nice. It's actually not right. That's a distortion. You've got to have kids. Kids are important to a woman because they actually give an extra training to a woman, to be a mother.

The president's remark, which was given further legitimacy after being defended by the ANC Women's League, reproduced the fantasy of the ideal (heteronormative) family within the nation-building project and the gender normative roles considered vital to its creation.[17]

HETERO-SOCIALISATION, CHILDREN AND RIGHTS

Traditionally, the law has been a key tool in facilitating and legitimising heteronormativity. Legal statutes and judgements that differentiate between individuals on the basis of sexual orientation have, according to Pierre de Vos (2008), been justified on the grounds that institutions such as the family are heterosexual in nature and perform an essential social function – that is, reproduction and child rearing. Furthermore, this social function is something that the state (according to heteronormative discourses) has an obligation and responsibility to protect and strengthen. De Vos further argues that differential treatment of queer persons has been based on a belief that homosexuality is morally and religiously reprehensible as well as being unnatural and dangerous, particularly to vulnerable individuals such as children, thus requiring the law to put in place measures to 'protect' them.

In the South African context, the legitimisation of heteronormativity through legislation and court decisions contradicts the spirit, purpose and objectives of the Constitution by undermining the basic right to equality. Moral and religious justifications pose a particular threat of infringing on diverse expressions and identities. In the *National Coalition for Gay and Lesbian Equality* v *Minister of Justice*, the Constitutional Court stated that 'the enforcement of the private moral views of a section of the community, which are based to a large extent on nothing more than prejudice, cannot qualify as such a legitimate purpose'[18] for limiting a person's right to equality. In other words, the courts cannot extend legal protection to institutions that facilitate prejudice. However, the enforcement and regulation of sexuality and/or gender identity within social institutions such as the family – which, in certain situations, could amount to a violation of a child's constitutional rights – often remains unacknowledged or overlooked.

All of the rights contained in the Constitution apply equally to children. As always, these rights can be subject to the Bill of Rights' limitation clause, but such decisions must be deemed necessary, justifiable and still 'based on human dignity, equality and freedom, taking into account all relevant factors'. Section 28 of the Constitution provides that 'Every child has the right to be protected from maltreatment, neglect, abuse or degradation' and specifies that a 'child's best interests are of paramount importance in every matter concerning the child'. It could thus be argued that a child, in accordance with his/her right to equality, always has the right to express and perform non-heterosexual desires or behaviours. Moreover, this right must be seen to still apply to non-heterosexual children in families where there is resistance, either expressly or tacitly, to queer identities and expressions on religious, cultural, ethical or moral grounds. The right to privacy is especially relevant to children (particularly those expressing gender-nonconformity or non-heteronormative sexualities) as it is essential for the development of a mature and stable personality. As G. E. Devenish (1999:135) correctly points out, the right to privacy is 'closely related to the right to dignity and has as its objective the preservation for each individual of the choice of when and how much he or she will allow interference with his or her mind or body or private activities'.

To successfully apply a limitation to a child's constitutional rights – whether related to sexual orientation, gender presentation or any other circumstance – the need for the limitation must be adequately demonstrated. Furthermore, the level of infringement must be justifiable according to the criteria set out in the provision for limitations. In cases where a court finds that differential treatment of a child based on his/her sexual orientation and/or gender presentation is legitimate, a decision must also be reached on the extent to which this applies. Given a child's innate right to equality and privacy (as discussed above), 'protecting' society by excluding or controlling non-heterosexual persons cannot be considered reasonable grounds for violating a child's constitutional rights.

Court decisions relating to queer identities, the family and the law tend to focus on the rights of LGBTI parents and the impact of their sexuality on their children.[19] This has resulted in the rights and interests of non-heterosexual children in heterosexual families being under-explored in the ambit of family law. This lack of critical attention is most likely due to the absence of a precedent-setting case on the rights of LGBTI children in a family where their gender-nonconformity is resisted by heterosexual parents. A case focusing on this could argue that parental resistance to the child's sexuality conflicts with the child's best interests by violating his/her right to equality and that he/she is being unfairly discriminated against on the grounds of sexuality and/or gender. It could further be argued that the child's right to privacy and human dignity is being denied.

It must be noted that children constitute a vulnerable group due to the unequal power dynamics within parent–child relationships. Parents enjoy majority status and are socially and legally vested with a right to raise their children as responsible citizens by exercising reasonable power and control over them. However, such socially condoned control does open up a space for potential abuses of power. The family context poses a considerable risk for abuses of power based on a child's sexuality, particularly in relation to a violation of that child's rights to equality and privacy. In terms of balancing the rights of parents and a non-heterosexual child, the existing uneven power relations in the parent–child relationship must be acknowledged. As Devenish (1999:135) observes, families 'assist in the production and perpetuation of hierarchies of subordination and control which are made to seem natural and inevitable. This, in turn, serves to obscure its oppressive nature and allows individuals and the state to rely on such values and institutions to protect the specific power hierarchy in society.'

The complex ways in which race and socio-economic status mediate children's vulnerability must also be acknowledged when considering children's rights as related to sexual orientation and gender identity. In other words, how the family is constituted in terms of economic and cultural capital will impact on a child's vulnerability in multiple ways, including the freedom to express queer identities. LGBTI children are at further risk of discrimination because of their age, which could exacerbate their inability to freely express a sexuality that does not conform to socially, traditionally or culturally accepted gender norms. What is critical, then, as Nira Yuval-Davis (2006:200) points out, 'is to analyse how specific positionings and (not necessarily corresponding) identities and political values are constructed and interrelate and affect each other in particular locations and contexts'.

The Constitutional Court has held that the family is an important social institution that provides security, support and companionship and that bears an important role in the rearing of children.[20] The court has further held that family care is an important feature of South

African life and that family life is essential for a child's wellbeing.[21] Section 28 of the Constitution also provides that every child has the right to family or parental care, which can be argued to extend to a right to emotional and psychological wellbeing resulting from such care. This right has been noted as operating against state institutions that take over the care of children so 'there seems to be no good reason why the right may not similarly operate against parents or guardians who expose the child to neglect or abuse' (Cockrell, 2000). The Child Care Act 74 of 1983 states that an indication that a child is in need of care is when that child 'lives in or is exposed to circumstances which may seriously harm his or her physical, mental or social wellbeing'. Likewise, Section 28 of the Constitution, discussed above, provides that every child has the right to be protected from maltreatment, neglect, abuse or degradation. By extension, it could be argued that an exercise of parental power that adversely impacts on a non-heterosexual child's freedom to express his/her sexual orientation and/or gender identity constitutes maltreatment or degradation. This should apply not only to direct or aggressive suppression, but also to indirect or tacit 'correction' of the child's sexual orientation and/or gender expression.

THE 'BEST INTERESTS OF THE CHILD'

The 'best interests of the child' criterion is paramount to all matters concerning the care, protection and wellbeing of a minor. This principle was demonstrated in the case of *Minister for Welfare and Population Development* v *Fitzpatrick and Others* in which the court ruled that the best interests of the child principle must take precedent over the other rights enumerated in Section 28 of the Constitution: 'Section 28(2) [the best interests of the child provision] must be interpreted to extend beyond those provisions. It creates a right that is independent of those rights specified in Section 28(1).'[22] The Children's Act 38 of 2005 (henceforth referred to as 'the Children's

Act') provides that, in applying the best interests of the child criterion, certain factors must be taken into account, including the child's gender and 'any other relevant characteristics of the child' – which surely includes sexual orientation and/or gender identity. It is essential that these factors are considered in light of the historical disadvantage that queer persons have experienced in South Africa and the persistent discrimination that they continue to face. Additionally, it is important that these considerations account for historical and contemporary effects of race and socio-economic status that always, but in different ways, mediate gender and sexuality.

The Children's Act is explicit in 'the need for a child to be brought up within a stable family environment and, where this is not possible, in an environment resembling as closely as possible a caring family environment'. Notions of a stable and caring family can be argued to require that non-heterosexual children are nurtured in a way that promotes their individual and natural development and their expression of sexuality regardless of whether this conforms to normalised standards or with the religious or cultural beliefs of the parents. The best interests of the child must take precedence over all other considerations. This criterion is, of course, open to diverse interpretations and subjective analysis. Be that as it may, this criterion should be assessed against human rights standards as provided for under the Constitution. Accordingly, the right to equality on the basis of sexual orientation should take precedence over parents' beliefs of what would serve as the best interest of the child.

Although South African law adequately seeks to address gender- and sexuality-based discrimination in theory, access to and implementation of such protections is often difficult or problematic. No matter how progressive the Constitution, the fundamental rights to equality, human dignity and freedom cannot be uniformly applied, particularly in the case of non-heterosexual children, as long as society enforces strict hetero-patriarchal gender roles that limit or deny a person's privacy or freedom of expression.

In January 2011, the Minister of Justice and Constitutional Development announced that his department is currently drafting an anti-racial discrimination and related intolerance Bill.[23] To date, no progress with the development of the Bill or its coming before parliament has been publically announced. It is likely that this Bill will create a space for lobbying and pressure for the government to include provisions that address discrimination suffered by non-heterosexual children within the context of the family. The Bill could also serve to amend the Children's Act to specifically address this issue. The inclusion of such a provision would serve as a means for the state to fulfil its constitutional duty to advance the rights of LGBTI children.[24]

CONCLUSION

This chapter has reflected on some of the ways in which hetero-socialisation operates within the family as an institution, and the law as an authority, with particular relevance for non-heterosexual children. The enforced hetero-socialisation of non-heterosexual children within normative families can constitute discrimination, and family resistance to a child's expression of same-sex desire must be understood as a gross violation of that child's constitutional rights. In a democracy founded on values of human dignity, equality and freedom, non-heterosexual children should be able to express their identities without fear of punishment; this is a right that *must* be protected. The ways in which LGBTI children experience their sexual and/or gender identities, as well as how 'the best interests of the child' concept is understood and applied, must also be considered in relation to other social positionings, such as the continuing effects of racialisation, socio-economic status, and community and family cultural value systems.

In South Africa, where the majority of citizens are of colour, there must also be a concerted effort on the part of researchers to document and analyse the experiences of non-heterosexual children of colour within normative heterosexual families. This research is critical in the production of knowledge around gender, race and sexuality, as well as in comprehensively applying the 'the best interests of the child' criterion. Indeed, it is a field of study that South African researchers working in the field of gender and sexuality must prioritise.

REFERENCES
Brady, A. (2011). 'Could This Women's World Champ Be a Man?': Caster Semenya and the limits of being human. *AntePodium, Online Journal of World Affairs*, Victoria University, Wellington. Available at http://www.victoria.ac.nz/atp/articles/pdf/Brady-2011.pdf
Butler, J. (1990). *Gender trouble: Feminism and the subversion of identity*. New York: Routledge.
Butler, J. (1991). Imitation and gender insubordination. In D. Fuss (Ed.), *Inside/out: Lesbian theories, gay theories* (pp. 13–31). New York: Routledge.
Cahill, S., Battle, J. & Meyer, D. (2003). Partnering, parenting, and policy: Family issues affecting black lesbian, gay, bisexual, and transgender (LGBT) people. *Race and Society*, *6*, 85–98.
Cockrell, A. (2000). *The law of persons and the Bill of Rights*. Available at http://www.mylexisnexis.co.za/nxt/gateway.dll/2b/zc/una/py9tb/0y9tb/7y9tb?f=templates$fn=default.htm$vid=mylnb:10.1048/enu
Currah, P. (1997). Continuing the civil rights struggles: Ends and means: Defending genders: Sex and gender non-conformity in the civil rights strategies of sexual minorities. *Hastings Law Journal*, *48*, 1363–1364.
Devenish. G. E. (1999). *A commentary on the South African Bill of Rights*. Durban: Butterworths.
De Vos, P. (2008). *Sexual orientation and the Bill of Rights*. Available at http://www.mylexisnexis.co.za/nxt/gateway.dll/2b/p6oda/e7oda/fak7a?f=templates$fn=default.htm$vid=mylnb:10.1048/enu

Dlamini, B. (2006). Homosexuality in the African context. *Agenda*, *20*(67), 128–136.

Gqola, P. D. (2010). *What is slavery to me? Postcolonial/slave memory in post-apartheid South Africa*. Johannesburg: Wits University Press.

Hate crimes in South Africa: A background paper for the Hate Crimes Working Group. (n.d.). Retrieved 24 January 2013, from the Consortium for Refugees and Migrants in South Africa (CORMSA) website, http://www.cormsa.org.za/wp-content/uploads/2010/07/hate-crimes-working-group-background-paper.pdf

Hill-Collins, P. (2005). *Black sexual politics: African Americans, gender, and the new racism*. New York: Routledge.

Lewis, D. (2011). Representing African sexualities. In S. Tamale (Ed.), *African sexualities: A reader* (pp. 199–216). Cape Town, Dakar, Nairobi and Oxford: Pambazuka Press.

Lubbe, C. (2007). Mothers, fathers, or parents: Same-gendered families in South Africa. *South African Journal of Psychology*, *37*(2), 260–283.

Magubane, Z. (2001). Which bodies matter? Feminism, poststructuralism, race, and the curious theoretical odyssey of the 'Hottentot Venus'. *Gender and Society*, *15*(6), 816–834.

Msibi, T. (2011). The lies we have been told: On (homo)sexuality in Africa. *Africa Today*, *58*(1), 54–77.

Nell, M. & Shapiro, J. (2011). *Out of the box: Queer youth in South Africa today*. The Atlantic Philanthropies.

Osha, S. (2004). Unravelling the silences of black sexualities. *Agenda*, *62*, 92–98.

Pillay, V. (2012). ANCWL defends Zuma after 'sexist' complaint. *Mail & Guardian*, 28 August. Available at http://mg.co.za/article/2012-08-28-ancwl-defends-sexist-complaint-against-zuma/.

Ratele, K. (2006). Ruling masculinity and sexuality. *Feminist Africa:*

Subaltern Sexualities, *6*, 48–64.

Reddy, V. (2006). Decriminalisation of homosexuality in post-apartheid South Africa: A brief legal case history review from sodomy to marriage. *Agenda*, *20*(67), 146–157.

Salo, E. & Davids, B. (2009). Glamour, glitz and girls: The meanings of femininity in high school matric ball culture in urban South Africa. In M. Steyn & M. van Zyl (Eds), *The prize and the price: Shaping sexualities in South Africa* (pp. 39–54). Cape Town: HSRC Press.

Sanger, C., Williams, J. & Arnott, J. (2011). *Know your rights: A simplified guide to LGBTI rights against unfair discrimination*. Cape Town: Women's Legal Centre.

Sanger, N. (2010). 'The real problems need to be fixed first': Public discourses on gender and sexuality in South Africa. *Agenda*, *83*, 114–125.

Steyn, M. & Van Zyl, M. (2009). *The prize and the price: Shaping sexualities in South Africa*. Cape Town: HSRC Press.

Tamale, S. (2011). *African sexualities: A reader*. Cape Town, Dakar, Nairobi and Oxford: Pambazuka Press.

Yuval-Davis, N. (2006). Intersectionality and feminist politics. *European Journal of Women's Studies*, *13*(3), 193–209.

Erased, Elided and Made Invisible? A Critical Analysis of Research on Bisexual Parenthood and Families

Ingrid Lynch

THE LAST TWO DECADES HAVE SEEN the emergence of a growing body of research focusing on reproductive decision-making among lesbian- and gay-identified parents, particularly around conception and related issues,[25] and on parenting experiences among lesbian- and gay-headed families.[26] Very few studies have, however, explored – or even acknowledged – the unique experiences of bisexual-identified parents. This is, in part, related to the broader invisibility of bisexuality both socially and within scholarly research. Historically, sexuality-related research has had an implicit focus on heterosexuality, with little consideration of other identity categories (Bullough & Bullough, 1997). As this research focus has expanded to consider diverse sexual expressions and identities, a heterosexual/homosexual binary – one that posits heterosexuality and homosexuality as the only legitimate categories of sexuality – has developed in terms of how sexuality is approached, discussed and analysed within academic works (Fox, 2004). Indeed, the monosexual assumption underpinning this binary has pervaded broader sexuality studies, and psychology specifically, to such a point that bisexuality is not easily conceived of as a legitimate category of sexual identification (Fox, 2004).

The theoretical preoccupation with monosexual identities is also reflected in many social science studies, with Rust (2000:5) noting that most research prior to the 1980s conceptualised bisexuality as 'a lesser degree of "homosexual" experience, as the intermediate range on a heterosexual-homosexual continuum, or as a matter of "diversity among homosexuals"'. As a result, data on bisexual individuals has often been 'forced' into a heterosexual/homosexual model, regardless of an individual's self-identification (Carr, 2006; 2011). The persistent organisation of sexuality into this dichotomy has led to bisexuality being, in essence, erased from social science research.

The small body of work that constitutes South African lesbian, gay, bisexual, transgender and intersex (LGBTI) psychology has followed the precedent set internationally, with almost no local research having being conducted specifically on bisexuality. Searches of the South African database SA ePublications and the international database PsycINFO yielded only three South African studies with a focus on bisexuality, a result that highlights the irrefutable silence around bisexuality in local research. The first of these studies, that of Blumberg and Soal (1997), uses a qualitative approach to explore notions of identity among self-identified bisexual women. The second, conducted by De Bruin and Arndt (2010), investigates attitudes towards bisexual men and women among South African university students. Finally, my own research (2012) explores South African self-identified bisexual women's accounts of their gendered and sexualised identities. While bisexuality itself might be a contested category of identity, this does not excuse the scarcity of South African-based studies investigating the experiences of bisexual-identified individuals. Furthermore, the limited scope of the studies listed above illustrates the crucial need for research that moves beyond an individual identity perspective to explore bisexual parenthood and family.

RESEARCH ON SAME-GENDERED REPRODUCTIVE DECISION-MAKING AND PARENTING

International research on LGBTI reproductive decision-making and parenting is similarly characterised by a silence around the experiences of bisexual individuals. While much international research on lesbian and gay parenting includes bisexual participants who are in same-gendered relationships, hardly any studies examine bisexual parenting specifically. For example, Bergstrom-Lynch's 2012 study of disclosure practices among prospective parents in same-gendered relationships includes five participants who self-identify as bisexual out of a total sample of thirty. However, in presenting her findings, Bergstrom-Lynch describes participants solely as lesbian or gay and offers no findings specific to her bisexual participants. Goldberg (2007) similarly declares a focus on lesbian, gay and bisexual parenting, but then elides bisexual parents within gay or lesbian parents' experiences throughout.

More recently, Ross et al. (2012:139) discuss briefly bisexual parenting but fail to offer substantial analysis, instead merely ascribing the invisibility of bisexuality in LGBTI parenting research to 'an implicit assumption that the experiences of bisexual parents will be the same as either heterosexual or gay/lesbian parents, depending on the sex of their parenting partner (if they have one)'. Goldberg (2009:7) also notes that studies on same-gendered parenting

> very rarely acknowledge, much less explore, the unique perspectives of bisexual men and women in their samples, as distinct from those of self-identified lesbian women and gay men. Rather, bisexual women and men in these studies are functionally treated as lesbian or gay by virtue of their membership in same-sex relationships.

Likewise, studies of individuals in other-gendered relationships typically assume heterosexual identification, again rendering the specific perspectives of bisexual individuals invisible.

In this chapter, I review the sparse accounts of bisexual parenthood and families in existing literature by outlining three themes identified using a deconstructive thematic analysis of these texts.

METHODOLOGY

Relevant texts for analysis were located through a systematic search of standard academic databases of published research, including PsycINFO, JSTOR, Family and Society Studies Worldwide, Social Work Abstracts and Academic Search Premier. The keywords used were 'bisexuality', 'mixed-orientation', 'queer', 'parenting', 'parenthood', 'families' and 'children'. Considering the lack of research on bisexual parenthood, I decided not to limit the inclusion criteria according to geographical context, date of publication, discipline or methodology.

The database search yielded one empirical study with a specific focus on the reproductive decision-making and/or parenting experiences of bisexual-identified individuals: a mixed-method study by Ross et al. (2012) that looks at the mental health of and support available to Canadian bisexual women during pregnancy. I continued to conduct an internet-based search using Google Scholar, which yielded another empirical study focused specifically on bisexual-identified individuals: a qualitative study by Eady et al. (2009) – again with a Canadian focus – that explores bisexuality and disclosure in the adoption system. I added to this my own study (Lynch & Maree, in press) on South African self-identified bisexual women's engagement with heteronormative marriage and family discourses. I also conducted a fruitless search of South African databases of unpublished theses and dissertations. Participants in the three studies selected for analysis are limited to self-identified bisexual women, with the exception of Eady et al. which includes two self-identified bisexual men.

A deconstructive thematic analysis, using Braun and Clarke's (2006) guidelines, was used to identify recurrent themes in the texts. This reiterative process entails producing general codes based on the data; assigning codes to themes and sub-themes; refining themes by relating them to data extracts and to the research question; and producing a narrative report explicating the themes. I did not limit the deconstructive thematic analysis to the selected texts but instead extended the frame of analysis to integrate theoretical insights from existing literature in the broader field of bisexuality studies. This synthesis was valuable in that it allowed for the themes identified in the sparse literature on bisexual parenthood to enter into conversation with texts related to bisexual identities and relationship configurations more broadly. In this manner, I was able to demonstrate how accounts identified in the literature relate to dominant discourses relating to normative relationship structures, parenthood and family.

In the discussion that follows I present three interrelated themes – the 'impossibility' of the bisexual family; other-gendered bisexual families and invisibility; and notions of bisexual individuals as untrustworthy partners – that not only impact negatively on the experiences of bisexual families but that also exclude such families from more research.

THE 'IMPOSSIBILITY' OF THE BISEXUAL FAMILY

Hegemonic understandings of what constitutes an acceptable and valued family invariably posit the ideal as a white, economically privileged family resulting from a heterosexual-identified man married to a heterosexual-identified woman. Pronatalist discourses prescribe a normative context within which reproductive decision-making and parenting 'should' take place and designate families deviating from this model as unfit (Morell, 2000). For heteronormative individuals, having children is generally taken for granted and often not seen as a deliberate choice – rather, it is regarded as a 'natural' progression in the heterosexual life-course (Morison, 2011). When reproductive decision-making and parenting occur outside of 'acceptable' family formations – such as within bisexual families – social sanctions often constrain such activities.

In many ways, bisexual-identified parents destabilise heteronormative constructions of marriage and family. Like all sexual categories, bisexuality is discursively constructed and is a site open to contestation, both in terms of meanings ascribed and social attitudes. A widely circulating discourse about bisexuality equates the category with non-monogamy. According to this discursive formulation, bisexual individuals can only identify as such if they remain involved with both men and women – that is, a bisexual identity is predicated on having concurrent relationships with both men and women (Klesse, 2005). As such, being in a monogamous relationship – be it with a man or a woman – is seen as destabilising, or even voiding, one's bisexual identity (Eadie, 1996). By equating bisexuality with non-monogamy, the possibility of loyalty to one partner becomes, in the minds of many people, unlikely or impossible (Eadie, 1996; Klesse, 2005). Such discourses around bisexuality, particularly its incompatibility with monogamy, have led to an entrenched belief that bisexual individuals cannot provide the 'ideal' outcome of a long-term union and family. This sentiment is reflected in the below quote from Lynch and Maree (in press), in which a participant reflects on her father's response to her identification as bisexual:

> My dad just wants the best for me, and he doesn't think that [a bisexual lifestyle] is the best. He doesn't see it as being any kind of option for having a good life, with children, a stable family, kids.

The entrenched association between non-monogamy and bisexual individuals has been challenged by some scholars, with McClellan

(2006) noting that relationship configurations for bisexuals include the same variety as those of lesbian, gay or heterosexual individuals. However, regardless of a bisexual person's relationship status and history, the strong social association with non-monogamy can constrain his or her ability to create or maintain a family. Jesse, a participant in research by Ross et al. (2012:148), describes how this common depiction of bisexuals limits her ability to disclose her sexual identification to other parents who do not identify as bisexual:

> [If you are] lesbian or gay, well, then they think at least you've made up your mind and you're not promiscuous... [being promiscuous] makes you unfit.

Eady et al. (2009) finds that the reluctance of bisexual individuals to disclose their sexual identification also impacts on people wishing to adopt, with some participants reporting a fear of being regarded as 'unsuitable' should they disclose their sexuality during the adoption process. In the following extract from Eady et al. (2009:126–7), a bisexual-identified single woman recounts her reluctance to correct her adoption case worker's assumption that she identifies as lesbian:

> I just felt like I would have had to explain more [if I came out to my worker] because then I would come across as more promiscuous. Of course this is me assuming, but I do believe there would have been more questions... I just felt like I didn't want to go there with her.

Josh and Miriam, a bisexual-identified couple from the same study, share a similar experience. Miriam recounts how a police background check during the adoption process led to their case worker questioning her partner's involvement in a LGBTI pride parade, seemingly out of concern that their bisexuality – and thus 'promiscuity' – would compromise their parenting abilities:

> [The case worker] started to question us about whether we were monogamous. He started to question what kind of same-sex relationships we had... it was clear that he thought that us being bisexual and Josh being at Pride meant that we obviously had relationships going on with same-sex partners... which would not be a good thing... So that was very clear: being a same-sex couple is one thing, but not being monogamous – forget it... I guess it goes together with his assumption that we weren't monogamous if we're bi. (128)

In addition to associations with promiscuity, a more general unintelligibility of bisexuality also contributes to invisibility within reproductive and parenting contexts. Disclosing an identity as bisexual is complicated by anticipated responses of educators, healthcare providers, other parents and family members. This closes off important potential sources of support, a concern articulated by a self-identified bisexual woman in Ross et al. (2012:146):

> Even with healthcare providers, I struggle to figure out how to tell them I'm bisexual... is it important, is it not important?

UNTRUSTWORTHY PARTNERS AND UNTRUSTWORTHY PARENTS? EXCLUSION IN LESBIAN AND GAY PARENTING CONTEXTS

A consequence of equating bisexuality with non-monogamy is that many bisexual individuals are confronted with distrust in lesbian and gay spaces and are subsequently excluded from potential sources of support within these communities (Israel & Mohr, 2004; Klesse, 2005). This relates to a second theme in the existing literature: the way in which the non-monogamous construction of bisexuality is drawn on in lesbian and gay spaces to depict bisexual individuals as untrustworthy partners. This leads to the commitment and loyalty of bisexual individuals often being doubted, and lesbian/gay individuals might fear that a bisexual partner will leave the same-gendered relationship for an opposite-gendered partner (Eliason, 2001; Ochs, 1996). Bisexuality is also at times understood as indicating a lack of commitment to being with a same-gendered partner, contributing to a lack of support for bisexual parents in lesbian and gay spaces (Ross et al., 2012). In a rare mention of bisexuality in South African research, Zubeida, a self-identified bisexual woman, echoes this experience:

> I guess I feel oppressed as a bisexual person. Most lesbian and gay organisations don't really cater for bisexuals – I think largely because bisexuals are even less visible than homosexuals. There is also so much distrust of bisexuals in the homosexual community. (Chan Sam, 1995:191)

Further to this, some bisexual individuals might find that the support they previously enjoyed in lesbian and gay spaces while in a same-gendered relationship is forfeited when entering an other-gendered relationship, often because heterosexual relationships can be seen as undermining the efforts of lesbian and gay groups to mobilise for recognition and equal rights. The successes achieved by many lesbian and gay activists, particularly in South Africa, were partly due to the manner in which such groups strategically deployed essentialist discourses of sexual orientation rather than those foregrounding the fluidity of sexuality (Epstein, 1998; Thoreson, 2008). Consequently, bisexual individuals are often viewed with suspicion because of their sexual ambiguity and their 'dubious' or unclear commitment to lesbian and gay movements (Blumstein & Schwartz, 1974; Rust, 1995). Carey, a self-identified bisexual woman in Ross et al. (2012:148), describes the lack of support she has at times encountered in the lesbian community:

> I think that I can certainly understand women who love women not

wanting to be with a woman who has been with men, or who has chosen to be with men. I think that a lot of them are sort of closed off, or not comfortable with that idea... [lesbians might think] maybe I don't really like women or I'm just, like, toying with the idea, or just experimenting.

A construction of bisexual individuals as untrustworthy not only impacts on the availability of potential sources of social support, it also shapes judgments around bisexual individuals' abilities to parent. A bisexual-identified woman in Eady et al. (2009:129) recounts the response of a case worker when learning about her sexual identification:

> They made this whole thing [out of it, saying], 'Well, you didn't tell us you were bisexual, and who's looking after the kids when you're out?'

OTHER-GENDERED BISEXUAL FAMILIES AND INVISIBILITY

The third theme identified in existing literature is that of bisexual individuals sharing in heterosexual privilege when in an other-gendered relationship. Däumer (1992:96) lists some of the social and material benefits of presenting as heterosexual in societies that remain overwhelmingly heteronormative: 'social endorsement and a certain visibility; legal and financial benefits (and) relative safety from homophobia'. Relevant to this is the notion of concealable stigma, whereby some potentially stigmatised markers of identity, such as sexual orientation, can be concealed more easily than others in order to avoid discrimination (Goffman, 1963; Herek & Capitiano, 1996). Unlike other social markers such as race or gender, sexual orientation is not always immediately obvious to others (Herek & Capitiano, 1996). Rust (1993) refers to the social belief that bisexual individuals can presumably present as heterosexual, and thus hide their 'otherness', more easily than lesbian women or gay men, consequently providing bisexuals with greater access to heteronormative privilege. This is based on an assumption that bisexual individuals are more likely to be normatively gendered than lesbian- and gay-identified individuals. This belief is also informed by the assumption that other-gendered relationships are necessarily heterosexual, without consideration for the individual sexual identification of each partner. Such an assumption can be troubling for bisexual individuals, with many self-identifying bisexuals reporting a sense of discomfort with being read as heterosexual when in an other-gendered partnership. A bisexual women in Ross et al. (2012:147) describes how 'passing' as straight renders a valued part of her identity invisible:

> I don't like looking heterosexual. I like being pregnant, but I don't like that automatically people just look at me and discount that part [of my identity].

The belief that bisexual individuals share in heterosexual privilege has many consequences for individuals' access to support structures and services. Indeed, bisexuals are often regarded as having access to resources in heterosexual spaces and therefore not needing the support lesbian and gay parenting communities could potentially offer (Rust, 1993). A sense of exclusion from LGBTI spaces, as discussed earlier in this chapter, often results in many bisexual individuals not easily integrating into lesbian and gay parenting communities (Rust, 1993). Further to this, the relative lack of an identifiable bisexual community (compared to more well-established lesbian and gay communities) means that significant support needs often remain unmet (Ault, 1996; Bradford, 2004). Cara, a participant in my earlier study (2012), refers to such a lack of a coherent and supportive bisexual community in South Africa:

It's difficult... The bi community is very small and very hidden; it's like an endangered species.

Similarly, Maria, a bisexual-identified woman in Ross et al. (2012:148), describes an unmet need for support and a sense of isolation resulting from not forming part of an identifiable community:

I wish I knew more women that were pregnant or had kids and were in a similar situation with me, and I could chat with them on a regular basis... I'm trying to reach out and hang around with those people, but I think it just takes time. And sometimes I feel like I don't have very much time.

NORMALISING STRATEGIES: A NEW VIOLENCE OF EXCLUSION?

Much of the research on same-gendered reproduction and parenting centres on a normalising project that aims to secure the same rights enjoyed by heterosexual individuals for lesbian and gay parents and prospective parents. To be afforded social and legal recognition as a family, it is widely believed that one must be married or in a recognised domestic partnership that approximates – as closely as possible – the heterosexual ideal. This approach has, however, been problematised by scholars such as Clarke (2003), who argues against normalising strategies for lesbian and gay individuals. In a South African study, Laing (2012) critiques normalising strategies as reinforcing heteronormativity. Such strategies are argued as excluding bisexual individuals who cohabit, polyamorous families and bisexual single parents thus limiting initiatives aimed at acknowledging family diversity (Clarke, 2003). Butler (1995) argues that advancing a new grounding through normalising accounts of same-gendered families – that is, simply replacing oppressive heteronormative groundings with revised but still restrictive ones – is a case of committing the same violence of exclusion that activists have worked to resist.

These critiques highlight the need for caution around advocating for a redefinition of marriage and family, especially when such re-articulations continue to exclude certain family configurations. Normalising strategies have political utility when deployed strategically to secure equal rights, but such undertakings must be accompanied by an awareness that *all* categories should be continually contested and treated as sites of 'permanent openness and resignifiability' (Butler, 1995:50). Thus, in arguing for the inclusion of bisexuality in discourses around reproductive decision-making, families and parenting, it is crucial that activists avoid doing so in a manner that perpetuates the marginalisation of groups still beyond the renegotiated requirements for social acceptance.

SOME IMPLICATIONS FOR POLICY AND PRACTICE

Considering the lack of support offered to bisexual parents within both heterosexual and non-heterosexual communities, there is a clear need for increased support structures for bisexual-identified parents and prospective parents. This could take the form of deliberate inclusion in lesbian and gay parenting spaces, where bisexual individuals have reported feeling excluded. Eady et al. (2009) argue that sharing resources and experiences with other LGBTI parents and prospective parents can be valuable for overcoming some of the challenges encountered by bisexual-identified individuals in heteronormative contexts.

Further to this, psychologists and other support professionals can help to increase visibility of issues specifically related to bisexual-identified parents. While bisexuality remains a contested identity in some contexts, it is a meaningful point of identification for those claiming this identification category (Klesse, 2005; 2011). By including bisexuality in debates around parenting, support professionals can advance the social recognition of diverse family formations. Education and awareness-raising campaigns that challenge stereotypes around bisexuality – such as the view that bisexuality is incompatible with marriage and, by extension, family – can assist in creating a more accepting social environment, one in which bisexual individuals can have children without facing multiple sites of marginalisation. However, in efforts to increase recognition of family diversity, support professionals must remain sensitive to the problematic nature of simply adding bisexuality as a category of identity, an approach that may in turn contribute to the exclusion of other less widely recognised or socially visible family configurations.

While there is a clear need for increased research focused on bisexual parents and prospective parents more broadly, there is also a need for a wider range of targeted studies. It is noteworthy that the research analysed in this chapter focuses almost entirely on women who self-identify as bisexual. It is thus essential that future studies address the near total absence of research into bisexual men and parenting. Finally, there is also a need for research identifying and assessing different strategies for increasing support available to bisexual-identified parents.

REFERENCES

Almack, K. (2006). Seeking sperm: Accounts of lesbian couples' reproductive decision-making and understanding of the needs of the child. *International Journal of Law, Policy and the Family*, *20*, 1–22. doi:10.1093/lawfam/ebi030

Ault, A. (1996). Ambiguous identity in an unambiguous sex/gender structure: The case of bisexual women. *The Sociological Quarterly*, *37*(3), 449–463.

Bergstrom-Lynch, C. A. (2012). How children rearrange the closet: Disclosure practices of gay, lesbian, and bisexual prospective parents. *Journal of GLBT Family Studies*, *8*(2), 173–195. doi:10.1080/1550428x.2011.623929

Blumberg, J. & Soal, J. (1997). Let's talk about sex: Liberation and regulation in discourses of bisexuality. In A. Levett, A. Kottler, E. Burman & I. Parker (Eds), *Culture, power and difference: Discourse analysis in South Africa* (pp. 82–95). Cape Town: University of Cape Town Press.

Blumstein, P. W. & Schwartz, P. (1974). Lesbianism and bisexuality. In E. Goode (Ed.), *Sexual deviance and sexual deviants* (pp. 278–295). New York: Morrow.

Bradford, M. (2004). The bisexual experience: Living in a dichotomous culture. *Journal of Bisexuality, 4*(1/2), 8–23.

Braun, V. & Clarke, V. (2006). Using thematic analysis in psychology. *Qualitative Research in Psychology, 3*, 77–101. doi:10.1191/1478088706qp063oa

Bullough, V. L. & Bullough, B. (1997). The history of the science of sexual orientation 1880–1980. *Journal of Psychology and Human Sexuality, 9*(2), 1–16.

Butler, J. (1995). Contingent foundations: Feminism and the question of postmodernism. In S. Benhabib, J. Butler, D. Cornell & N. Fraser (Eds), *Feminist contentions: A political exchange* (pp. 34–56). London: Routledge.

Carr, C. L. (2006). Women's bisexuality as a category in social research. *Journal of Bisexuality, 6*(4), 29–46. doi:10.1300/J159v06n04_03

Carr, C. L. (2011). Women's bisexuality as a category in social research, revisited. *Journal of Bisexuality, 11*(4), 550–559. doi:10.1080/15299716.2011.620868

Chabot, J. M. & Ames, B. D. (2004). 'It wasn't "let's get pregnant and go do it"': Decision-making in lesbian couples planning motherhood via donor insemination. *Family Relations, 53*(4), 348–356.

Chan Sam, T. (1995). Black lesbian life on the Reef. In M. Gevisser & E. Cameron (Eds), *Defiant desire: Lesbian and gay lives in South Africa* (pp. 186–192). New York: Routledge.

Clarke, V. (2003). Lesbian and gay marriage: Transformation or normalisation? *Feminism & Psychology, 13*(4), 519–529.

Däumer, E. D. (1992). Queer ethics; or, the challenge of bisexuality to lesbian ethics. *Hypatia, 7*(4), 91–105.

De Bruin, K. & Arndt, M. (2010). Attitudes toward bisexual men and women in a university context: Relations with race, gender, knowing a bisexual man or woman and sexual orientation. *Journal of Bisexuality, 10*(3), 233–252. doi:10.1080/15299716.2010.500955

Distiller, N. (2011). Am I that name? Middle-class lesbian motherhood in post-apartheid South Africa. *Studies in the Maternal, 3*(1), 1–21.

Donovan, C. & Wilson, A.R. (2008). Imagination and integrity: Decision-making among lesbian couples to use medically provided donor insemination. *Culture, Health & Sexuality, 10*(7), 649–666. doi:10.1080/13691050802175739

Eadie, J. (1996). Being who we are (and anyone else we want to be). In S. Rose, C. Stevens & The Off Pink Collective (Eds), *Bisexual horizons: Politics, histories, lives* (pp. 16–20). London: Lawrence and Wishart.

Eady, A., Ross, L., Epstein, R. & Anderson, S. (2009). To bi or not to bi: Bisexuality and disclosure in the adoption system. In R. Epstein (Ed.), *Who's your daddy? And other writings on queer parenting* (pp. 124–132). Toronto, ON: Sumach Press.

Eliason, M. (2001) Bi-Negativity: The stigma facing bisexual men.' *Journal of Bisexuality, 1*(2/3), 137–154.

Epstein, S. (1998). Gay politics, ethnic identity: The limits of social constructionism. In P. M. Nardi & B. E. Schneider (Eds), *Social perspectives in lesbian and gay studies: A reader* (pp. 134–159). London: Routledge.

Fox, R. C. (2004). Introduction. In R. C. Fox (Ed.), *Current research on bisexuality* (pp. 1–6). Binghamton: Harrington Park Press.

Goffman, E. (1963). *Stigma: Notes on the management of spoiled identity*. Englewood Cliffs: Prentice-Hall.

Goldberg, A. E. (2007). Talking about family: Disclosure practices of adults raised by lesbian, gay, and bisexual parents. *Journal of Family Issues, 28*(1), 100–131. doi:10.1177/0192513X06293606

Goldberg, A. E. (2009). *Lesbian and gay parents and their children: Research on the family life cycle.* Washington, DC: American Psychological Association.

Hemmings, C. (2002). *Bisexual spaces: A geography of sexuality and gender.* New York: Routledge.

Herek, G. M. & Capitanio, J. P. (1996). 'Some of my best friends': Intergroup contact, concealable stigma, and heterosexuals' attitudes toward gay men and lesbians. *Personality and Social Psychology Bulletin, 22*(4), 412–424.

Israel, T. & Mohr, J. J. (2004). Attitudes toward bisexual women and men: Current research, future directions. *Journal of Bisexuality, 4*, (1/2), 119–134.

Klesse, C. (2005). Bisexual women, non-monogamy and differentialist anti-promiscuity discourses. *Sexualities, 8*(4), 445–464. doi: 10.1177/1363460705056620

Klesse, C. (2011). Shady characters, untrustworthy partners, and promiscuous sluts: Creating bisexual intimacies in the face of heteronormativity and biphobia. *Journal of Bisexuality, 11*(2/3), 227-244. doi:10.1080/15299716.2011.571987

Laing, B. (2012). *A discourse analysis of gay men's identity constructions in a same-sex marriage.* Paper presented at the International Congress of Psychology, July 2002, Cape Town, South Africa.

Leiblum, S. R., Palmer, M. G. & Spector, I. P. (1995). Non-traditional mothers: Single heterosexual/lesbian women and lesbian couples electing motherhood via donor insemination. *Journal of Obstetrics and Gynaecology, 16*, 11–20.

Lewin, E. (1994). Negotiating lesbian motherhood: The dialectics of resistance and accommodation. In E. N. Glenn, G. Chang & L. R. Forcey (Eds), *Mothering: Ideology, experience, and agency* (pp. 333–353). New York: Routledge.

Lynch, I. (2012). *South African bisexual women's accounts of their gendered and sexualised identities: A feminist poststructuralist analysis*. (Unpublished doctoral dissertation). University of Pretoria, Pretoria.

Lynch, I. & Maree, D. J. F. (in press). Negotiating heteronormativity: Exploring South African bisexual women's constructions of marriage and family.

McClellan, D. L. (2006). Bisexual relationships and families. In D. F. Morrow & L. Messinger (Eds), *Sexual orientation and gender expression in social work practice: Working with gay, lesbian, bisexual, and transgender people* (pp. 243–262). New York: Columbia University Press.

Morell, C. (2000). Saying no: Women's experiences of reproductive refusal. *Feminism & Psychology, 10*(3), 313–322.

Morison, T. (2011). *'But what story?' A narrative-discursive analysis of 'white' Afrikaners' accounts of male involvement in parenthood decision-making*. (Unpublished doctoral dissertation). Rhodes University, Grahamstown, South Africa.

Ochs, R. (1996) Biphobia: It goes more than two ways. In B. Firestein (ed), *Bisexuality: The Identity and Politics of an Invisible Minority* (pp. 217–239). Thousand Oaks, California: Sage Publications.

Ross, L. E., Siegel, A., Dobinson, C., Epstein, R. & Steele, L. S. (2012). 'I don't want to turn totally invisible': Mental health, stressors, and supports among bisexual women during the perinatal period. *Journal of GLBT Family Studies, 8*(2), 137–154.

Rust, P. C. (1993). 'Coming out' in the age of social constructionism: Sexual identity formation among lesbian and bisexual women. *Gender & Society, 7*(1), 50–77.

Rust, P. C. (1995). *Bisexuality and the challenge to lesbian politics*. New York: New York University Press.

Rust, P. C. (2000). Criticisms of the scholarly literature on sexuality for its neglect of bisexuality. In P. C. Rust (Ed.), *Bisexuality in the United States: A social science reader* (pp. 5–10). New York:

Columbia University Press.

Strah, D. (2003). *Gay dads: A celebration of fatherhood*. New York: J.P. Tarcher.

Thoreson, R. R. (2008). Somewhere over the rainbow nation: Gay, lesbian and bisexual activism in South Africa. *Journal of Southern African Studies, 34*(3), 679–697. doi:10.1080/03057070802259969

SECTION 2

Portraits and Voices: Representing Diversity

Home Affairs: A Photographic Essay Celebrating Family Diversity

John Marnell

IN 2008, GAY AND LESBIAN MEMORY in Action (GALA), in association with TRACE Exhibition Group, launched Home Affairs: About Love, Family and Relationships, a travelling exhibition exploring the diversity of families within the Rainbow Nation. The material was collected and curated by a team of people, including Sharon Cort, Anthony Manion, Mark Gevisser and Sibusiso Kheswa.

    The exhibition was inspired, in part, by the many significant legislative reforms – or, more accurately, the resistance that accompanied these – that had occurred during the preceding decade. The debates leading up to the adoption of the Civil Union Act in 2006 revealed that, despite South Africa having one of the most liberal constitutions in the world, the idea of same-sex marriage – and, by extension, same-sex families – remains highly contentious. Indeed, to this day there exists a climate of hostility, and in many cases of violent opposition, to non-heterosexual identities, expressions and relationships. Of course, this ongoing opposition stems from a range of intersecting social, cultural and environmental factors, many of which actively silence the experiences of lesbian, gay, bisexual, transgender and intersex (LGBTI) people. For GALA, one of the most effective ways of combating discrimination and violence is education, be it through direct advocacy work, knowledge production or, as in this case, exhibitions that introduce the broader public to LGBTI lives and experiences.

Since there are a multitude of family formations that have evolved in South Africa – a consequence of cultural, political and economic conditions as well as personal choices – GALA decided to frame same-sex relations within a broader context of family diversity. Instead of solely recording the experiences of lesbian and gay parents, the decision was made to feature, among others, multi-racial relationships, families formed through adoption, transgender partners and matriarchal family structures. The curators firmly believed that only by displaying these portraits side by side could the exhibition effectively convey the myriad family formations and practices in this country and, significantly, the commonalities between them.

From the outset it was clear that the exhibition also needed to capture how the participants themselves understood and felt about their families. Each family was thus asked to share and reflect on their experiences, on their relationships with each other and on the challenges they face. Extracts from these interviews were then displayed alongside the portraits, both to contextualise the images and to invite viewers to go beyond a simple 'happy family' reading. By combining these strong, positive and affirming portraits with first-person accounts, the exhibition created a space for viewers to consider how families – no matter the gender, sexuality or race – share basic values.

For this photo essay (see picture section), we have chosen six portraits and interviews: Nonhlanhla and Her Family; Nhlanhla and Fanney; Robert and His Family; Bev and Her Family; JP and Paul;

and Richard and His Family. These were selected not only because they provide an insight into the very different experiences of LGBTI people in contemporary South Africa, but also because *as a whole* they challenge the notion of the 'normal' family. Despite the obvious cultural, economic and racial differences between the subjects, there is a unifying theme running through the portraits and interviews: it is not marriage or children or blood ties or playing by the 'rules' that make a family – it is, rather, love. As the interview extracts make clear, there are many other qualities – commitment, respect and trust, to name a few – that also play an integral role in creating a healthy and stable family environment, but at the core of these families is one thing: love.

The limited space available in this book means that it is impossible to depict the countless permutations of family formations in South Africa, and as a result we have had to leave out many striking and thought-provoking portraits. Given the central thrust of the publication, the decision was made to leave out the heterosexual – but by no means definitively heteronormative – families. We acknowledge that, in many ways, this decision undermines the original motivation behind the project, but we hope that the selection featured here will still prompt readers to 'rethink' families, to challenge their own assumptions and beliefs, and to reflect on their experiences. It was also not feasible to print the interview extracts alongside the portraits, leading to an unavoidable disconnect between the exhibition materials. Rather than read straight through the interviews, I strongly encourage you to move between the text and images, as this will help to surface the ideas and emotions that bind these families together.

The Home Affairs exhibition would never have been possible without the generosity of the participants. Their willingness to invite viewers into their lives and to share their experiences allowed GALA to create a unique snapshot of LGBTI life in contemporary South Africa. Of course, it is not easy to open up one's private life to the public, and GALA is truly grateful for the courage and honesty of those who took part in the project. It is also necessary to acknowledge the work of Sabelo Mlangeni, whose stunning portraits so beautifully captured each family.

As the last two decades have sadly shown, it takes more than constitutional and legislative reforms to create a society free from discrimination. GALA doesn't for a moment think that an exhibition will suddenly change the lives of those LGBTI people who continue to face marginalisation and violence, but we do believe passionately that increasing visibility while simultaneously emphasising our common humanity is one vital – albeit small – step in the right direction.

Home Affairs Interview Extracts

NONHLANHLA AND HER FAMILY

Nonhlanhla is a human rights activist. She has three daughters: Mphakiseng, Nhlakanipho and Mpumi. During the apartheid era, she was in the ANC underground, and it was then that she first realised she was attracted to women. She now lives with her partner, Nozipho, a social worker and daughter of a well-known prophet and writer. Nonhlanhla's daughters live with her grandmother, Alinah. Her birth mother is Matlakala, but she grew up believing her aunt, Thabile, was her mother.

Growing Up

'I was raised by my grandfather and grandmother as well as my aunt and my uncle. My grandfather passed away when I was very young. For me, he was my father; he was the main person I was very close to. I ended up being with my grandmother a lot. She was a domestic worker, so during school holidays I went with her to where she worked. My aunt would only come on Saturdays. I grew up believing that she was my biological mother.'

Nonhlanhla

'I was brought up in a family of sangomas who are staunch believers in cultural customs. My father is a sangoma who has made a lot of predictions. I have never really followed in this work, but I really appreciate my father. He does not discriminate among his children; we are all the same. But I believe I am his favourite. My father is beautiful in my eyes, more than all other fathers.'

Nozipho

Nonhlanhla Finds out Why She Wasn't Raised by Her Mother

'When I finally asked why I was not raised by my mother, I was told my father never wanted me as his child and did not want to marry my mother. My grandparents did not want me to live with my mother while she was living with a man who wasn't my biological father. Customarily, my grandfather had to slaughter a goat and introduce me to the Zwane ancestors so they would welcome me as their own child. Then I was able to be called a Zwane. My biological father's surname was Zondo.'

Nonhlanhla

Nonhlanhla Meets Her Biological Mother

'I realised my aunt was not my biological mother when she fell pregnant. Everybody was saying, "That's nice: you are going to have your first-born". I started asking myself, "What am I then?" I was upset. I did not want this child to steal my mother, who did everything for me. When they realised I knew something they took me to my mother and told me who she was.'

Nonhlanhla

Nonhlanhla Meets Her Biological Father

'One day there were some people in a car in my street looking for me. One was claiming that he was my father. My aunt got furious, and we went to ask who they were. A man said, "I am your father." I hid behind my aunt, saying "I already have a father" – my aunt's boyfriend. No one explained to me. [My biological father] also came other times, and once he brought me dungarees. I was so excited that I finally had someone that I could call a father.'

Nonhlanhla

Nonhlanhla's Children Move in with Her Mother

'My children live with my grandmother. I was working to be able to feed them so sent them to live with my mother. But because I am an only child, my mother is very jealous. She said, "Now these are my children. You have to go and find your own children". It is also a traditional thing, because you cannot go with your children if you get somebody new in your life. They try to protect them.'

Nonhlanhla

Nonhlanhla Realises She is Attracted to Women

'In 1995, when I had joined MK [Umkhonto we Sizwe, the ANC's armed wing], I saw a woman passing by, and I said to my comrade, "There is this feeling that I feel for this woman – what am I supposed to do?" She said, "Just go after her and tell her that you love her." I went to her, proposed to her, and she told me it is okay and we fell in love.'

Nonhlanhla

The Comrades React

'The comrades who I told did not have a problem. But the day that we surrendered arms we had a big party. They told us to bring our partners and I was kissing a woman. One comrade, a man, said, "I am not going to tolerate this shit." That night I missed being hit by three bullets. The next day there was a meeting and even the top rank said, "You cannot choose for our comrades whether they are gay or not. It is our comrade and we have to respect each other." Now my comrades do not have a problem.'

Nonhlanhla

Being a Gay Mother
'My kids do not ask too much. We were very close until the twins were victims of a hate crime. I blamed myself because of my sexual orientation. I was not able to protect them; I would rather die. If you touch my children, you have touched me. But I said, let the law take its course, but it never happened that way.'

Nonhlanhla

Nozipho Enters the Family
'I mainly work with children and thought that no one just accepts a person. I thought, "I am not going to fail". I decided to introduce myself to the children one by one. When I asked the twins, "How do you feel with your mother dating other women?" They simply answered, "What's wrong with that, sis Nozipho?" So I figured I was not the first and that the kids were used to it.'

Nozipho

'This child is not like the lion she had before. She knows how to have respect; she feels at home. When you look at it, it's like it's not what we are talking about, this thing of girl to girl. It's like they are friends.'

Alinah

'I love being part of a unit. I love seeing family support each other through thick and thin. But even here in Nonhlanhla's home, I feel that I have found another family. From their side, they must accept me. They must be honest: if there is something wrong that I am doing, they must call me to order. For me they are a good family.'

Nozipho

'For me, family is always there, even if I am sick or something happens. But family is anyone who is close that you treat as your sibling. It can be your friend who is very close to you; then you treat them as part of your family.'

Mpumi

NHLANHLA AND FANNEY
Nhlanhla and Fanney have been romantic partners for thirteen years, though at the time of this interview they had been in a relationship for eight years. They are also business partners and run their own film company. Both live in Soweto – Nhlanhla with his parents and Fanney with his brother. They spend a lot of time at their office. Although they do not live together, each sees the other as his family.

Growing Up
'I was brought up in Soweto. I have two sisters and three brothers. I'm the last one. I left my parents when I was sixteen, and I was living around with my sisters and my aunt. I grew up ambitious, but my mother was very strict. So I thought: let me give her a break. Also, I wanted to be independent.'

Fanney

'I grew up with my parents in Soweto. My father was a political activist, so he sent my two older sisters out of the country. My parents were very protective because of my father's background. They had to know my every move. It was prison-like, but it was a prison with love. My father is very macho, so that created a gap between us; I'm rebellious towards him.'

Nhlanhla

Fanney and Nhlanhla Meet

'I first saw him on TV, dancing, and I thought wow! But at the time I didn't even know there was such a thing as gay. I don't know how, but I got to meet him and I thought, "Great personality!" He was very light. A lot of people in the gay circles are heavy. But because I liked him so much, I kept running away from him.'

Nhlanhla

'He was kind of like shy. I think that's what most attracted me to him. He's very, very neat, but it's not easy to approach a guy and say because you are neat, you must be gay. You need to get to know a person. We started talking about the movie *Punked* and we just clicked. It was like wow, you know, he is very intelligent. We started to be friends.'

Fanney

Fanney and Nhlanhla Create a Family

'In these eight years I have learned a lot from Nhlanhla, and I think he has learned a lot from me. With Nhlanhla I can talk about anything. Also, if you're from the township you live by rules. But with Nhlanhla I can fight for a remote, I can eat, sleep, watch a movie and no one complains *ukuthi* [that "Why are you watching TV in the morning?"]. It's very flexible.'

Fanney

'I think the difference between the family I have with Fanney and my biological family is that I can express myself when I'm with Fanney; I can speak my mind without any restrictions. If we do break up, we'd still be there for each other because we're more than just a couple – we're family. It is a much stronger bond than just being a couple.'

Nhlanhla

Working Together and Sharing a Vision

'We have a film production company. We want to make films that represent gay people. I watch *Generations* and I say, "Why don't they put a gay character into *Generations*?" It's real, it's there! So we do the kind of movies that we do because we're not represented. But at times when we ask for funding, people are reluctant to fund gay movies. I think we need some "edutainment" to educate people about homosexuality.'

Nhlanhla

'Out in Africa [film festival] is trying so hard to create workshops to tell gay stories .When they represent gay people on television, it's like you're slutty and you die. It's like five seconds of the stereotypical gay thing. We have real stories – love stories – that we are trying to represent.'

Fanney

Fanney and Nhlanhla's Relationship with Their Families

'My family is very understanding and very close. I can't do anything without Nhlanhla because any time I say I'm going somewhere they'll say, "Where's Nhlanhla?" We don't have issues and we talk about everything, but not about my sexuality.'

Fanney

'My family is very conservative, very strict, and everything has got to be played by the rules: girls date boys and boys date girls. They are very supportive but not when it comes to my relationship. My father said, "It's not something that I will support, but it's something that I will accept because I wouldn't want to change you."'

Nhlanhla

Dealing with the Outside World

'The guys that stay around my place want to hang around with me.

They want to know how I live my life; they're very curious. They are not sure whether I'm gay or bisexual or straight, because I think I fit in everywhere. They know where I come from, my family; no one will touch me.'

Fanney

'I have experienced a bit of hate crime, but a long time ago. Some guys wanted to beat my friend and me up. When we ran they fired at us. Now the most stressful thing for me is for people to always be pointing at me in the work environment and saying, "Oh, it's the gay one".'

Nhlanhla

ROBERT AND SALLY

Robert is a female-to-male transperson. Three years before this interview, at the age of thirty-seven, Robert began his gender transition, a process that he undertook with the encouragement of his partner, Sally. As well as undergoing hormone therapy, which caused a range of physical changes to Robert's body, he has also had surgery to remove his breasts. His mother, Estelle, his aunt Rina and cousin Ellenor have all supported Robert during his journey, as have Sally's sister, Cathy, and father, Tom. Since taking part in this project, Robert and Sally have married.

Growing Up

'I grew up in a typical white working-class family. My parents got divorced when I was eighteen months old and my mother remarried. We weren't a very touchy-feely family. My stepfather was a very cold, aloof person. The dinner table was not a very warm, communicative place. We would criticise rather than protect each other. My mother tried to keep it together as much as she could, and to make a success of the family she made after having a divorce.'

Robert

'We were a happy family when the children were smaller: Robert, or Adele as she was then called, was like a magnet, and all the children were drawn to her. In high school, she was deputy head girl. But I realised she was different from an early age. As soon as she could tell me what she wanted to wear, she would go straight to the boys' department. It came as no surprise to me when she told me she was gay.'

Estelle

'I grew up in a typical white South African nuclear family. We were middle class; we had a house and a pool. My mum is a strong but quiet person. She is the glue that holds us together. My father is more expressive and explosive. He has always considered himself a champion for the underdog. I think that is where I got my initial education about what it means to be someone who doesn't have power or who isn't taken care of.'

Sally

Robert Meets His Father

'When I was five, my mother told me that my biological father was gay. He didn't play much of a role in my childhood. I met him properly when I was sixteen and suddenly I could understand why I looked the way I do. Also, we had an absolute and immediate comfort in communicating; I felt like I was looking into a mirror. I observed him as the classical gay person who is pained and who could not come to his potential because he was homosexual. I understood the weight that it carried when formulating my own identity, and I was determined not to let that happen to me. Of course, I was born in a better time so it was easier for me to make my own decisions.'

Robert

Robert and Sally

'I met Sally at a party. I think it was then that I decided that I wanted her, but we had a few other paths in our lives before that happened. Even though she was just a friend, she always loved me and showed an interest in me. She was always real, never judgmental. I only pursued her seven years later. Eventually she said yes, and a while later she agreed to marry me. Marriage for me is a very romantic thing with Sally. Also, because I am a transgender person now and living my life as I want, I totally allowed myself to feel the romance that I'd suppressed before, ironically, as a woman.'

Robert

'We are not in a straight or a same-sex relationship. Robert is a transman. So, we first have to deal with my long-time close friends being a little taken aback because they think that I am leaving the "club", the [safety] of being lesbian. I do not think I am doing that. I think it is interesting for me because I realised how much we rely on our friendships and our community for safety. I think a lot of people felt a little afraid, or a little unsure about where my identity was going to go. But I think they're working through it. And they are all unequivocally, completely happy about us getting married.'

Sally

Robert Comes Out as Transgender to His Family

'My mother struggled with the concept of her child altering her/his body. But once she worked through that she has been great. She doesn't have any issues anymore. She has struggled through things like names and pronouns, but on a core level she has totally acknowledged my life as it is.'

Robert

'My aunt has always been a really big support in my life: I never felt her love was ever conditional. She was always there for me in every way she could be. She totally supported the transition from the beginning till now. She is less threatened by other people's identities, as her own identity is very strong. She doesn't feel that what I do bares any reflection on her. She just wants me to be loved.'

Robert

'Whenever Robert comes to Port Elizabeth, he stays with me. To me, he will always be a special person: he is fabulous and I really adore him. This year he will be with Sally's family over Christmas and I will really miss him. I can't imagine Christmas without him.'

Rina

'Years ago there was a programme on *Carte Blanche* about somebody who transitioned. It was a failed operation and he battled to be accepted by society. So when Robert started the process I was worried that he would be hurt as a result of prejudices. But times have changed, and because he is more comfortable within himself now, he naturally attracts a lot of people.'

Ellenor

'The men in my family have been spectacularly awful about my transition. I think my brother and stepfather both suffer from being disempowered white males. If a woman in the family whom they consider weaker than them or they have authority over decides to now declare herself a male; I can imagine how that plays into all their identity stuff.'

Robert

Robert and Identity
'I am a transman, meaning I am a female-to-male transsexual. I'm busy with my transition. I prefer women sexually, although if I really have to state my absolute sexual preference, it would probably be bisexual as I find men sexually interesting too. But I partner with women. Necessarily, up to now I have led the life of a lesbian, which I'm happy about. I always say, "I used to be a lesbian." I think of

myself as queer, but a lot of people see me as a heterosexual man.'

Robert

Sally and Identity
'Gender-wise I am happy with my femaleness. I identify myself as a dyke, which means more than just my sexual orientation to me: it's a political orientation. It means that I place myself in a realm of alternative sexualities and identities. Politically, I am also a feminist. I've had a lot of questions from very good friends about how I can identify as a dyke and be involved with Robert. The lesson I have learned in being with Robert, and in previously being Robert's friend rather than his lover, is that identities are fluid. You can [inhabit] different spaces at the same time. I think often our identities are more about our alliances – who we choose to align ourselves to.'

Sally

BEV AND HER FAMILY

Bev is a television director and a lesbian activist. She grew up in a family of women, including her grandmother, Gladys; her mother, Eaglette; her sister, Tebogo; and her two aunts, both named Elizabeth. Over the years, Gladys and Eaglette's Soweto home has become a safe place for lesbian and gay people needing support, such as Thabo.

Growing Up in a Matriarchal Home
'My father never played any role. My mother made sure I was educated. Whatever I needed was from my mom. My father's family is and was very aloof. They distanced themselves from us. The only one who stayed with us was my father's younger brother. All the others did not like my mother because they said she was too white.'

Eaglette

'Growing up I was scared of my grandmother; everything had to be just so. If you cleaned, it had better be sparkling! We would try and make her laugh and she would shout at us that there was no time to play. I understand her a lot more now: she had a really hard time growing up, and at fourteen had to drop all her dreams to raise her eight brothers and sisters.'

Bev

Bev and Her Mother
'Women have always been at the centre of this family. We didn't wait around for the men to pay. I was a singer, and I went on the road to help support us. It was a problem because my mum had to make sacrifices and I did not raise my kids. But when I wasn't travelling, I was with them.'

Eaglette

'My mum was a big superstar, but she didn't earn very much. To be a singer in the apartheid days was not fun and games: she never got any royalties. When I did get her attention, it was wonderful. By the time I got to my teens, we would get into All Stars and jeans and take a walk in town; I would be her best friend. We have become more like friends than mother and daughter.'

Bev

Bev and Her Father
'My kids have different fathers. Bev's father was a Putco bus driver. When Beverley was born, her father did everything for her, bought everything for her. Then after that, because he was a very silly man, he had about fourteen kids with fourteen different women. He was very naughty, and we parted.'

Eaglette

'I subsequently found out about my father's other kids. I am slowly getting in touch with many of them. They are blood. But our relationships haven't been tested in terms of having to rely on each other or knowing that the other person will be there for you.'

Bev

Bev Tells Her Family that She is Lesbian

'I first used the word "gay" to talk about myself through Boy George. He was the first gay man I heard of who had no shame about saying "I love men". I told my family over Sunday lunch that I was gay. It was as if I had said, "I eat babies". I would ask my grandma and my mum why I couldn't say I was gay. They would say that it is just a white thing.'

Bev

Bev Takes an Overdose

'One day I found that Bev had taken an overdose of tablets. She left a note that nobody loves her. I went to see a psychiatrist and I said, "I know such people to have [genital] organs and I've washed Bev since she was a baby and she is a girl." She said, "It's not that they have two organs, but that they are born with that feeling that they are the opposite sex." I felt hurt because my child nearly died. My priest said that as long as she is respectful and is not up to mischief, then it is okay. From there, we welcomed her.'

Gladys

'I had to learn to accept that Bev is gay. I'm proud of her. If she wants to get married, I'd be happy for her. She is a very respectful child and she doesn't just do things. But for me, marriage is about togetherness and not about a piece of paper – whether you are gay or lesbian or straight.'

Eaglette

Bev Finds a Group of Gay Friends

'I felt very alone, and there was no one to talk to. One day my friend from across the road told me that he was gay too. I used to say that I was going to marry him because he was the only boy I felt comfortable with. We started hanging out with these flamboyant boys. The seven of us would walk down the street; when we were together we didn't care what other people thought. I belonged somewhere for the first time. They count as my first chosen family.'

Bev

Bev is Attacked by a Group Of Men
'I was walking alone and I heard a gang of men talking and saying, "Is it her? Let's get her". I slipped into the barbershop and the guys in the barber escorted me out. As we looked up, my grandmother comes up the street with her hair flying. As she is walking, she's picking up the rest of the neighbours and she's got this huge iron rod. The gang saw what was coming and left. I was overwhelmed by the support.'

Bev

'My sister, Tebogo, is three years younger than me. She is the only sibling I grew up with. I have always been very protective of her. In high school some guy tried to sexually assault her. I beat him up. Oh, did I beat him up! He must have been twice my size, but my rage was so great.'

Bev

An Open Home
'When I grew up, people used to come here and have breakfast, lunch and supper, even the musicians from Babsy Mlangenis, Gordon Morara. Even the priest used to come and eat breakfast, lunch and supper here. We had no money, but God provided. I love to share with people because I never grew up with a brother or sister. My family, to me, is everybody – it's not only my blood.'

Eaglette

'I love many people the same way that I love my family. If I see that people are suffering near me, in my street, I try to share with them. What I love most is when the family is together here at home, for me to talk to them and explain what life is about and how a person should carry themselves.'

Gladys

'My grandmother didn't understand me being a lesbian. I ran away to my father's place and had the same problem there. I was afraid to go home, so I came here. My grandmother used to come here and insult me to them, and tell Bev that she's the one that taught me to be gay. Bev's grandmother knows about lesbians, and she went to my grandmother and tried to put some sense into her. I did eventually go home, but I've been coming to Gladys and Eaglette for twelve years now. I love them so much. They are my family no matter what.'

Thabo

JP AND PAUL

JP is a former priest in the Anglican Church and Paul is a minister in the gay Hope and Unity Metropolitan Community Church (HUMCC), which he helped to establish in South Africa. They met when they were running a soup kitchen for street children in Hillbrow, Johannesburg. JP's wife had left him, and his and Paul's friendship grew into love. JP and Paul have been together for over a decade and, in 2008, they were married under the Civil Union Act. JP now works for INERELA+, an international network of religious leaders – lay and ordained, women and men – living with or affected by HIV.

Desire to Marry

'I want to marry Paul. He has given me the ten most blissfully happy years of my life. Must I forever deny Paul the commitment of my life because my church can't deal with it? It's a hard decision because I know that God has put a calling on my life to be a priest, but he has also put a calling on my life to be in a committed relationship with Paul.'

JP

'After four years, JP started talking about marriage, but it was the last thing on my mind. We were already committed. I have always taken his son as my own real child. He's part of me; he's part of my family. But when JP was sick in hospital and I wasn't allowed to visit him because they said I wasn't family, it was an eye opener. I also started to worry about my own future and security.'

Paul

Views on Each Other
'Paul has an incredible generosity of spirit; I love the way he is protective of people. I love his gentleness with me. I love the way he blusters and shouts and cavorts around without ever meaning a word.'

JP

'JP is a very spiritual person: he is loving and understanding; he's open-minded and willing to sit and listen. I'm very difficult, and he tolerates all my nonsense.'

Paul

Religion and Faith
'When we were first involved, Paul's mom asked me, "How can you live with being a homosexual considering what the Bible says?" This actually gave me a chance to talk to her about what is really recorded in scripture and some of the differences in translation and interpretation. We often bring our own prejudices to scripture. From that day on she has never questioned me and has only supported me.'

JP

On the HUMCC

'We have always done unions, even before the Civil Union Act. If this is what people want, it would be sinful for us to deny them this right. The Civil Union Act is important because of the legalities, but still people feel there is a gap if they do not have a religious wedding. It is something that is sacred to them.'

Paul

RICHARD AND HIS FAMILY

Richard is a specialist standards writer. He had three sons before coming to terms with being gay and deciding to end his marriage. His sons chose to live with him following the divorce. Seven years later, he met William, who moved into their home. His sons Jeremy and Mark are married, and Paul lives with his partner Mia. Richard and William have married under the Civil Union Act. Louise, William's mother, lived with them when this family portrait and interview took place. Louise has since passed away.

Richard Tells His Family He is Gay

'I remember the night my father came out to my mother. The fight was horrendous. My father felt an incredible amount of guilt and remorse, but ultimately he had to come to terms with who he was.'

Jeremy

'I'd only once ever before seen my parents fight – over some furniture or something. I tried to run away to my friend's house because I felt safe there. I think I was quite devastated, because my family was being stripped apart, more than because of my dad coming out.'

Paul

The Boys Move in with Richard

'Jeremy was very angry at first because the family was breaking up, but then our relationship resurfaced and he came to live with me.

After coming out, I really took off as an individual. I started painting again, did a master's degree, got involved in gay activism, and so there was a real buzz in the house.'

Richard

'I have very little time for my extended family, except my grandmother, because they took it upon themselves to convince me that my dad was evil. And this was a period when my mother broke down and couldn't look after me. I mean, how do you take a seven-year-old kid and confuse him like that?'

Paul

'Living with my mother, who was going through a particularly difficult time, was draining. My father was in a better position, both financially and emotionally, to take care of us, so we moved in with him.'

Mark

The Boys' Mother
'My early remembrance is that she was really a wonderful woman. Obviously she took [Richard's coming out] badly and never really managed to find her own kind of strength. We communicate, but not very well.'

Jeremy

'I don't think my mother has any more resentment towards my father. I think what upsets her is that she doesn't feel like she is part of the family. Now I am seeing her more regularly, but again it's not like she is an integrated part of the family.'

Paul

'My ex-wife comes to our major celebrations like Christmas and birthdays. She's not part of the immediate circle but more like part of the extended family.'

Richard

Challenges at School
'Throughout my schooling, I was terrified of people finding out [about his father's sexuality] and being ostracised or beaten up. When I went to Woodmead, I made a rule for myself that if I was going to be friends with somebody, they must know.'

Paul

'At Woodmead, [the children] had a wonderful set of friends and a supportive staff. I got on very well with the other parents because they were very liberal – that's why they sent their children there. The children would have been given hell in a government school for having a gay father.'

Richard

'When I was fourteen, we took part in a TV programme about our family story. There were some snide and ignorant comments at school, but by then I was strong-headed enough to stand up for myself or to ignore those who weren't worth engaging with.'

Mark

Raising Children
'My ideas about raising children had nothing to do with me being gay. I gave my children a lot of freedom because I wanted them to be independent. I wanted there to be closeness not because of blood ties but because of respect for one another. Although we were happy, I did worry whether I was doing the right thing. If I had met William earlier, it would have made my life a lot easier because I would have had some moral support.'

Richard

William Moves in with The Family

'I was a little worried about how my sons would handle it. I was worried that William would find us overwhelming as a family, find us to be a little closed clique. I think he did find it like that sometimes, but he never said so.'

Richard

'I am also a very shy person: usually people have to work very hard to relate to me. But we just allowed it to develop naturally. We were all tolerant with one another. It was about being in a supportive role to Richard and to the boys if they needed it. But it was in the background.'

William

'By the time William joined the household, we were completely comfortable with my dad having boyfriends. But some of his previous relationships had been emotional rollercoasters for him, so there was some apprehension at first. However, having William in the household has over time become the most wonderful and natural thing ever.'

Mark

Richard and William Get Married

'After we had been together for a number of years, we decided we wanted to formalise our relationship. We had contracts drawn up, invited a few friends over, signed the contracts and had a little party.'

Richard

'The actual experience at Home Affairs was quite horrible: we battled and waited, and there were these insecurities that came up that we might be discriminated against. But being recognised by the state and by society – that was a nice feeling! I did not expect it to change the way that we feel towards one another, but actually we feel much closer.'

William

'I couldn't be happier or prouder. They had already been in a long-term happy, stable relationship, so it made complete sense. I am just glad they have had the opportunity to cement their relationship and to give it both the symbolic and legal status it deserves.'

Mark

'For me, it was really just a ceremony that confirmed what I already knew. But I think they came full circle, because my dad couldn't come out for a very long time and was very screwed up about it. He had an abusive father and it was such an oppressive society. Now, finally, the state has admitted it is okay, and that is amazing.'

Paul

'Now that they are married, I actually feel better, because now there is a real connection between the two of them. There's more security, and I think they've reaped the benefit of what happened.'

Louise

Being Part of this Family
'Growing up in this family has taught me, first and foremost, not to judge. It has taught me to be fiercely independent, to stand up for who I am and what I believe. It has taught me to have empathy for people who are in difficult situations. It has shown me very strongly that society changes and that you have to be open and willing to except those changes. And it has shown me that the one true common denominator in a family is love, and one should always be open to that.'

Jeremy

'We are unconventional in many ways. We have basically made up our own religion. I have worked with mysticism and various other systems, so I have worked out a philosophy. We are free thinkers, but if we have opposite points of view, it doesn't cause friction. But we also do the usual things; we are supportive of each other, loving and tolerant, and we give each other space to develop our own interests.'

William

'I've been living here on and off for a year and they are lovely. I feel very at home because I am a very neat and tidy housewife and I like it to be just right, and I find it the same here. It's such a well-organised situation.'

Louise

'Paul's dad let me stay with them when I was having a hard time. Having such a warm, stable daily existence really helped me. They are very loving people.'

Mia

M/Other Families: Some Introductory Comments to the Project

Natasha Distiller and Jean Brundrit

M/OTHER FAMILIES WAS A PROJECT that took place in 2011 under the auspices of the Institute for the Humanities in Africa (HUMA) and the Department of Fine Art, both of the University of Cape Town. It was funded in collaboration with the Women and Gender Studies Department at the University of the Western Cape. With respect to the photographs, the work is based upon research supported by the National Research Foundation. The project comprised a series of interviews with, and portraits of, lesbian-parented families, most of whom live in Cape Town. We represent some of the portraits here, after a brief commentary on the thinking behind the project.

M/Other Families intended to record – and in doing so to engage with the complex issues of representing – what some lesbian-parented families might 'look like'. We also wanted to question visually the viewer's experiences of families and thus his/her expectations of what constitutes a 'family portrait'. Additionally, by displaying extracts from the interviews alongside the life-size photographs, we were able to introduce the families' senses of themselves. Indeed, the ways these families felt – and have experiences being seen as – 'different' and the ways they felt 'the same as' heteronormative families came into focus through the photographs and accompanying text (see picture section).

Almost a decade ago, pioneering scholars of American queer studies compared 'the liberal recoding of freedom as… domesticity, and marriage' to Bush's war on terror, religious fundamentalism, xenophobia, the collapse of the welfare state and so on (Eng et al., 2005:2). They suggest that the move to claim heteronormative privileges for queers is one of the political ills of recent times. Eng et al. (2005:2) ask:

> If mainstream media attention to queer lives and issues has helped to establish the social and legal foundation for the emergence of gay marriage, family, and domesticity, what are the social costs of this new visibility? And how does the demand for marriage and legal rights affect, run counter to, or in fact converge with conservative promotion of traditional marriage?

Here, these scholars are invoking the familiar feminist concern that to demand access to rights as they exist within the current legal and socio-economic framework is a capitulation to – or, more correctly, an endorsement and shoring up of – a patriarchal heteronormative world. But in South Africa, what Eng et al. designate as 'queer liberalism' – the inclusion of people with non-normative sexual identities into the very system that seeks to damn them and thus, to some extent, leading to both a legitimation of that system and a co-option of non-normativity – may be differently inflected.

In South Africa, same-sex-attracted people have the right to marriage. However, we do not currently have the 'problem' of mainstreaming the idea of same-gender families to the point that African lesbian and gay individuals are at any risk of normativity.[27] Rather, we have, despite de jure protection, the opposite problem: the increased vilifying of same-sex love as, by definition, outside of the realm of the human and therefore of the nation. This attitude is clearly endorsed by our leaders. In 2006, a few years before his ascension to the presidency, then-deputy president Jacob Zuma made several homophobic comments at a Heritage Day event, including advocating violence against gays. He told the *Sowetan* newspaper that same-sex marriages are '"a disgrace to the nation and to God"' ('Zuma invokes gay wrath', 2006). In 2009, under Zuma's leadership, Minister of Arts and Culture Lulu Xingwana walked out of an exhibition of women artists at Constitution Hill, Johannesburg. Among the images she objected to were photographs by internationally acclaimed lesbian artist Zanele Muholi. The minister said in a statement after the event that the exhibition was 'immoral, offensive and going against nation building' ('Minister slams "porn" exhibition', 2010).

It is relevant to point out the complicitous potential in working with heteronormativity. But the South African context provides one illustration of why the claiming of human, legal and other existing rights by non-heterosexual citizens might be valuable and important. In our case, it works specifically against the murderous denial of the basic humanity of South Africans who are not heterosexual. This denial is expressed most perniciously in the assertion that homosexuality and other non-heteronormative identities and practices are 'un-African'. In this context, 'queer liberalism' is not at all a right-wing approach: it is an assertion of a recognisable humanity, an intelligibility – *pace* Judith Butler (2004) – in the only terms available to demand recognition by fellow citizens. Such recognition is, for some, a matter of life and death.

The study of what is sometimes called queer families (although the terminology of the Western academy is not seamlessly applicable in South Africa) has over the past forty years developed into a vast international interdisciplinary area. There is an interesting ideological tension in this literature. While feminist analyses of the meanings of queer (usually lesbian-parent) families celebrate the anti-patriarchal nature of such families, much of the empirical literature has tended to focus on how queer (again, usually lesbian-parent) families are not *really* different to heterosexual families in that they produce gender-normative and usually heterosexual children.[28]

There is a clear political investment in such a position: since the study of lesbian-parent families began in the 1970s, a period when courts needed guidance on custody issues, the reassurance that queer parents will not by definition produce queer children was necessary to secure first legal and, later, socio-political rights for these families.[29] It has been important to assert the respectability of families with children parented by (mainly female) homosexuals, although the playing field is increasing, with other kinds of Other families are becoming more viable.

A limitation of the international literature, often noted by its writers, is that it has accessed samples of people who are overwhelmingly middle class and, in almost all cases, white. These individuals have also usually chosen to become parents. Thus, the kinds of families whose functioning has been under international review are far removed from the majority of queer or same-sex-loving South African parents, especially women. Locally, Carien Lubbe (2007; 2008) has begun to chart the implications of the international work already done for the South African situation.[30] There is still much work to be done, especially in capturing the experiences of the majority of same-sex-loving South Africans, before we can begin to make sense of the local situation.

But in the context of our history and current social climate, insisting on the existence and legitimacy of same-gender families in the same terms in which the human rights of others have been argued for is an important political tool. Same-gender families with children are not the only kind of 'alternative' family to deserve legitimacy, of course. But given the politically dominant discourses of reified African identity in circulation, to challenge the component parts of the 'normal' becomes an activist imperative.

The homosexual with children is inserted into society in specific ways. S/he challenges the commonsense assertion that homosexual relationships, because apparently non-reproductive, are fundamentally different in kind from heterosexual partnerships, where the function of relationships – and, by extension, the definition of family – is presumed to be the production and care of children. This reclaiming of the realm of reproduction has specifically local resonances. Henriette Gunkel (2010:30) has summarised how, within the racialising project of apartheid, the policing of sexuality as heterosexuality was crucial: 'The securing of the purity of the "white race" is directly linked to reproduction, and thus to heterosexuality, and... the heterosexual institution: the family.' Asserting that homosexual people can and do reproduce, especially within the recognisable context of the family, offers what is, in fact, a radical challenge to dominant assumptions.

Same-gender families with children stand not only for queer capitulation to the status quo, but also as an unarguable symbol of the ways that homosexuals and other sexual Others should be recognised as equally human, equally African and equally deserving of inclusion in communities. There is always the possibility that the recognition of lesbian and gay rights within the logic of a human rights framework – and as a result the incorporation of people who are not heterosexual into the nation – can serve not to re-inscribe heteronormative structures but to queer them. In the case of South Africa, the successful granting of rights has been read not only as an appropriation but as the realisation of a queerness inherent in the state since the Freedom Charter of 1955 (Oswin, 2007). This reading sees the national recognition of the citizenship of its sexually non-normative members not as a political loss but as a kind of guerrilla warfare.

In 1996, Carl Stychin was already identifying the tensions between the limiting, constitutive nature of rights-based activism and the importance of rights for creating spaces for marginalised people, a tension subsequently confirmed in the South African context by Van Zyl (2009) and Gunkel (2010), among others. This tension is raced and classed. Stacey and Meadow (2009) have pointed out the ways in which the rights of citizenship articulated through the human rights framework mostly accrue to wealthy white individuals. At the same time, Stychin (1996) also points to the importance of the human rights framework for the South African majority, given our history. He emphasises how a discourse of rights ensures the protection of minority rights, even if these do not reflect majority sentiment. In South Africa, lesbian and gay rights are certainly not supported by majority sentiment.

Homosexuality has a history of being constructed as 'outside the nation' (Gunkel, 2010:27), regardless of what that nation is, and a particular history of being constructed as 'un-African'. These are more reasons why it is important to demand recognition for homosexuals in terms of national belonging. The fact that homosexual families, especially if they have children, live inescapably in the nation makes them particular nodal points for arguing the necessity of their citizen rights. Indeed, we suspect it is mostly only elite queers who can afford to refuse this recognition and who can revel in liminality and subversion rather than be oppressed by it. Homosexual nuclear families may endorse the heterosexual norm, as may homosexual life-partnerships formalised in the model of marriage, but they may also simultaneously subvert the very content of the normal.[31] Regardless, the reality of living intelligible lives, especially in the context of raising children, means that access to state-sanctioned rights is not a political or philosophical bone of contention – it is what is necessary to make life livable. The concrete responsibilities of looking after children insert the parents into ordinary, normative daily life in an inescapable way: no matter your politics, when you have to negotiate maternity wards and playgroups and schools, the reliance on the acceptance of the wider community becomes inescapable. The need for social recognition of one's family, of one's status as a parent, of the structure and legitimacy of one's child's life, makes it clear that social intelligibility and the legal protections that follow are exceedingly precious commodities.

This is why we wanted to render intelligible the lives of same-sex-loving South Africans in terms that ensure their rights to life, livelihood and, indeed, family. This 'homonormative' framework is not the only way to understand queer identities and lives in South Africa, or elsewhere, and we would not wish to argue that it should replace alternative identities and life choices. But it is one way to use the system to insist on a recognition of the humanity of queer South Africans in the face of murderous hatred.

M/Other Families is one tiny – and, of course, limited – step in a very long journey; it explores just some of the contours that are mapped above. Most of the families represented in this project are white and middle class. This was partly a function of the theoretical foundations of the project: it grew from an analysis of the international literature on lesbian family functioning. Since we were in some ways doing a small comparative study, white, middle-class lesbians were an obvious starting point. Additionally, the complexities of reaching non-white South African families – from issues of their safety if they participated, to issues of how most same-sex-loving South African women self-identify – meant that this important work needs to wait for a bigger and more inclusive version of this project. We acknowledge that the representation of white, middle-class lesbians is not a representation of the lives or experiences of most South African women who love women. In order to do more fully some of the work we aspire to, this project must expand to include other South Africans, not all of whom will necessarily identify as lesbian or who will be in these nuclear set-ups, or who will have chosen to have children through the fertility clinic systems or adoption. We look forward to working with friends and allies to make this happen.

REFERENCES

Butler, J. (2004). *Undoing gender*. New York and London: Routledge.

Bos, H. M. W., Van Balen, F. & Van den Boom, D. C. (2005). Lesbian families and family functioning: An overview. *Patient Education and Counselling, 59*, 263-275.

Brewaeys, A. & Van Hall, E. V. (1997). Lesbian motherhood: The impact on child development and family functioning. *Journal of Psychosometric Obstetrics and Gynecology, 18*, 1-16.

Child abuse rate at zero per cent in lesbian households: New report finds (2010). *Huffington Post*, 10 October, from http://www.huffingtonpost.com/2010/11/10/lesbians-child-abuse-0-percent_n_781624.html

Clarke, V. (2008). From outsiders to motherhood to reinventing the family: Constructions of lesbian parenting in the psychological literature 1886-2006. *Women's Studies International Forum, 31*, 118-128.

Eng, D., Halberstam, J. & Munoz, J. E. (2005). What's queer about queer studies now? *Social Text, 23*(3-4), 1-17.

Gabb, J. (2004). Crucial differentials: Querying the incongruities within research on lesbian parent families. *Sexualities, 7*(2), 167-182.

Golombok, S., Spencer, A. & Rutter, M. (1983). Children in lesbian and single-parent households: Psychosexual and psychiatric appraisal. *Journal of Child Psychology & Psychiatry, 24*(4), 551-572.

Gottman, J. S. (1990). Children of gay and lesbian parents. In F. Bozett & M. Sussman (Eds), *Homosexuality and family relations*. New York: Harrington Park Press, 177-196.

Gunkel, H. (2010). *The cultural politics of female sexuality in South Africa*. New York: Routledge.

Hoeffer, B. (1981). Children's acquisition of sex-role behaviour in lesbian-mother families. *American Journal of Orthopsychiatry, 51*(3), 536-544.

John, N. (1994). 'Pretended families': On being a gay parent. In M. Gevisser & E. Cameron (Eds), *Defiant desire: Gay and lesbian lives in South Africa*. Johannesburg: Ravan, 342–347.

Lubbe, C. (2007). Mothers, fathers, or parents: Same-gendered families in South Africa. *South African Journal of Psychology*, *37*(2), 260–283.

Lubbe, C. (2008). The experience of children growing up in lesbian-headed families in South Africa. *Journal of GLBT Family Studies*, *4*(3), 325–359.

Marcus, S. (2005). Queer theory for everyone: A review. *Signs*, *31*(1), 191–218.

Minister slams 'porn' exhibition (2010). *Times Live*, 2 March, from http://www.timeslive.co.za/local/article332784.ece

Oswin, N. (2007). The end of queer (as we knew it): Globalization and the making of a gay-friendly South Africa. *Gender, Place and Culture: A Journal of Feminist Geography*, *14*(1), 93–110.

Park, A. (2010). Study: Children of lesbians may do better than their peers. *Time*, 7 June, from http://www.time.com/time/health/article/0,8599,1994480,00.html

Patterson, C. (1994). Children of the lesbian baby boom: Behavioural adjustments, self-concepts, and sex-role identity. In B. Greene and G.M. Herek (Eds), *Lesbian and gay psychology: Theory, research and clinical applications*. London: Sage, 156–175.

Stacey, J. & Meadow, T. (2009). New slants on the slippery slope: The politics of polygamy and gay family rights in South Africa and the United States. *Politics & Society*, *37*(2), 167–202.

Stacey, J. & Biblarz, T. J. (2001). [How] Does the sexual orientation of parents matter? *American Sociological Review*, *66*, 159–183.

Steckel, A. (1985). *Separation-individuation in children of lesbian and heterosexual couples*. (Unpublished PhD dissertation). The Wright Institute Graduate School Berkeley. Available at http://www.apa.org/pi/lgbc/publications/lgpstspec.html, accessed August 2007.

Steckel, A. (1987). Psychosocial development of children of lesbian

Mothers. In F. Bozett (Ed.), *Gay and lesbian parents*. New York: Praeger.

Stychin, C. (1996). Constituting sexuality: The struggle for sexual orientation in the South African Bill of Rights. *Journal of Law and Society, 23*(4), 455–483.

Tasker, F. & Golombok, S. (1997). *Growing up in a lesbian family: Effects on child development*. London and New York: Guilford.

Van Zyl, M. (2009). Beyond the Constitution: From sexual rights to belonging. In M. van Zyl & M. Steyn (Eds), *The prize and the price: Shaping sexualities in South Africa*. Cape Town: HSRC Press.

Zuma invokes gay wrath (2006). *News24.com*, 26 September, from http://www.news24.com/SouthAfrica/News/Zuma-invokes-gay-wrath-20060926

M/Other Families Interview Extracts

C & D

C: Just before she gave birth there were people saying to us, oh, you know, 'Ooh god, get your rest now', 'Just you wait', that kind of thing, but no one tells you the level of joy that you have, when you have them. No one tells you the extent of the work and no one tells the extent of the joy.

D: I think that we always knew that we wanted to be moms, and, and for us it was always about the question of how we were going to go about it. And initially I thought that us going for artificial insemination wasn't going to be the best option for her because if she wanted to know where her biological other half was coming from then she should have the right to know that.

C: So we made a choice to try the process with a friend of ours. We tried the natural route… But then all of a sudden it felt really as if we had a third person in our relationship. Eventually it just became way too much for me. So we stopped doing that, and that's when we explored the option of going for artificial insemination… I had to get my head around that, because I was the one that was very adamant that I wanted A to know the other biological half, and in a way I still feel as if I've robbed her of being able to, when she might want to, when she's older… The way that we've satisfied ourselves is to say well, later on when we have the conversation with her, to be able to say to her, 'You know what, my girl, we tried that route, because we wanted to give you that option, but it wasn't going to work, and we had to go this route.'

C: We as lesbians have to work so much harder than straight people to have children, and I think that's the one thing that gets me the most angry when you see people who just basically have them and then don't want them, or don't care about them. It just makes me so sad, because you know you have this group of people out there who have the argument, 'Oh you know, gay people shouldn't have children', and in actual fact, you say to yourself, 'My god, how dare you judge me, and how dare you say that to me, because we're going to make fantastic parents. 'Cos we're gonna want them.' We want them and we're going to invest energy and time and effort into our children. I mean, we really want our kids, we really do, and we have to go through so much, try so much harder and pay so much money and, and go through all the horrible drugs to get them and all the comments and all the people judging and that kind of thing, and then at the end of the day we end up with the most wonderful, wonderful children.

D: When I brought A to C's work and the woman said, 'Oh so who's the mom?', and I said, 'No, we're both moms'. 'Ja but who's the mom?' And she wouldn't let up until I said, 'Okay, I'm the mom'.

C: I feel a bit sad, and I feel like, you know, as if they don't acknowledge me as her mom as well, then I feel I've become invisible in the whole equation and in society. So it does make me feel sad, and I won't say it makes me angry, 'cos I just don't allow those things to make me angry, but it makes me sad because, I mean you know, she's my pride and joy.

NA & NI

Na: D's got four mothers that for her play different roles. Yeah, like that is not very normal kind of family according with the rules of what is a family. And ja, is a very beautiful but complicated situation to understand. For us it's very easy, and very clear, but for the rest of the people it's complicated. Can you imagine L in the school, telling to the teachers and to the friends, 'That was my mother and my other mother. [And] my sister is Columbian, and my sister's got another sister from the other mother, and my sister's got another mother that is living in Cape Town but is my aunty'. That is a little bit difficult to understand [*laugh*].

Ni: If she does an oral, in the class, she'll speak about her family and she'll speak about it like it is, and up till now it looks like the teachers have been quite, almost protective. They don't allow kids to make fun of it, but she's also quite assertive, so up till now she's not raised any issue. But that's up till now, we don't know how, as she gets older, what... She's ten.

I was married before, and I divorced my husband and that's when I started living with Na. So she's got a dad.

Na: I adopt D with my ex-husband but she didn't have contact with him, because we have split when she was like six months old. And it was no contact with him. Not because my decision, was more because his decision. And D grow with no father. And I promise you, looking L, and looking D, their development is not different. The development is the context like you make for them, like the life and the clarity of the life, and the total security to know that they belong to a family and they can account with that family for what everything they need. I think that is the most important thing. I don't think, D's got different problems because she didn't grow with the father, or she didn't have a father figure.

Na: That is true. And we can't change the social concept about what is a family, but we can give the strength to the children to deal with that. And that is what we try to do.

Na: I enjoy the situation, because our family got many different things. We are many different races in the family, we have different languages. We've got different surnames. Each of us has a different surname. Like that our family's totally different like whatever family you can find, but like a different kind of nuclear family too, because we are together and we look after each other. And that is something that is very strange for people. But what we are finding, more than rejection is admiration. For example, the thing of internal roles in the family in the house, how to deal with the day-to-day in the house, they say that we are lucky because in the house everyone share everything and it's not that I need to be in charge of only these things, even if in the background each of us have some clear responsibilities.

Ni: I don't know, maybe all of us want some kind of unit, and we've had to work at it. I mean we've all had to do something very clear and very consciously. For me it certainly was my first real experience of working at building a family. You know it was always just there or you took it for granted, and here none of that could be done, it couldn't be done like that, it was something we had to work at.

Na: In all our different interactions, I think the strongest one is D and L. They are sisters, and nobody can argue about that and they look after each other, and they fight when they want to fight, but we can't do anything to L, because D jump to defend L. We can't say anything bad about D, because L kill us! They act like real sisters, and they are very proud of each other. But like I said to you, this nice situation that we are here, now, was not for free, we need to work about that. But it's not impossible.

N & L

N: One of the reasons getting pregnant was so unpleasant is because, it's a fertility clinic and the whole medical system is set up for people with problems. Where there's something wrong that has to be fixed. I don't have a fertility problem. What's wrong and needs to be fixed is that I'm gay. So, I went through the whole thing with this feeling like, you know, the thing that's wrong here, or the thing that isn't right, or the thing that needs intervention is my sexuality.

L: I'm just thinking at the same time, if you gonna go with that metaphor, what you're fixing is the fact that I can't put sperm in you, that's what you're fixing, and, you know that's, ja, I mean, that is a weird thing for me, because I do believe that the biology thing – gay's not natural – is bogus, but when it comes to the thing of having children, biologically, you need the sperm.

And I was very adamant that I actually didn't want the same sperm across both children, because for me that made the donor more significant, and I really wanted the donor to be kind of irrelevant in our lives. But then I actually had an interesting shift after the birth of J. When he was one year old, I just suddenly realised he's not insignificant, the donor. I had this feeling of gratefulness towards the donor, and that was quite a shift for me.

L: You know, for me, it's right that you should work very, very hard to get a child, because it needs to be that much of a considered process. Pretty much I'm glad that it was a considered and difficult process, and maybe that's the way it should be for everyone.

N: We really, really wanted these kids. You have to really [*laugh*] want them to go through it.

L: There's no blaming the child in this instance because you know they had absolutely nothing to do with the fact that they're here, you know, you very much invoked them.

L: I had a connection with J, I honestly believe, long before he came out of the womb. That's been the same with both the boys. I'm very, like, I'm able to engage and be there and whatever and, ja, so I am a mother. You have made this conscious decision, and now it's your job to make sure that this child is as safe from all the bad things in the world as they can be, as it is every person's job, every parent's job. So, there is this huge responsibility.

You end up having to say over and over, you have to declare who you are and that's tiring, that's very tiring, but you also have to do it for the sake of the children, 'cos you don't want them to feel invisible, or hidden or that your family's invisible or hidden. It goes against my personal grain of who of I am, 'cos I'm private and quiet.

Once I took J to the doctor when he was about eight months old or so, and we were sitting in the waiting room, and the receptionist looked and, 'Oh cute' you know how they always coo and, and she said, 'He's so his mother's son, it's unmistakable'. I let, I let it slide you know, it's like I passed.

N: You know, I used to think it was weird to talk about 'my wife', and

I used to think it was aping something and used to be quite hostile, like it's not something I'd ever want to do, but actually L is my wife, that feels like what she is, and I often want to say 'my wife' and I don't because I'm worried that people will laugh at us. I mean it seriously, and I don't want it not to be taken seriously, I don't want people to think it sounds weird, so that's why I tend not to use it except to people who I know will take it seriously.

SECTION 3

Negotiating Parenthood: Expectations, Processes and Experiences

'Two Women Can't Make a Baby': South African Lesbians' Negotiation with Heteronormativity around Issues of Reproduction

Natalie Donaldson and Lindy Wilbraham

EMERGING FAMILY FORMS

HISTORICALLY, THE 'FAMILY' IS AN institution constructed along heteronormative terms, where biological reproduction positions one parent as the male father and the other as the female mother (Dalton & Bielby, 2000). This view of the 'traditional' family has been difficult to deconstruct, since it is entangled in patriarchal cultural assumptions about gender and sexuality. Hegemonic understandings of family, gender and sexuality are based on what is considered natural and normal, where 'natural' and 'normal' are determined by biological processes (Dalton & Bielby, 2000; Lubbe, 2007; Neophytou, 1994). However, since the considerable gains of the feminist movement towards equal rights in education, employment and reproduction, many women have been able to construct families where, in some cases, a man is not included as one of the parents (Dunne, 2000). Related to equal rights are the biomedical advances in assisted reproductive technologies (ARTs), developments that have given individuals the opportunity to conceive children without 'engaging in any sexual activity at all with a member of the opposite sex' (Lubbe, 2007:273). The increased availability of ARTs, both locally and internationally, has meant that there are now more options available for single men and women, as well as same-sex couples, leading to more freedom regarding how they will conceive. Within the South African context, additional factors – for instance, the death of biological parents due to HIV/AIDS, or recent legislation allowing same-sex couples to adopt and co-parent children – have also meant that traditional views and caretaking practices of the family are being displaced by more 'non-traditional' family formations (Lubbe, 2007; 2008). Thus, it has become difficult for researchers to speak of one dominant family structure, since families in South Africa now take on many forms (Bozalek, 2006; Lubbe, 2007; 2008; Sunde & Bozalek, 1995).

Dunne (2000:11) contends that same-sex couples choosing to become parents 'presents a radical and radicalizing challenge to heterosexual norms that govern parenting roles and identities'. Put simply, in same-sex couples choosing to become parents, the biological imperative that dictates there be one male father and one female mother is destabilised, thereby challenging the assumption that heterosexual parenting is the only 'natural' and 'normal' means of conceiving and raising a child. Arguably, it is lesbian couples using anonymous donor insemination who present the greatest challenge to heteronormativity, since the physical presence of a male figure is removed (Chabot & Ames, 2004; Dalton & Bielby, 2000; Dunne, 2000). The South African post-apartheid Constitution of 1996 is the first in the world to explicitly prohibit discrimination on the basis of sexual orientation (Reddy, 2006; Van Zyl, 2011). This inclusion of this protection has led to the legalisation of same-sex marriage along with equal benefits for same-sex couples, rights to adoption and co-parenting rights. However, South Africa is still deeply heteronormative in terms of its views on sexualities and gender.

Indeed, even with this liberal constitutional framework, dominant family ideologies still posit the 'traditional' Western, middle-classed model as the ideal, and it is against this standard that other family units are measured (Bozalek, 2006; Lubbe, 2007). As a result, even though few families conform to this nuclear structure, there exists a 'familist ideology' (Sunde & Bozalek, 1995:26) that positions the nuclear formation as the most desirable and effective family structure for meeting the social, economic, emotional and psychological needs of individuals within capitalism. What this means is that all other family forms (for instance, single-parent families or lesbian/gay-headed families) are pathologised as 'missing' something or someone vital and essential for a child's healthy development (Bozalek, 2006; Kruger, 2003; 2006; Lubbe, 2007; 2008).

DISCOURSES AROUND SAME-SEX SEXUALITIES IN SOUTH AFRICA

While lesbian/gay-headed families are becoming increasingly visible and, to some extent, more acceptable, heteronormative discourses still exert considerable influence on the cultural acceptance of lesbian and gay individuals and, as a result, on how same-gendered families are perceived. These heteronormative understandings predominantly manifest within religious and cultural discourses in which religious and cultural prescriptions are used to determine what is moral, natural and normal. Lubbe (2007:267) argues that religious discourses, specifically Christian discourses, are "probably the most deeply entrenched discourse[s]" within South African society. A telling example of these religious discourses was found in an exploratory study conducted by Sanger and Clowes (2006) with ten heterosexual men and women in the Western Cape. Sanger and Clowes found that participants drew on religious discourses to justify and legitimise their arguments that same-sex relationships were amoral, unnatural and abnormal. In putting forward arguments such as 'not in the plan of God' and 'not what God intended for creation' (Sanger & Clowes, 2006:41), participants positioned heterosexuality as the only moral, natural and normal way to be. Similarly, traditional African cultural discourses have constructed same-sex sexualities as 'un-African', and thereby unacceptable, illegitimate, abnormal and unnatural (Reddy, 2006). What makes religious and cultural arguments so convincing is that they contain an emotive power that serves a 'performative operation because it articulates a call to action' (Reddy, 2002:167). By arguing that same-sex sexualities are practices that originate from colonial European or 'Western' countries, same-sex sexualities are strongly positioned as being foreign and, by extension, dangerous in that they challenge and pollute the taken-for-granted ways of doing things in local contexts. The result is that same-sex sexualities become seen as practices that need to be eradicated in order for the country to sustain itself and to progress (Reddy, 2002). Therefore, it is through this emotive power that culture and religion are able to 'act as a barrier in the fight against patriarchal and heteronormative notions of sexuality' (Bhana et al., 2007:135).

Given the conservative heteronormative cultural context of South Africa and the predominant view that same-sex sexualities are amoral and unnatural, it is inevitable and unsurprising that lesbian-/gay-headed families would create tension. It is also safe to assume that this heteronormative culture would affect the reproductive decisions that lesbian women make when they decide to become parents. The question that needs to be asked then is how heteronormative rules for reproduction and child rearing inform the reproductive decisions that same-sex couples make. In other words, what factors are involved in the decision-making processes of same-sex couples when talking about the various options for conception, in a context that still deems same-sex sexualities as abnormal and abhorrent?

SAME-SEX COUPLES AND REPRODUCTIVE DECISION-MAKING

For same-sex couples, becoming parents is often a deliberate process that is 'multilayered and complex' (Chabot & Ames, 2004:348) in terms of the decisions involved. Lesbian couples, for example, need to decide whether to adopt or use ARTs. If they choose to use ARTs, then the couple needs to decide which partner will carry the child, whether a known or anonymous donor will be used, whether to tell friends and family about the method of conception, and how they will handle questions around paternity when the child is old enough to ask (Chabot & Ames, 2004; Dalton & Bielby, 2000; Dunne, 2000; Touroni & Coyle, 2002). The process of reproductive decision-making for lesbian women has received considerable research attention in the United States and the United Kingdom. Studies have found that many lesbian couples opt for donor insemination since this is deemed by them to be the easiest and quickest means of forming a family when compared to the legalities of adoption (Chabot & Ames, 2004; Gartrell et al., 1996; Patterson, 1998; Touroni & Coyle, 2002). In addition to the concerns around legal rights, some of the lesbian women in a study conducted by Chabot and Ames (2004) argued that donor insemination was chosen because they did not feel that they should be excluded from the experience of giving birth. Research has also found that same-sex couples who chose an anonymous donor made this decision to avoid legal battles should the male donor later want contact with the child, while those who chose a known donor did so in order to have a male role model for their child (Chabot & Ames, 2004; Gartrell et al., 1996; Patterson, 1998; Touroni & Coyle, 2002).

More qualitative research has focused on the experiences of lesbian couples around parenting and reproductive decision-making within contexts that are still very heteronormative.[32] Dalton and Bielby (2000) conducted interviews with lesbian mothers in California and found that these women attempted to actively challenge heteronormative understandings of reproduction and parenting. For example, the women argued that the term 'mother' should not be limited by biology and that motherhood encompasses more than just giving birth and sharing a genetic connection to a child. Also, because two women were the primary caregivers for the child(ren), this meant that parenting responsibilities were shared and not allocated according to the gender or sex of the parent. Similar conclusions were found by Dunne (2000) in her interviews with lesbian women in the UK. However, the primary discourses used by the women in both these studies often reinforced heteronormative understandings of reproduction and parenting. For example, donors were often referred to as 'fathers', which further reinforces the association between gender, reproduction and parenting (Dalton & Bielby, 2000). Furthermore, the majority of women believed that a male 'father figure' still needed to be present in the lives of the child(ren) for healthy social, emotional and psychological development (Dunne, 2000). Hequembourg's (2004) study looked specifically at the strategies used by lesbian mothers in New York when dealing with the difficulties they face within a heteronormative social context. The most common strategy employed by these women was to make their families appear as 'normal' as possible, where 'normality' was measured against heterosexual familial norms. For instance, the women in this study would formalise their families through commitment ceremonies, events that often resembled heterosexual weddings, and second-parent adoptions. Hequembourg concluded that there appeared to be very little desire to challenge heteronormativity, but rather a strong need to be assimilated into existing social structures and to not be seen as different to heterosexual counterparts.

Locally, lesbian parenting and reproductive decision-making has not received as much scholarly attention. While research exploring the experiences of same-sex sexualities in South Africa is growing, only a small portion of this research focuses on the experiences of lesbian/gay parents.[33] Furthermore, research looking at the reproductive decision-making processes of same-sex couples who wish to become parents is virtually non-existent. This chapter therefore contributes to the local and international body of research in the area of lesbian women's reproductive decision-making. In doing this, it is important to look at how heteronormativity 'shapes the experiences, identities, and discourses' (Oswald et al., 2009:45) of lesbian women and how lesbian women appropriate, negotiate and resist heteronormativity when making decisions around reproduction and parenting. This chapter thus makes a significant contribution to the field of lesbian and gay research by exploring the discourses lesbian women draw on in an attempt to achieve a sense of social acceptance and normalcy in a culture that still regards lesbian sexualities as deviant and unnatural.

METHODOLOGY

This chapter is drawn from a discursive study that used three focus-group discussions to investigate how a self-identified lesbian audience interprets and talks about fictional representations of lesbian women in two South African televised dramas: *Society* and *The Mating Game*.[34] *Society* featured representations of black lesbian women, while *The Mating Game* featured a representation of a white lesbian woman. There is limited lesbian representation in South African fictional television programmes, and these two examples were chosen as they were the only fictional programmes featuring lesbian characters at the time the research commenced. The media representations themselves were not analysed, but rather used as a means of generating discussion. According to Hall (1997a:9), representation – how an event, object or person is described, portrayed, depicted or symbolised in various media – is constitutive of events, objects and people, in that there is never 'one, true meaning'. Rather, meaning depends on the meaning that individuals give to the event, object or person. However, meaning can only be attached to the images presented by the media if and when audience members are able to position themselves in relation to the image (Hall, 1997b). In other words, representations hold a socially conventional identity claim, and the media makes available various subject positions for individuals to appropriate, negotiate with and/or resist. Hall (1997b) argues though that individuals 'subject position' themselves within a discourse that makes the most sense to them and, by doing this, the individual becomes subject to the meanings, power and regulations of largely hegemonic discourses.

Using Wetherell's (1998) critical discursive psychology approach, the broader research explored how young self-identified lesbian participants appropriate, negotiate and resist the lesbian subject positions presented in three clips from the two television programmes. Wetherell's critical discursive psychology explores the context-specific nature of discourse as well as the wider social, cultural and institutional context within which discourse is produced. This approach was chosen as it would provide insights into how and why the participants utilised certain discourses within the context of the focus-group discussion, as well as the wider social and cultural implications of these discourses for lesbian women. There are three important analytical tools in Wetherell's approach: (1) identifying the subject positions made available in participants' discourse; (2) identifying and analysing the interpretative repertoires – the everyday language, clichés, metaphors or anecdotes – that the participants use in arguing, describing and evaluating the subject positions made available; and (3) identifying and analysing the ideological dilemmas that occur when participants draw on contradictory discourses and find themselves occupying a troubled position that they need to work to repair. The ideological dilemmas present moments of crisis and instability in meaning that could reproduce heteronormative ideologies and power relations or that could work to unsettle, undermine, resist and transform these ideologies and power relations.

Two of the three focus groups used in the broader research included black and white lesbian participants. However, the pilot focus group, from which the excerpt used in this chapter is drawn, comprised five white self-identified lesbian women between the ages of twenty and twenty-six. All of the women in the pilot focus group were reading towards undergraduate degrees in the social sciences and came from middle- to upper-class backgrounds. What will be shown in the excerpt and discussion that follows is how participants used heteronormative discourses in their group discussion around reproduction and lesbian sexualities.

THE UNNATURAL AMORAL LESBIAN

In choosing which clips to use for the focus group the researchers drew on the advice of various discourse researchers (Parker, 1997; Puchta & Potter, 2004; Wilbraham, 2006). The suggestions were to choose clips that include subject positions that would generate interesting discussions and, most importantly, would aid in answering the research questions. The excerpt featured below forms part of a discussion that took place in response to a clip from *The Mating Game*. This clip was chosen because it was controversial and the researchers felt that it would generate interesting group discussions. Furthermore, it would answer the research question of how lesbian women are positioned in fictional South African television programmes and how a lesbian-identified audience negotiates with these subject positions. The clip presented the character Sara, a white lesbian medical doctor, in an intimate situation with a man who had been a patient of hers. It becomes clear in the scene that Sara's intention was to have unprotected sex with the man and, without his knowledge or consent, to get pregnant.

This clip generated much discussion and heated debate – that is, ideological dilemmas and troubled positions – with participants vehemently resisting this representation. Participants first argued that the representation was positioning lesbian women as deceitful and as the stereotypical lesbian predator. However, as the discussion progressed and participants were asked to relate this to their own experiences, or to the experiences of lesbian women they knew, this resistance moved towards negotiating with this representation. This excerpt was chosen for this chapter as it provides some insight into how the participants talked about reproduction and parenting in relation to lesbian sexualities.

> Tarryn: She was heartbroken and desperate, and all she wants is a family. I don't know. I guess she has the money, she could've done it other ways, I guess, but–
>
> Jessica: Maybe she wants natural conception though, not everybody–
>
> Stephanie: Ja, but what lesbian in their right mind would want a guy to give her natural conception?!
>
> Jessica: Because not everyone, not all lesbians believe in being insemin–, being artificially inseminated–
>
> Marie: Ja, maybe it's not about the actual act.
>
> Jessica: I, I always thought my whole life that I, I was gonna get artificial insemination and now I'm like, but can you play God? Is that okay to play God? Like, I don't know: God created, or whoever or whatever created, the fact that people have sex, that's our natural thing, that man and a woman have sex. We're designed that way: to have sex, to have a baby. That's how we were made – two women can't make a baby–
>
> Stephanie: That's because then all women would be lesbians.
>
> Jessica: But [*laugh*] ja, I just feel that if I wanted to have, if I honestly wanted to have a baby, I would sleep with a guy, perhaps like the same way as like Tina and Bette [referring to *The L Word*, an American television drama series] wanted to have a threesome, make it about all of us creating a baby together. Personally, that is my opinion, like, I wouldn't, I always thought that I'd go the other way, but I, I don't think that I actually would, like, I don't wanna tell my kids how I created them–

Tarryn: Okay, but then also, what about straight couples who can't(!) have children and they have artificial insemination, then is it the same argument, you playing God, is it?

Jessica: I'm not saying it's an argument, I'm just saying some people, some lesbians(!) could have the same idea that it's not right to, to say okay now I'm gonna have a baby, I'm gonna have artificial insemination. Some might say, be like, yes I don't want to sleep with a man, I don't, you know what I mean, but I wanna have bab–, a baby, and I agree with natural conception. It's not about lesbians in the right mind, it's just, when it comes to your child, what's the best thing to do?

An ideological dilemma occurred in the participants' attempts to understand why the lesbian character would voluntarily have unprotected, penetrative sex with a man in order to conceive a child when there are alternative reproductive options available to her as a wealthy (white) woman. In South Africa there are a wide variety of options available, such as adoption and ARTs, for women who want to have children. The talk in this group, however, did not include any discussion around the option of adoption, but rather speculating on why the character chose the heterosexual penetrative method and why this method was better than using ARTs. It is clear then that, from the outset of this discussion, heteronormativity was the participants' primary discursive resource in engaging with the representation in the clip.

Tarryn attempts to provide an explanation using emotive language such as 'heartbroken and desperate'. Tarryn's repetition of 'I guess' works as a rhetorical strategy known as hedging, which is employed to make the meaning of an argument unclear and provisional and to avoid offence (Puchta & Potter, 2004). The use of 'I guess' also indicates uncertainty and demonstrates that Tarryn is struggling to make sense of this scene. Jessica provides a solution to this confusion, arguing that maybe Sara wanted to have a baby through 'natural conception'.

The dominant subject position made available in Jessica's argument is that lesbian women who have children through 'alternative' means (i.e. 'artificial insemination') other than heterosexual sex (i.e. 'natural conception') are 'playing God' and are, therefore, unnatural and amoral. An ideological dilemma is created by Stephanie's immediate challenge of Jessica's argument by exclaiming 'what lesbian in their right mind would want a guy to give her natural conception?!' Jessica is then met with a potentially embarrassing situation and is forced to justify her comment and repair the troubled position that her comment has created. In the process of attempting to repair this troubled position, Jessica uses three discursive strategies: discourses of nature, of religion and of the concept of the 'good mother'. All three discursive strategies work to reinforce heteronormative understandings of gender, reproduction and parenting.

CONFLICT BETWEEN NATURE, RELIGION AND LESBIAN SEXUALITIES

In talking about reproduction, the lesbian women in this study ascribed to the culturally pervasive idea of biological reproduction and heterosexual sex as 'natural conception'. This is evident in Jessica's distinction between natural conception and artificial insemination. In South Africa, from both a biomedical and legal perspective, all forms of ART are considered legitimate methods for women to conceive children. With fertility rates dropping significantly over the past couple of decades, the use of various ARTs has increased, especially among middle- to upper-class women and couples who have the necessary financial resources (Palamuleni et al., 2007; Van Balen & Gerrits, 2001). This said, it appears in the above excerpt that heteronormativity is rooted in popular social discourses that refer to ARTs as 'artificial insemination'. While this term is a lay understanding of ARTs, Farquhar (1996:45) argues that the word 'artificial' in relation to ARTs has a 'naturalizing effect'. Clarke

(2001:561) agrees with this, adding that the use of 'naturalness' as a rhetorical device includes issues of morality and has implications for what is considered 'good, healthy and virtuous'. Jessica explicitly positions heterosexual sex as natural in her continuous use of the phrase 'natural conception' and in arguing that men and women are 'designed' to 'have sex to have a baby' and that 'two women can't make a baby'. The positioning of heterosexual sex as natural and normal implies that any other means of conceiving a child – including heterosexual women who cannot get pregnant without ARTs – is abnormal and unnatural (Farquhar, 1996). Jessica includes a religious discourse in her argument through her repetitive questioning around whether it is acceptable to 'play God'. This religious discourse is one that is rooted in fundamentalist Christian understandings of reproduction, where human beings are viewed as predominantly biological creatures created through heterosexual sex, and any human interference with biological processes is considered unnatural and meddling with God's creation. In assimilating nature and religion, Jessica draws on two emotive and powerful rhetorical strategies that work to place her in a position of moral authority over what is considered 'right' and 'wrong' (Peck, 1994). As Clarke (2001) argues, the moral imperative is clearly evident in the use of phrases such as how it is meant to be, or as in Jessica's argument of 'that's how we're made'.

Positioning ARTs as artificial insemination is a rhetorical strategy that Jessica employs to add credence to her argument and is an attempt to repair the troubled position she has created. However, in using the term artificial insemination and pushing it up against 'natural' conception, Jessica's discourse works to reinforce the heteronormative ideology that procreation outside of heterosexual sex is unnatural and, therefore, wrong and immoral. Jessica's argument also resembles the arguments used in Sanger and Clowes' (2006:41) study, mentioned earlier, where heterosexual participants used similar arguments such as 'not in the plan of God' to justify their positioning of same-sex sexualities as unnatural and abnormal. In social and cultural debates, individuals and institutions who oppose lesbian/gay parenting often use the biological argument that 'men and women are designed to procreate' (Clarke, 2001:561). Thus, it is interesting that Jessica would use a heteronormative framing of reproduction that has served to oppress and discriminate against a social group that she is part of. However, heteronormativity is so pervasive in our social and cultural worlds that it also works to dominate in 'unconscious or inconspicuous ways' (Lubbe, 2007:264).

Jessica is clearly dealing with an ideological dilemma in trying to negotiate between powerful discourses around nature and religion, and her own sexuality. This is not surprising, since religious or spiritual challenges are 'at the heart of the gay or lesbian experience' (Buchanan et al., 2001:436). In interviews conducted with lesbian women in Johannesburg, Smuts (2011) found that one of the primary challenges faced by lesbian women who also consider themselves religious or spiritual is an internal struggle to reconcile their faiths with their sexualities. The participants either avoided religious practices, viewing them as sites of heterosexist discrimination and prejudice, or they did not disclose their sexualities out of fear of being rejected and isolated. For many participants, attempting to reconcile their lesbian sexualities with their religious beliefs or upbringing tended to create feelings of guilt and shame (Smuts, 2011). Same-sex sexualities go against many fundamentalist Christian teachings, so in advocating for natural conception, Jessica is able to make a kind of compromise whereby she gets to accept her lesbian sexuality while also allaying possible feelings of guilt and shame. As Buchanan et al. (2001:437) argue, in a culture or society where particular religious beliefs are considered paramount, an individual will often use those religious beliefs to 'achieve acceptance, societal status, or personal desires for security'. Here it seems as if Jessica is using a heteronormative understanding of reproduction to achieve some form of social acceptance and 'normalcy'. That is, in adhering to doctrines around

Home Affairs Exhibition Materials

Nonhlanhla and Her Family

© Sabelo Mlangeni – GALA

L to R (standing): Mphakiseng, Nozipho, Nonhlanhla, Nhlakanipho, Mpumi
L to R (seated): Thabile, Alinah, Matlakala
Interview extract on page 93

Nhlanhla and Fanney

L to R: Nhlanhla and Fanney
Interview extract on page 97

Robert and Sally

Robert and Sally holding photographs of
L to R (top): Cathy and her children; Robert and Estelle; Sally and Cathy
L to R (bottom): Ellenor and George; Rina and Ellenor; Tom and grandchild
Interview extract on page 100

Bev and Her Family

L to R (seated): Elizabeth, Elizabeth, Bev, Gladys and Eaglette
On floor: Thabo and Tebogo
Interview extract on page 104

JP and Paul

L to R: Paul and JP
Interview extract on page 108

Richard and His Family

L to R (standing): Jeremy and Richard
L to R (seated): Louise, William, Mia and Paul
Interview extract on page 110

M/Other Families exhibition materials

Portrait of C and D's Family

Interview extract on page 126

Portrait of Na and Ni's Family

Interview extract on page 128

Portrait of N and L's Family

Interview extract on page 130

reproduction set out in fundamental Christian texts, Jessica is able to position herself as moral and, therefore, normal and acceptable.

Stephanie, in response to Jessica's support of 'natural' conception, attempted to use humour as a means of re-establishing a light-hearted context, joking that 'all women would be lesbians' if they did not have to rely on men to conceive children. Jessica laughs at this comment, but the joke appears to be mostly ignored and brushed off. Wetherell (2001) refers to matters of 'stake' in social interaction, which affect how a speaker is viewed by those s/he is speaking to. Stephanie's joke indicates to Jessica that she has not yet finished repairing the troubled position she has found herself in and Jessica needs to rectify this in order to regain a positive presentation in the group. Following this, she attempts to repair this position by explaining how she envisions an ideal method of conception. Jessica argues that a possible ideal way of conceiving a child would be through a 'threesome' where a lesbian couple has sex with one another and a man. In doing this, Jessica positions a threesome as more natural than artificial insemination. Jessica's religious and natural argument is on shaky ground here since many religions would not condone a threesome since it involves sex outside of a monogamous relationship. However, Jessica's argument seems to be a form of compromise, of hiding behind powerful heteronormative imperatives for sex and reproduction. A threesome would enable a woman to reconcile the expectation of natural conception while ensuring the acceptance of a lesbian sexuality, as if they are all 'creating a baby together'

The threesome also conforms to heteronormative representations of lesbian sexualities seen in pornography and some contemporary Hollywood films. Representations of women's sexualities are predominantly constituted within the male gaze and threesome representations play into the stereotypical heterosexual male fantasy of watching women having sex, a positioning that serves to keep lesbian sexualities non-threatening in a heteronormative world (Diamond, 2005). Diamond argues that this explicit representation of lesbian sexualities can be seen as a representation of women's sexual freedom, where women are now being positioned as able to want and enjoy sex with different kinds of people. However, drawing on the feminist theory of Rich (1980), such representations of lesbian sexualities mean that 'compulsory heterosexuality' is left unchallenged. So, in Jessica using a threesome as the ideal way of conceiving a child, heterosexual sex is still regarded as the benchmark for normality, morality and naturalness. Jessica's argument implies that, since there is a man involved who will impregnate one or both of the women, this is deemed more natural and more acceptable than ARTs.

Tarryn challenges Jessica's argument by removing lesbian sexualities out of the equation and relating this to heterosexual couples who use ARTs because they are having trouble conceiving. This makes it clear to Jessica that she has not quite repaired the troubled position she created and so she moves to using a different rhetorical strategy: a heteronormative interpretation of the 'good mother'.

LESBIAN PARENTING AND GOOD MOTHERHOOD

It is through using the argument of a 'good mother' that Jessica is finally able to repair her troubled position. Jessica's use of the concept of a good mother is demonstrated in her use of the phrase 'when it comes to your child, what's the best thing to do?' In asking this rhetorical question, Jessica uses taken-for-granted potential psychological and emotional effects that the method of conception would have on a child to justify her position that natural conception is the ideal method for conception. In drawing on a heteronormative understanding of what constitutes a good mother, Jessica positions *all* women (not just lesbian women) as needing to put aside their own desires and needs in order to meet the needs of their children, even before these children exist.

According to Kruger (2003:198), motherhood has always 'been

invested with ideological meaning and cultural significance'. This is due to beliefs around what is normal and natural being rooted in the discourse of motherhood (Kruger, 2006). In Youngleson's (2006:29) thematic analysis investigating the dominant discourses on motherhood with ninety-two 'coloured' women in a semi-rural South African community, she found that an overriding belief was that a good mother 'operates in a nuclear family setup', where the child(ren) have been conceived 'naturally'. It was believed by participants that any other means of conceiving or raising a child would result in psychological harm. In addition to this, one of the dominant discourses used was the need for mothers to be self-sacrificing and focused on meeting the needs of their child(ren). While some South African research in the area of mothering has attempted to understand women's own, often contradictory, experiences of motherhood (Jeannes & Shefer, 2004; Kruger, 2003, 2006), the view that a mother is primarily responsible for the child(ren)'s needs is still strongly promoted in social, cultural and popular discourses (Bozalek, 2006; Kruger, 2003). Therefore, Jessica uses this discourse of motherhood in order to regain a positive presentation in the group. This strategy works well because the discourse of the self-sacrificial mother is almost always presented in a positive way, where the self-sacrificing mother is positioned as 'caring, honourable and good' (Youngleson, 2006:34). 'Needs' discourse also carries authority since it originates from a wealth of psychological literature, and is condoned and promoted in many religious texts focusing on 'good mothering' techniques (Kruger, 2003, 2006; Lawler, 1999; Wilbraham, 2008). Furthermore, 'needs talk' appeals to a moral and ethical obligation, since the word 'need', unlike the word 'want' or 'desire', implies that something must be met or negative consequences will result.

The implication of the good mother discourse is that it works to reinforce heteronormative gender roles, where psychological and emotional support for the child(ren) is the sole responsibility of the female mother. However, the appeal to children's universal 'needs' and the expectation of mothers to do the 'best thing' for their children is one that would be extremely difficult to argue against, and so Jessica was able to repair the troubled position she occupied in the group. In addition to this, it appears that Jessica uses this argument of the 'good mother' as a way of compromising with the struggle she faces in attempting to reconcile same-sex sexualities with religion and nature. In other words, in advocating for natural conception, which she argues is the best choice for a child, Jessica is able to position herself as belonging to a group of good, natural and self-sacrificial women, while at the same time avoid being marked with the stigma of selfishness or sexual deviance. In doing this, she is able to achieve a sense of normalcy and social acceptance in a world where social and cultural beliefs are predominantly heteronormative.

CONCLUSION

Heteronormativity permeates most societies and cultures and is used to promote conservative gender norms and the belief that heterosexuality and the nuclear family are natural and ideal (Bozalek, 2006; Clarke, 2002; De Vos, 2004; Dunne, 2000; Lubbe, 2007). In light of this, Jessica's discourse works to transform heteronormative notions of nature and religion to include her, as a lesbian woman. That is, in transforming heteronormativity to include her, Jessica is able to accept her own lesbian sexuality *and* gain some recognition of being normal and moral. This demonstrates how same-sex sexualities often internalise heteronormative ideals and regulate their own behaviours and practices according to these ideals in order to achieve a sense of social acceptance and normality in a social world that rejects and marginalises same-sexualities.

Eves (2004) and Wetherell (1998) both argue that heteronormative ideologies are so pervasive that individuals do not have alternative discursive resources to draw from when talking about their own identities and experiences, even if their own genders or sexualities do not fall within the boundaries of heteronormative acceptability. Therefore, it can be argued that even in attempts to resist the heteronormative subject positions of the clip's lesbian character, the lesbian women in the group discussion still had to use heteronormative discourses in their negotiation with these subject positions. However, Butler (2004:39) argues that the norms within societies and cultures construct 'livable' and 'unlivable' lives, where 'what makes a life livable, [are] certain normative conditions that must be fulfilled for life to become life'. In cultures where heteronormativity dominates, a livable life is one that adheres to dominant norms around gender and sexuality. One would expect that constitutional protection and the guarantee of equality for same-sex sexualities would create livable lives for same-sex sexualities. However, 'the guarantee of equal rights has proved inadequate to ensure livable lives' (Van Zyl, 2011:335) within the social and cultural contexts of South Africa. Therefore, while negotiation and compromise can be seen as transforming heteronormativity to include lesbian sexualities, conforming to heteronormative ideals (such as monogamy, marriage and having children) is still seen as the only way to have a livable life.

It appears that Jessica is attempting to find a way to have a 'livable life' within this focus group context. In other words, she is attempting to conform to the heteronormative conditions promoted in the outside social world, while at the same time needing to be accepted by the lesbian women in the group. This was not an easy task for her, as her use of heteronormative arguments did not go unchallenged by other participants. However, it is clear that it became a question of finding the *right kind* of argument to use and the *right kind* of 'moral' and 'normal' position to take within this focus group. As shown, Jessica had to go through a process of using at least three different arguments before her suggestion for natural conception was accepted by the lesbian women in the group. In eventually finding the 'right' heteronormative repertoire of the 'good mother' and appealing to the socialised gendered notion of the child(ren)'s needs, Jessica was able to achieve a 'livable life', regain a positive self-presentation in front of the other participants, and achieve a sense of social acceptance and normality within a broader heteronormative world.

Research into how and why heteronormativity is used, resisted and reinforced by same-sex sexualities within different contexts and social interactions is much needed. Furthermore, how heteronormative ideals, values and morals affect how same-sex sexualities are lived and how they operate in South Africa is needed. This chapter is a small but significant step in this direction. Since this focus group comprised only a few participants, all of whom were middle- to upper-class white lesbian women, there is much scope for expanding this kind of research to incorporate a diversity of races, ages, classes and sexualities.

REFERENCES

Bhana, D., Morrell, R., Hearn, J. & Moletsane, R. (2007). Power and identity: An introduction to sexualities in southern Africa. *Sexualities, 10*(2), 131–139.

Bozalek, V. (2006). Analysing a text on the prevailing paradigm of 'family' in the 'psy' professions. In T. Shefer, F. Boonzaier & P. Kiguwa (Eds), *The gender of psychology* (pp. 151–164). Cape Town: University of Cape Town Press.

Buchanan, M., Dzelme, K., Harris, D. & Hecker, L. (2001). Challenges of being simultaneously gay or lesbian and spiritual and/or religious: A narrative perspective. *The American Journal of Family Therapy*, (5), 435–449.

Butler, J. (2004). *Undoing gender*. New York: Routledge.

Chabot, J. M. & Ames, B. D. (2004). 'It wasn't "let's get pregnant and go do it"': Decision-making in lesbian couples planning motherhood via donor insemination. *Family Relations, 53*(4), 348–356.

Clarke, V. (2001). What about the children? Arguments against lesbian and gay parenting. *Women's Studies International Forum*, *24*(5), 555–570.

Clarke, V. (2002). Sameness and difference in research on lesbian parenting. *Journal of Community & Applied Social Psychology*, *12*(3), 210–222.

Dalton, S. E. & Bielby, D. B. (2000). 'That's our kind of constellation': Lesbian mothers negotiate institutionalized understandings of gender within the family. *Gender Society*, *14*(1), 36–61.

De Vos, P. (2004). Same-sex sexual desire and the re-imagining of the South African family. *South African Journal on Human Rights*, *20*(2), 179–206.

Diamond, L. M. (2005). 'I'm straight, but I kissed a girl': The trouble with American media representations of female-female sexuality. *Feminism Psychology*, *15*(1), 104–110.

Donaldson, N. (2011). *Lumberjacks and hoodrats: Negotiating subject positions of lesbian representation in two South African television programmes.* (Unpublished master's thesis). Rhodes University, Grahamstown.

Dunne, G. A. (2000). Opting into motherhood: Lesbians blurring the boundaries and transforming the meaning of parenthood and kinship. *Gender and Society*, *14*(1), 11–35.

Eves, A. (2004). Queer theory, Butch/Femme identities and lesbian space. *Sexualities*, *7*(4), 480–496.

Farquhar, D. (1996). *The other machine: Discourse and reproductive technologies.* London: Routledge.

Gartrell, N., Hamilton, J., Banks, A., Mosbacher, D., Reed, N., Sparks, C. H. & Bishop, H. (1996). The national lesbian family study: 1. Interviews with prospective mothers. *American Journal of Orthopsychiatry*, *66*(2), 272–281.

Hall, S. (1997a). Introduction. In S. Hall (Ed.), *Representation: Cultural representations and signifying practices* (pp. 1–11). London: Sage.

Hall, S. (1997b). The spectacle of the 'other'. In S. Hall (Ed.),

Representation: Cultural representations and signifying practices (pp. 223–330). London: Sage.

Hequembourg, A. (2004). Unscripted motherhood: Lesbian mothers negotiating incompletely institutionalized family relationships. *Journal of Social and Personal Relationships, 21*(6), 739–762.

Jeannes, L. & Shefer, T. (2004). Discourses of motherhood among a group of white South African mothers. *JENdA: A Journal of Culture and African Women Studies, 5*, 1–21.

Kruger, L. (2003). Narrating motherhood: The transformative potential of individual stories. *South African Journal of Psychology, 33*(4), 198–204.

Kruger, L. (2006). Motherhood. In T. Shefer, F. Boonzaier & P. Kiguwa (Eds), *The gender of psychology* (pp. 182–197). Cape Town: University of Cape Town Press.

Lawler, S. (1999). Children need but mothers only want: The power of 'needs talk' in the constitution of childhood. In J. Seymour & J. P. Bagguley (Eds), *Relating intimacies: Power and resistance* (pp. 64–88). London: MacMillan.

Lubbe, C. (2007). Mothers, fathers, or parents: Same-gendered families in South Africa. *South African Journal of Psychology, 37*(2), 260–283.

Lubbe, C. (2008). The experiences of children growing up in lesbian-headed families in South Africa. *Journal of GLBT Family Studies, 4*(3), 325–359.

Neophytou, V. (1994). Lesbian mothers. *Agenda: Empowering Women for Gender Equity, 10*(22), 24–28.

Oswald, R. F., Kuvalanka, K. A., Blume, L. & Berkowitz, D. (2009). Queering 'the family'. In S. Lloyd, A. Few & K. Allen (Eds), *Handbook of feminist family studies* (pp. 43–55). Thousand Oaks, CA: Sage.

Palamuleni, M., Kalule-Sabiti, I. & Makiwane, M. (2007). Fertility and childbearing in South Africa. In Y. Amoateng & T. B. Heaton (Eds), *Families and households in post-apartheid South Africa:*

Socio-demographic perspectives (pp. 113–134). Cape Town: HSRC Press.

Parker, I. (1997). Discursive psychology. In D. Fox & I. Prilleltensky (Eds), *Critical psychology: An introduction* (pp. 284–298). London: Sage.

Patterson, C. J. (1998). The family lives of children born to lesbian mothers. In C. J. Patterson & A. R. D'Augelli (Eds), *Lesbian, gay, and bisexual identities in families: Psychological perspectives* (pp. 154–176). New York: Oxford University Press.

Peck, J. (1994). Talk about racism: Framing a popular discourse of race on *Oprah Winfrey. Cultural Critique*, (27), 89–126.

Puchta, C. & Potter, J. (2004). *Focus group practice*. London: Sage.

Reddy, V. (2002). Perverts and sodomites: Homophobia as hate speech in Africa. *South African Linguistics and Applied Language Studies*, 20, 163–175.

Reddy, V. (2006). Decriminalisation of homosexuality in post-apartheid South Africa: A brief legal case history review from sodomy to marriage. *Agenda*, 20(67), 146–157.

Rich, A. (1980). Compulsory heterosexuality and lesbian existence. *Signs*, 5(4), 631–660.

Sanger, N. & Clowes, L. (2006). Marginalised and demonised: Lesbians and equality – perceptions of people in a local Western Cape community. *Agenda: Empowering Women for Gender Equity*, 20(67), 36–47.

Smuts, L. (2011). Coming out as a lesbian in Johannesburg, South Africa: Considering intersecting identities and social spaces. *South African Review of Sociology*, 42(3), 23–40.

Sunde, J. & Bozalek, V. (1995). (Re)presenting 'the family': Familist discourses, welfare and the state. *Transformation*, 26, 63–77.

Touroni, E. & Coyle, A. (2002). Decision-making in planned lesbian parenting: An interpretative phenomenological analysis. *Journal of Community and Applied Social Psychology*, 12(3), 194–209.

Van Balen, F. & Gerrits, T. (2001). Quality of infertility care in poor-resource areas and the introduction of new reproductive technologies. *Human Reproduction, 16*(2), 215–219.

Van Zyl, M. (2011). Are same-sex marriages un-African? Same-sex relationships and belonging in post-apartheid South Africa. *Journal of Social Issues, 67*(2), 335–357.

Wetherell, M. (1998). Positioning and interpretative repertoires: Conversation analysis and post-structuralism in dialogue. *Discourse Society, 9*(3), 387–412.

Wetherell, M. (2001). Themes in discourse research: The case of Diana. In: M. Wetherell, S. Taylor & S. J. Yates (Eds), *Discourse theory and practice*: *A reader* (pp. 14–28). London: Sage.

Wilbraham, L. (2006). *Governing mother-child communication about sex in HIV/Aids epidemic: Positioning Lovelines.* (Unpublished doctoral dissertation). University of Cape Town, Cape Town.

Wilbraham, L. (2008). Parental communication with children about sex in the South African HIV epidemic: Raced, classed and cultural appropriations of Lovelines. *African Journal of AIDS Research, 7*(1), 95–109.

Youngleson, A. (2006). *The impossibility of ideal motherhood: The psychological experiences and discourse on motherhood amongst South African low-income coloured mothers in the Kylemore community.* (Unpublished master's thesis). University of Stellenbosch, Stellenbosch.

Planned Lesbian Parenting in South Africa: Reflections on the Process of Clinically Assisted Donor Insemination

Carien Lubbe-De Beer

ADVANCES IN REPRODUCTIVE TECHNOLOGIES, along with significant legislative reforms, have opened a space for lesbian women in South Africa to start families within the ambit of their relationship. This chapter seeks to contribute to the growing body of literature on lesbian couples who use, or plan to use, clinically assisted donor insemination against the backdrop of the variety of ways in which lesbian families are formed. Despite a proliferation of international research on lesbian-headed families, there has been scant scholarly work done on the phenomenon within South Africa. Such research is urgently needed, as local experiences might have some unique characteristics to offer the international landscape. Changes to South Africa's political and legislative framework since 1994 have made it possible for lesbian couples to create their own families and to become increasingly visible. However, the paucity of local research calls for an exploration of the reasons why lesbian couples consider conceiving a baby, the decision-making process involved and their thoughts on the possibility of becoming/being parents.

South Africa's constitution is regarded as one of the world's most progressive in terms of human rights, and it has been internationally lauded for its Equality Clause, which – among other protections – prohibits discrimination on the basis of sexual orientation (Cock, 2003). Changes to the Human Tissue Act of 1997, which now recognises the right of single women (irrespective of sexual orientation) to undergo donor insemination, have made it possible for lesbian couples to access such services and to create families (Pantazis & Bonthuys, 2007). Furthermore, the introduction of the Civil Union Act in 2006 guaranteed equal parental rights to both partners in a lesbian relationship, thus creating a more positive legal environment for same-gender couples to create a family (*Civil Union Act, 2006*).

Despite these significant legislative reforms, South Africa remains a conservative and heteronormative family-based society in which the traditional family is powerful, visually present and highly valued (Lubbe, 2007). Most parents encourage their children – especially as adolescence and sexual maturity approaches – to date opposite-sex individuals, to marry and, eventually, to have children (Hunter & Mallon, 2000). Even the knowledge and values that are socially constructed in educational settings are done so along heterosexual lines and are bound up with the organisation and regulation of the heterosexual family.

Heterosexism and heteronormativity are the dominant discourse through which the traditional family is idealised and privileged. However, the 'traditional' family is not a static notion or formation: throughout history, conceptions and practices relating to families have changed and taken on different forms, and they continue to develop. Moreover, with the current high divorce rate for heterosexual marriages, the narrow definition of the nuclear family is coming under ever closer scrutiny. Research by the South African Institute of Race Relations shows that only a third of children live with both their biological mother and father, and that nine million children

(48 per cent) are growing up without a biological father figure (living but absent). Such figures suggest that the Western nuclear family of today may be an illusion, while also underscoring that many communities adopt, and function within, a philosophy of extended families – for example, an uncle or grandfather may act as a father figure, or a variety of elders act as parents.

Furthermore, parental roles, duties and functions can be performed in a wide variety of ways that are not linked to gender stereotypes. Gender and parenting should be regarded as fluid variables that shift and change to suit different contexts at different times (Lubbe, 2007). So, what are the implications of this for parenting? This fluidity offers people who want to be parents the possibility of choosing, forming and performing their own individual identities as parents in a way that brings their unique abilities, strengths, skills and talents into play. It challenges society to disregard the stigmas of the past. Is it inherently significant if the mother of a family changes a light bulb or services the car? Or if the father cooks, minds the children and takes care of the garden? Or indeed if all these functions are efficiently performed in a lesbian-parented family in which the children are loved, nurtured, cared for and protected? It furthermore raises the question of why society finds it difficult to disregard gender roles and why some people persistently argue that it matters who cares for and nurtures children. As recent research suggests, it is the quality of relationships in a family that is more important than the family's form or structure (Lubbe, 2007).

INTERNATIONAL RESEARCH FINDINGS
Research on planned lesbian-parented families began to emerge in the 1990s (Mitchell, 1996; Patterson, 1994). The earliest studies compared heterosexual couples, lesbian couples and single women (Wendland, Byrne & Hill, 1996), or lesbian and single heterosexual mothers (Golombok, Tasker & Murray, 1997; Chan, Raboy & Patterson, 1998), and this style of comparative study remains

popular (Borneskog et al., 2012). One of the first extensive studies was that of Pies (1989), which uses qualitative research techniques to explore lesbian couples' reasons for wanting children, their choice of donor, the planning and coordination of the process, internalised homophobia, the way in which family members were told, practical considerations such as how the women's careers were affected, and how couples maintained their relationship.

A key focus in the international literature has been the way in which lesbians choose to become pregnant – that is, whether they opt to conceive through heterosexual intercourse, through self-insemination or through clinically assisted donor insemination (Brewaeys et al., 1995; Haimes & Weiner, 2000; Touroni & Coyle, 2002). Research on the choice between a known and unknown donor is also now well established (Gartrell et al., 1996; Leiblum, Palmer & Spector, 1995), as is the choice between an identity-release donor or a permanently anonymous donor, depending on the legal context of the country in which the procedure occurred (Scheib, Riordan & Rubin, 2005; Smith, 2012). Studies also include an exploration of participants' desires and motivations for having children as well as the accompanying decision-making processes (Gartrell et al., 1996; Mitchell, 1996; Patterson, 1998; Tasker & Golombok, 1997). Research shows that heteronormative considerations raise several concerns for prospective lesbian parents, including fears that the child will be subjected to discrimination and hostility, and the possibility of less support – both for the parents and for the children – from significant others (Gartrell et al., 1996; Hare, 1994; Bos & Hakvoort, 2007). A significant observation to emerge from this research is that prospective lesbian mothers reflect considerably on the conceptualising of their family identity as well as on their parenting practices (Bos, Van Balen & Van den Boom, 2003; Breshears, 2010; Donovan & Wilson, 2008; Dunne, 2000).

Despite the plethora of research in recent years, no South African-focused studies (based on personal investigations of local and international databases) have been published on the formation of *planned* lesbian-parented families, despite it being well over a decade since the law regulating assisted reproductive technologies was amended. It was due to this knowledge gap that a small-scale qualitative study was undertaken to investigate the issues surrounding the creation of planned lesbian families. This chapter reports on some of the findings from the aforementioned study, which investigated six couples' desire to have a baby, the accompanying decision-making process, the identification of the donor and the donor insemination process itself. Relatively few studies have been conducted with a specific focus on decision-making and donor-related processes in planned lesbian-parented families, especially from a qualitative perspective.[35]

METHODS
Design
The present research followed a qualitative approach using a case-study design interwoven with narrative principles in order to gain rich and in-depth perspectives on the experiences of participants. The primary research question guiding the study was 'what are the experiences of lesbian couples in their transition to parenthood?'

Selection of Participants
Snowball sampling, along with a request on a lesbian baby website, was used to invite lesbian couples who were considering pregnancy or who had recently conceived through donor insemination. Eight couples were interviewed, with six of these constituting the database for this study. The other two couples were unsuccessful in their attempt to conceive, and their interview material was therefore not included. Pseudonyms are used throughout the below analysis.

The background of the couples, at the time they were interviewed, is provided below.

- Alicia and Christine (together for nine years; after nine years Alicia gave birth to a girl; at the time of the first interview Alicia was pregnant)
- Jane and Juliette (together for eleven years; after eleven years Juliette gave birth to a boy; at the time of the first interview Juliette was pregnant)
- Janet and Susan (together for eleven years; after ten years they conceived a girl, with Janet being an egg donor to her partner, Susan, whom they termed the birth mother)
- Megan and Katherine (together for seven years; after seven years Katherine gave birth to a boy; at the time of the first interview they were in the process of artificial insemination)
- Stephanie and Maggie (together for six years; entered into their relationship when the first-born (boy) was one month old; the second child, a girl, was conceived three years later, (with Maggie as the birth mother of both children)
- Tina and Lorraine (together for ten years; after five years Lorraine gave birth to a boy)

All of the participants can be categorised as white and middle class. At the time of the study, they all lived in Pretoria, South Africa, in an urban setting. All the couples could afford to plan and proceed with having a child through their access to high-quality private medical care, thus testifying to their middle-class socio-economic status. A need therefore exists for similar research involving members of other population groups, as well as interracial couples. Permission to conduct the research was granted by the Faculty of Education Research Committee of the University of Pretoria, and each participant gave her consent prior to the interviews.

Data Generation
Interviews of between one-and-a-half and two hours were conducted to capture in-depth descriptive and explanatory accounts of the

participants' experiences. The interviews were conversation-based and took place in the comfort of the participants' homes, where they were asked to relate their stories of parenting. Follow-up questions were also put to participants either in the same interview or at a later stage with second or third interviews.

Data Analysis
A thematic analysis was conducted using the categorical-content approach of Lieblich, Tuval-Mashiach and Zilber (1998). This entailed a thorough reading of the field texts in order to form an overall impression of each couple's story. Key words and phrases were highlighted and coded, and tentative themes were identified inductively in an attempt to understand the interwoven parts of each unique story. A cross-case analysis was then performed to identify key themes across the cases (Patton, 1990) and to cross-check across all interviews if new or divergent themes emerged.

Methodological Criteria
Qualitative research criteria such as trustworthiness, authenticity, credibility, dependability and reflexivity were respected, and the research was conducted in terms of an interpretivist paradigm (Terre Blanche & Durrheim, 1999). Knowledge is, of course, relative, plural and subjective, with researcher and participants co-creating this knowledge. An understanding of another person's inner reality can be obtained by carefully and systematically examining the person's views, meanings, experiences, accounts, actions and significant events in his/her life.

FINDINGS AND DISCUSSION
This paper discusses two broad themes: (1) the couples' desire to become parents, often involving a complex decision-making process, and (2) the role of the donor and the donor insemination process.

Theme 1: The Desire to Become Parents

A lesbian/gay lifestyle has long been associated with a childless life and an inability to create a nurturing and caring parenting environment. Research over the past decade indicates, however, that children conceived through assisted reproductive technologies are, by the very nature of the procedure, wanted and are thus born into favourable circumstances. This applies to heterosexual as well as lesbian couples (Parry, 2005), but is a particularly important consideration for those creating a non-traditional family unit within a heteronormative social environment (Bos et al., 2003). Despite such findings, the desire for a child cannot be automatically assumed for both partners in a relationship, and the ultimate decision to undergo clinically assisted donor insemination can be complex for some couples.

Alicia and Christine's story exposes the complex and difficult process that couples often go through before reaching an agreement. Alicia declared that she has always wanted to have a child; Christine, on the other hand, indicated she would rather have had 'a horse than a baby'. One of the catalysts for thinking about pregnancy was the birth of a close friend's baby, who had been conceived through assisted insemination. This incident strengthened Alicia's resolve to have a baby, but after a year without progress on the matter, she believed she may never have a chance to become pregnant. No specific decision was reached during this period, as the two women did not speak openly about the subject. The silence did not give Alicia any hope, but she eventually reached a kind of acceptance and peace: 'I really, really had peace in my heart, or so I thought'. In hindsight, Christine wonders if this 'no pressure' period made it easier for her to come to a decision. She described a kind of epiphany that took place in church:

> A little girl in front of me turned around and looked at me. I didn't open my eyes, but I knew she was looking at me. And I just got a feeling, and the feeling told me: 'Wow, it is going to be so nice to have your own daughter.' So I thought, 'Why not?' But I kept it to myself,

and the next morning I woke Alicia up at 5 am and said, 'I have been thinking, this child thing... let's do it!'[36]

This extract highlights the complexity of the decision-making process: while having a child may be an easy decision for one partner, the other person may not share this desire, and the process of deciding may take months, even years. In this case, the final decision was reached almost impulsively, but – from the way in which the story was told – the researcher sensed a significant spiritual aspect that was coupled with the belief that having a child might contribute to a more meaningful and purposeful life.

For Tina and Lorraine, the decision was far easier. Tina described the process as follows:

> I always wanted to have a child, but we didn't talk about it much. And when we met, I was under the impression that she didn't want to have children. If her mum would ask her, [Lorraine] would immediately tell them that we are not going to have children. But one night, when we were lying in bed, I told her I wanted to have a child because we have enough love to love someone else. And when I'm old, one day, I would love to have a child that visits and lots of grandchildren, and all the nice things that normal families have. She told me she doesn't have a problem with that as long as she doesn't have to carry a child. I think if you are a woman, you want to be a mother.

Two significant discourses emerge from Tina's narrative: the heteronormative ideal of a 'normal' family, and the notion that every woman wants to be a mother – that is, the prevalent association of womanhood with motherhood. According to Tina, her key motivation was love: she felt the couple's love would be enough to embrace a child in their lives. It is also interesting that Tina envisaged pregnancy in terms of an extension of her life, specifically into the following generation.

Most of the birth mothers in this study indicated an overwhelming desire to fall pregnant and to experience childbirth, which confirms Parry's (2005) finding that many women want to experience the physical sensation of pregnancy. Katherine: 'I want to be pregnant. I want to feel the baby growing inside me; we wanted to have our own. We wanted to have a baby – a child is an extension of our love, and emphasises the love that there is between a couple.' Juliette: 'I wanted to have my own, and I love being pregnant, and I'm going to miss it. I mean, if this is the last one, this is the last time that I'm going to have it. I need to see it from that viewpoint – it's the last time I'm having this experience.' And Alicia: 'If it's your own, it's different.'

Like Tina and Lorraine, it was relatively easy for Stephanie and Maggie to reach a decision. Maggie had a son from a previous heterosexual marriage, and both she and Stephanie wanted more than one child. They considered adopting but were warned by social workers that it might be a lengthy and complex process, so they decided to pursue the route of assisted reproduction. Stephanie, like Lorraine, had never felt a desire to carry a child but still wanted to be a parent, thus it was logical for Maggie to again be the biological mother.

Neither Jane nor Juliette initially wanted a child, but this changed for Juliette, and her longing to have a baby put a lot of pressure on their relationship. Their story again reveals the complex negotiation process that some couples go through. In Juliette's words:

> In my late twenties I never ever wanted to have children: it just seemed [like] too much responsibility. Then, somewhere in my early thirties, I felt as if my body told me something, and I told Jane that I wanted to have a child, but she didn't want to fall for this concept at all. And I just persisted, and I told her: 'even if I do it without you'. But she kept on saying that she doesn't want to have a child, that children are noisy, and she doesn't want to have screaming kids around her.

We were on holiday and there were lots of kids playing on the beach, and I just told her that I really wanted to have a child. I told her: 'Really, I want to have a child. I want to have one.' We chatted, and this time she wasn't totally negative... so I asked Jane if we could look into the possibilities of how one should go about it and she said: 'Yes, okay'. And for me that was a green light. So we talked to this couple about everything, the pros and cons and all the rest, and when we were driving home I told Jane that this is what I wanted: I want to have a baby. And then we decided together that we will do it.

Then my cycle didn't work out, as the insemination would take place over Christmas. We went back in January, but it didn't work. It was extremely emotional, and I didn't want to go again; it was clinical and emotional. In March we went to Disneyland, and when we came back Jane said she didn't want to have kids anymore... we had some ructions, as I wanted to go [to the clinic], and I had to dig deep in myself to have the courage to go again. But she didn't want to, so we went for counselling. We spoke about our differences and I made the decision that it's me and a baby or nothing. I did not want to lose her, but I wanted the baby at the same time. She wanted me but without a baby, and it took us a long time but in the end we made the choice that we will stay together, I will have the baby and if she can't cope, she can walk out. She supports me in my decision, but it's my baby. And that was the reality, and we told everyone so that no one would point fingers if it doesn't work out.

Jane explained her point of view as follows:

Life for me is about options, and if there are not choices then life isn't flexible and I cannot cope. It is not as if I have to choose a certain option, but just knowing that I have a choice makes it okay. It is important how I look at it: I am not excited about the baby, but it is an extension of Juliette, and I need to see if I can value that extension of her. And I am sad that I am not excited for her, but I am a realist.

> My work demands a lot of me and I travel a lot overseas, so we need to put the issues on the table. So I took it step by step: let's see if we can get you pregnant, then let's get through the pregnancy, then let's see how the first six months are and then we can take it from there. I don't want to let my life end because I'm having a baby – I want flexibility and choices.

As with the earlier examples, this account reveals the complexity of the decision-making process. Experiences such as the one described above also highlight the critical need for practitioners to be aware of the intricacies of each partner and the way in which motivations, desires and decision-making can frequently change.

Janet and Susan's story has a different tone – both wanted to fall pregnant and have children. Janet was explicit about her yearning to have a child: 'I've always wanted children; it's always been an absolute desire of mine, I've always been broody. I'm the oldest of eighteen cousins, so I grew up with babies all my life.' However, because Susan has fertility problems, it was decided that she would act as the birth mother using Janet's fertilised egg. Janet described the decision as follows: 'She's older, and she had a lot of fertility issues, so we chose for her to carry. Because of the fertility problems that she had, the doctors recommended that we use my eggs… it would have been nice to have done both, but unfortunately that wasn't possible.' The idea of not being biologically related to the child was something that Susan initially had to work through.

> There was a sense of loss for me… I had to grieve that I'm not going to have my own flesh and blood, but honestly, in having her and having her in my body, made no difference whatsoever to how I felt when I was pregnant. I was absolutely besotted from the moment I was pregnant. And, when she came out, I was crying my eyes out the whole time. [Not being biologically related] didn't make any difference whatsoever, nothing mattered, nothing else other than my

child. I mean, when I look at her, I see me, even though I know… the funniest thing is that most people say she looks like me.

The above reference to a 'sense of loss' is an important point, particularly with respect to some of the unique issues lesbian couples might face. Grief can be part of the complex mix for non-biological mothers and it is often unspoken about because women feel uncomfortable acknowledging sadness at a time they are expected to be feeling joy.

The five accounts above testify to the unique life circumstances of each couple and the complex nature of the decision-making process. This finding is supported by recent research that has shown that the decision to have a child is a carefully considered process for lesbian couples (Bos et al., 2003; Donovan & Wilson, 2008; McNair et al., 2002; Pies, 1989; Touroni & Coyle, 2002). Renaud (2007) lists three major factors when people consider parenthood: effort, expense and emotional commitment, and the interplay of these factors are evident in the above quotes. An exception is Jane, as she seems to be able to use the fact she has no biological connection to the child to distance herself from the situation and to remain disconnected from the pregnancy. This might be unique to lesbian couples.

In addition, the accounts described above are indicative of the internal couple dynamics about wanting or not wanting to have a child. For some of the women, the desire to have a child was associated with a biological – and perceived 'natural' – longing to be a mother; for others, it was a long, contemplative process culminating in a reading of the child as an extension of their love; for others, it was about giving their partner the freedom and choice to fall pregnant, as they themselves desire the freedom not to become part of the family if that is what they decide; for others, the decision was relatively easy, as both partners wanted to have children. This diversity of experience must inform the approach of professionals counselling lesbian couples, specifically around avoiding assumptions about the reasons for wanting to become parents. Practitioners working with same-gender couples can enhance their own empathic and caring engagement by being mindful of the complex process that went on behind the scenes long before the couple contacted them.

Theme 2: Donors and the Insemination Process

All of the couples in this study indicated a strong preference for anonymous donors so that they could raise their children without the threat of third-party interference and to strengthen the status of the non-biological mother. Similar reasoning is also present in international research on lesbian clinically assisted reproduction (Bos & Gartrell, 2011; Ben-Ari & Livni, 2006; Touroni & Coyle, 2002).

Once the decision to have a child has been made, the couple must consider the actual process of conception. All of the couples in this case study opted for clinically assisted insemination. Accordingly, the role and meaning of the donor, as well as the actual insemination process, emerged as prominent themes in the participants' narratives. Stephanie and Maggie, for instance, recalled a conversation with their gynaecologist:

> What the doctor told us is that the medical profession protects the donor. The doctor told us some general things like that the donor is a golfer, and that the donor can potentially have five children from different women… but there is no personal connection, there's no emotion there, so it doesn't matter, or worry me at all.

The doctor shared this information in an unemotional and detached manner, creating the impression that the donor was insignificant for Stephanie and Maggie (except, of course, for the medical procedure itself). In South Africa, only the physical characteristics, including the race of the donor, are usually disclosed, although some fertility clinics offer further details such as hobbies and fields of study.

Tina shared her and Lorraine's decision-making process regarding the choice of donor characteristics: 'For us it was important that [the donor] looks like Lorraine, especially since she is not biologically related to [the child], so we took her features into account when we chose the donor.' Other couples, however, chose characteristics similar to those of the birth mother. Megan and Katherine, for example, said: 'They give the criteria and you can only fill in the specifics – it's only colour of the eyes, hair, skin tone, height and blood group, so we chose as close to Katherine as possible.' Janet and Susan described a more extensive process:

> So basically we got faxed through a list, and then I guess it's just a case of reading it through. We tried to choose someone we had sort of biological characteristics or similar, to both in some way. And then just from the description, somebody you thought that you could… the donor was a musician, and my dad is a musician, so it kind of – I don't know – resonated. Then we had a shortlist of about two or three, and then we went out one evening with some of our friends, and we're like, read these three and what do you think, and everybody sort of chose the same one. I mean, it's not a huge selection, but I actually think that is easier. If there was too much of a selection it would have been a very, very long process to actually find a person. I found it actually… there were enough different types of people that you could pick up in what they wrote about themselves and that definitely attracted us I think.

Initially, Katherine and Megan were under the impression that their experience would be similar to that of Janet and Susan. However, each clinic follows a different approach with no clear structure available to lesbian couples embarking on the process. As Megan explained: 'We had [heard] this story with the choice of the donor, what we wanted. We had this vision where we will go through the files and almost get a vibe of who the person is, but then we couldn't – they chose for us.' Katherine continued: 'And the woman was sort of homophobic. She just said: "You don't have a choice", and when I asked her to think of us when she chooses, she just said bluntly: "Well, if I remember you".'

Ryan and Berkowitz (2009:163) maintain that lesbian couples who 'construct non-biological families have a unique opportunity to consciously create what their families will look like'. They conclude that 'whether the desired characteristics of the sperm donor lie in the sameness of the non-biological mother or the birth mother, the guiding reason is analogous: to create the appearance of a genetic family' (164). Similarly, Jones (2005) found that the participants in her research preferred donors who resembled the non-biological mother, due to a desire to have physical similarities between the child and the non-biological mother. In South Africa, all donor information is non-identifiable, a point raised by Janet and Susan:

> It's an anonymous donor so... there's not much choice, really. We don't know anybody that we would want to have [as a donor] and I don't really like to have somebody... external, honestly... I think, had the choice been there for an identifiable donor, I probably would have gone for that option, but it is expensive given that it comes from overseas. So it is an anonymous donor, selected from what was available at the time [*laugh*]. And yes, things just work out beautifully.

For some of the couples, having an unknown donor was important. Lorraine commented:

> I went to a sperm bank and bought the sperm like you go to a shop and buy groceries – it's the same thing. [The donor] doesn't need to know, because there is no way that I would allow a third party anywhere near my child. This is my child, I raised him, and that dad has nothing of him. He sold his sperm for money. It is as easy as that.

Her partner, Tina, cited the experiences of other couples who had chosen a known donor: 'We know someone who made use of a known donor and now, after eight years, they still struggle. I didn't want to bring a third party into our relationship.' Lorraine then exclaimed: 'I don't share my wife, and I don't share my child!'

Some of the other couples also based their decision on the stories of others. Megan and Katherine relayed what their gynaecologist had told them:

> She told us how she did extensive research and someone that she knows used a known donor. It is almost ten years later and they are still caught up in ongoing court battles, and they lost their house and everything due to the court fees. She actually advised us to stay away from even considering that option.

Jane and Juliette also shared a story about one of their friends who opted for a known donor:

> I think the anonymous donor thing is just less complicated. Friends of mine did it: [they] had a baby as a single mom with a gay man. But in the end his partner had huge issues with the little girl; he didn't want anything to do with the child. And the dad opened up trust funds for the kid and it caused quite an upset, as he was quite wealthy. Later on there were huge issues in his life and he committed suicide, and the will was contested by the partner, as he left everything to the little girl. In the end they settled, but it was such an emotional rollercoaster: she lost a friend and her daughter's dad.

While discussing their choice of an unknown donor, some couples spontaneously reported what they would tell their child. Lorraine: 'I am not interested to know who he is. My child does not need to know who his dad is, because he doesn't have dad. There are ways to tell a child something, but if we give him enough love he will be able to live with it.' Tina: 'If one day he is asking who his dad is, then I will explain to him that we couldn't have a child together, but we wanted him so bad and there was someone who cared enough to make it possible for other people'. Jane and Juliette: 'It is a special present: it was a man that gave us a special present, namely you/this child. And he is not part of the scenario: the donor is a special person, so the donor is not a daddy, just a donor.' Katherine and Megan: 'We are the parents, there is just a donor. We wanted to have the child as a union, and that is what we needed to have: a child. Luckily we live in an age where we are able to create our own family.'

These imagined responses are similar to those recorded by Stevens et al. (2007) in their qualitative study of the way lesbian mothers planned to tell, or had told, their children about their conception. Where the information was appropriate for the child's age, the unknown donor was referred to as 'a nice man, her donor daddy, gave me a seed and I had an egg and we made a baby' or 'a very kind man because he made it possible for me to have [a child]'. Another response was that 'she knows she doesn't have a daddy, and she knows she has got a [co-mother] instead, it's like you didn't have daddy, you got [co-mother]' (357).

The actual insemination process was described by most of the couples as a highly emotional experience. The current literature on planned lesbian families does not say much about the often painful process when insemination fails, so the reflections and insights from this study provide much-needed data of the experience. What is important to reiterate is that all couples interviewed were successful in their efforts, which raises the point that there is a lack of information given to these women prior to trying and that there might be misapprehensions between expectations about how the process works and the reality of assisted conception.

Tina: 'We went twice for insemination, and then I told [Lorraine] if it doesn't work this time then I am not going again, because it is emotionally draining'. This is similar to the experience of Juliette:

'But it didn't work. It was extremely emotional, and I didn't want to go again; it was clinical and emotional... I had to dig deep in myself to have the courage to go again.' Megan also talked about their first unsuccessful experience: 'Our doctor said such a true thing: when you go for the process you already have a baby in your mind – it is already there. So if it doesn't work out you've lost the baby; it's like a miscarriage.' Alicia's account shows not just how daunting the process can be but also the dearth of information available for lesbian couples embarking on the process:

> I first contacted Cape Town, because I could choose a donor from a list. But the second time the sperm was not available anymore, so I phoned Johannesburg, also from a list. And I drove to Johannesburg and back to Pretoria, but only then I found out that you're supposed to do a sonar to see how the egg cells are, etc. Then the next time, the day fell on a Sunday and my gynaecologist was not available, so I phoned the fertility clinic and the doctor said he would help me.

Where the process was successful, the response was – understandably – more positive: 'Things just work out beautifully' (Janet and Susan); 'I just knew in my heart I wasn't afraid or anything, and I just knew' (Alicia and Christine); 'but then we were so lucky to have him, we can't imagine our lives without him' (Tina and Lorraine); 'I made an appointment with the gynaecologist and waited one month and was successful the first time' (Maggie and Stephanie); 'Janet and I sort of prayed to God and asked for guidance and whatever... and, um, and then I fell pregnant with her' (Susan and Janet). Statements such as 'things just work out beautifully' reflect the acceptance and contentment felt when the insemination process is successful; months, and sometimes years, of contemplation, choices and decisions make way for a new life phase of pregnancy, the anticipation of childbirth and becoming a family.

LIMITATIONS

This study endeavoured to present a rich description of planned lesbian parenthood, yet its generalisability and representativeness can be questioned. The study represents only one depiction of planned lesbian-parented families filtered through the interpretive lens of one researcher. The study is also limited by what participants chose to report. The interview subjects' willingness to participate in the study could be interpreted as bias in favour of a positive outcome to their situation as lesbian parents – there could be negative implications for parents in a marginalised group if they did not report favourable or positive experiences (Donovan & Wilson, 2008).

CONCLUSION

The above findings contribute to the literature on planned lesbian-parented families by capturing rich descriptions of the highly reflective and contemplative process of wanting children. Qualitative research that provides in-depth data about the decision-making process can be of immense value to professionals working closely with lesbian couples. For instance, practitioners might be keen to understand more about the unique issues lesbian couples face that other couples do not (with the caveat that not all issues will affect all lesbians the same way).

This study indicates that the desire for a family among lesbian couples can be intense and, by extension, that parenthood is a carefully considered process. Because lesbian families have to contend with the complexity of negotiating a heteronormative landscape, the decision to have a baby is generally recounted repeatedly to family, friends and teachers in the ensuing years. The significance of this constant re-telling is worth considering, as it might reinforce in a child the feeling of being different or, conversely, of being 'really wanted'.

The data here suggests that clinicians must understand that lesbians often make decisions about parenting with ideals about families and family life that are similar to heterosexual couples. However, these couples also face unique challenges in terms of achieving this ideal, such as having to negotiate biological/non-biological parenting within a couple relationship, having to make serious decisions about how to get pregnant (a known versus unknown donor) and also having to go through a process of conception that inevitably involves external people (either a known donor or a clinic) and an often invasive and expensive insemination procedure. These processes may create huge tensions within a relationship, particularly in cases where one partner wants the child more than the other.

Practitioners fulfil various roles such as being networkers, collaborators and facilitators between individuals, families, communities and formal institutions, and they therefore need to possess a thorough understanding of, among other things, the experiences, needs, desires, relationship dynamics, personal histories, support systems and friendship networks of lesbian couples considering starting a family through assisted reproduction. Professionals can help couples understand how they relate both to the outside world and to each other, as well as the possible impacts of internalised homophobia. Moreover, understanding and compassion based on scientific research may help psychologists, nurses, medical doctors, fertility specialists, gynaecologists and related professionals to interrogate their own prejudices about same-sex parenting and assisted insemination. This will help them to successfully facilitate challenging situations, particularly those in which perceived differences may elicit prejudice and discrimination.

REFERENCES

Almack, K. (2005). What's in a name? An exploration of the significance of the choice of surnames given to the children born within female same sex families. *Sexualities, 8*(2), 239–254. doi:10.1177/1363460705050857

Almack, K. (2006). Seeking sperm: Accounts of lesbian couples' reproductive decision-making and understandings of the needs of the child. *International Journal of Law, Policy and the Family, 20*, 1–22. doi:10.1093/lawfam/ebi030

Ben-Ari, A. & Livni, T. (2006). Motherhood is not a given thing: Experiences and constructed meanings of biological and nonbiological lesbian mothers. *Sex Roles, 54*, 521–531. doi:10.1007/s11199-006-9016-0

Borneskog, C., Skoog Svanberg, A., Lampic, C. & Sydsjö, G. (2012). Relationship quality in lesbian and heterosexual couples undergoing treatment with assisted reproduction. *Human Reproduction, 27*(3), 779–786. doi:10.1093/humrep/der472

Bos, H. M. W. & Gartrell, N. (2011). Adolescents of the US National Longitudinal Lesbian Family Study: The impact of having a known or an unknown donor on the stability of psychological adjustment. *Human Reproduction, 26*(3), 630–637. doi:10.1093/humrep/deq359

Bos, H. M. W. & Hakvoort, E. M. (2007). Child adjustment and parenting in planned lesbian families with known and as-yet-unknown donors. *Journal of Psychosomatic Obstetrics and Gynaecology, 28*, 121–129. doi:10.1080/01674820701409793

Bos, H. M. W., Van Balen, F. & Van den Boom, D. C. (2003). Planned lesbian families: Their desire and motivation to have children. *Human Reproduction, 18*(10), 2216–2224. doi:10.1093/humrep/deg427

Breshears, D. (2010). Coming out with our children: Turning points facilitating lesbian parent discourse with their children about family identity. *Communication Reports, 23*, 79–90. doi:10.1080/08934215.2010.511398

Brewaeys, A., Devroey, P., Helmerhorst, F. M., Van Hall, E. V. & Ponjaert, I. (1995). Lesbian mothers who conceive after donor insemination: A follow-up study. *Human Reproduction, 10*(10), 2731–2735.

Chan, R. W., Raboy, B. & Patterson, C. (1998). Psychosocial adjustment among children conceived via donor insemination by lesbian and heterosexual mothers. *Child Development, 69,* 443–457.

Civil Union Act, 2006, no. 17 of 2006. Republic of South Africa.

Cock, J. (2003). Engendering gay and lesbian rights: The equality clause in the South African Constitution. *Women's Studies International Forum, (26)*1, 35–45. http://dx.doi.org/10.1016/S0277-5395(02)00353-9

Donovan, C. & Wilson, A. R. (2008). Imagination and integrity: Decision-making among lesbian couples to use medically provided donor insemination. *Culture, Health and Sexuality, 10*(7), 649–65. doi:10.1080/13691050802175739

Dunne, G. (2000). Opting into motherhood: Lesbians blurring the boundaries and transforming the meaning of parenthood and kinship. *Gender and Society, 14*(1), 11–35.

Gartrell, N., Hamilton, J., Banks, A., Mosbacher, D., Reed, N., Sparks, C. H. & Bishop, H. (1996). The national lesbian family study: 1. Interviews with prospective mothers. *American Journal of Orthopsychiatry, 66,* 272–281. doi:10.1037/h0080178

Golombok, S., Tasker, F. & Murray, C. (1997). Children raised in fatherless families from infancy: Family relationships and the socioemotional development of children of lesbian and single heterosexual mothers. *Journal of Child Psychology and Psychiatry, and Allied Disciplines, 38*(7), 783–792. doi:10.1111/j.1469-7610.1997.tb01596.x

Haimes E. & Weiner K. (2000). Everybody's got a dad... Issues for lesbian families in the management of donor insemination. *Sociology of health & illness, 22* (4), 477–499. doi:10.1111/1467-9566.00215

Hare, J. (1994). Concerns and issues faced by families headed by a lesbian couple. *Families in Society, 32,* 27–35.

Hunter, J. & Mallon, G. P. (2000). Lesbian, gay and bisexual development: Dancing with your feet tied together. In B. Greene & G. L. Croom (Eds), *Education, research and practice in lesbian, gay, bisexual and transgendered psychology* (pp. 226–243). California, London, New Delhi: Sage.

Jones, C. (2005) Looking like a family: Negotiating bio-genetic continuity in British lesbian families. *Sexualities, 8*(2), 221–237. doi:10.1177/1363460705050856

Kranz, K. C. & Daniluk, J. C. (2006). Living outside of the box: Lesbian couples with children conceived through the use of anonymous donor insemination. *Journal of Feminist Family Therapy, 18*, 1–33. doi:10.1300/J086v18n01_01

Leiblum, S. R., Palmer, M. G. & Spector, I. P. (1995). Non-traditional mothers: Single heterosexual/lesbian women and lesbian couples electing motherhood via donor insemination. *Journal of Psychosomatic Obstetrics and Gynaecology, 16*(1), 11–20. doi:10.3109/01674829509025652

Lieblich, A., Tuval-Mashiach, R. & Zilber, T. (1998). *Narrative research*. California, London, New Delhi: Sage.

Lubbe, C. (2007). Mothers, fathers, or parents: Same-gendered families in South Africa. *South African Journal of Psychology, 37*(2), 260–283.

McNair, R., Dempsey, D., Wise, S. & Perlesz, A. (2002). Lesbian parenting: Issues, strengths and challenges. *Family Matters, 63*, 40–49.

Mitchell, V. (1996). Two moms: Contribution of the planned lesbian family to the deconstruction of gendered parenting. In J. Laird & R. J. Green (Eds), *Lesbians and gays in couples and families: A handbook for therapists* (pp. 343–357). San Francisco, CA: Jossey-Bass.

Pantazis, A. & Bonthuys, E. (2007). Gender and sexual orientation. In E. Bonthuys & C. Albertyn (Eds), *Gender, law and justice* (pp. 120–157). Cape Town: Juta.

Parry, D. (2005). Women's experience with infertility: The fluidity with Conceptualizations of 'family'. *Qualitative Sociology, 28*(3), 275–291.

Patterson, C. J. (1994). Children of the lesbian baby boom: Behavioural adjustment, self-concepts and sex-role identity. In B. Greene & G. Herek (Eds), *Psychological perspectives on lesbian and gay issues: Vol. 1. Lesbian and gay psychology: Theory, research and clinical applications* (pp. 156–175). Thousand Oaks, CA: Sage.

Patterson, C. J. (1998). The family lives of children born to lesbian mothers. In C. J. Patterson & A. R. D'Augelli (Eds), *Lesbian, gay, and bisexual identities in families: Psychological perspectives* (pp. 154–176). New York: Oxford University Press.

Patton, M. Q. (1990). *Qualitative evaluation and research methods*. Newbury Park, California, London, New Delhi: Sage.

Pies, C. A. (1989). Lesbians and the choice to parent. *Marriage and family review*, *14*(3–4), 137–154. doi:10.1300/J002v14n03_07

Renaud, M. (2007). We are mothers too: Childbearing experiences of lesbian families. *Journal of Obstetric, Gynecologic, & Neonatal Nursing, 36*(2), 190–199. doi:10.1111/j.1552-6909.2007.00136.x

Ryan, M. & Berkowitz, D. (2009). Constructing gay and lesbian parent families 'beyond the closet'. *Qualitative Sociology*, 32, 153–172. doi:10.1007/s11133-009-9124-6

Scheib, J. E., Riordan, M. & Rubin, S. (2005). Adolescents with open-identity sperm donors: Reports from 12–17 year olds. *Human Reproduction, 20*, 239–252. doi:0.1093/humrep/deh581

Smith, L. (2012). Tangling the web of legal parenthood: Legal responses to the use of known donors in lesbian parenting arrangements. *Legal Studies*. doi:10.1111/j.1748-121X.2012.00248.x

Stevens, M., Perry, B., Burston, A., Golombok, S. & Golding, J. (2003). Openness in lesbian-mother families regarding mother's sexual orientation and child's conception by donor insemination. *Journal of Reproductive and Infant Psychology*, *21*(4), 347–362. doi:10.1080/02646830310001622141

Tasker, F. & Golombok, S. (1997). *Growing up in a lesbian family:*

Effects on child development. New York: The Guilford Press.

Terre Blanche, M. & Durrheim, K. (Eds). (1999). *Research in practice: Applied methods for the social sciences.* Cape Town: UCT Press.

Touroni, E. & Coyle, A. (2002). Decision-making in planned lesbian parenting: An interpretative phenomenological analysis. *Journal of Community and Applied Social Psychology, 12,* 194–209. doi: 10.1002/casp.672

Wendland, C. L., Byrne, F. & Hill, C. (1996). Donor insemination: A comparison of lesbian couples, heterosexual couples and single women. *Fertility and Sterility, 65,* 764–770.

Resistance and Re(Production): Becoming Lesbian Parents through Assisted Reproductive Technologies

Karl Swain and Kerry Frizelle

BACKGROUND

Recent legislative changes, and accompanying shifts in social trends and attitudes, have brought about a critical need for society (and especially those in the helping professions) to acknowledge the variation of family formations, structures and experiences in South Africa. In one of the first local studies into same-sex families, Lubbe (2007a) notes that homosexual partnerships have traditionally been linked to a childless lifestyle, or at least one that does not place a premium on children and families. The last decade has, however, seen a steady increase, both locally and internationally, in the number of lesbians becoming parents, with this growth often ascribed to improved access to adoption and assisted reproductive technologies (ART), as well as an increase in custody claims for children from earlier heterosexual relationships.

This chapter reports on a qualitative case study conducted in KwaZulu-Natal. The study aims to provide a detailed portrait of a lesbian couple's experience using ART and to explore the various issues they encountered while undergoing this process within a heteronormative social environment. A heteronormative society dictates that the ideal family unit consists of a heterosexual mother and father who have conceived children through 'natural' procreation. Consequently, any family structures deviating from this traditional model are positioned as the 'other' and framed as inferior or abnormal. Heteronormative standards are thus value infused and play a critical role in shaping the experiences of same-sex families.

The findings of this case study illustrate how the decision to create a family, the process of using ART and the experience of raising children are all socially mediated. Far from being an entirely personal or private experience, the family-creation process recounted by this lesbian couple reveals the intricate ways in which experiences are embedded in 'a complex web of intimate and larger social relations' (Gilligan, 1992, as cited in Mauthner & Doucet, 1998:125). The case study also highlights what Mauthner and Doucet (1998:125) refer to as 'relational ontology', a reading that places emphasis on understanding people in relation to their social context and 'exploring the 'duality' of social structures and human agency'. By acknowledging this duality it becomes possible to explore the powerful ways in which this particular couple's experiences are relationally and socially mediated while at the same time characterised by agency and resistance.

METHODOLOGY

The following analysis is based on a series of interviews conducted with a lesbian couple, B and J, who conceived using ART. The analysis employs the feminist voice-centred relational methodology developed by Mauthner and Doucet (1998) to translate their interest in relational ontology into a method of data analysis. This methodological approach seeks to explore 'individuals' narrative accounts in terms of their relationships to the people around them and their relationships to the broader social, structural, and cultural contexts within which they live' (126).

The analysis involved four readings of the data. The first reading examined the main plot and sub-themes, as well as recurrent images, words and contradictions that emerged during the discussion. The second reading focused on how the participants experienced, felt and talked about themselves. The third reading focused on how the participants spoke about their interpersonal relationships. The final reading attempted to place the participants' experiences within the broader socially, culturally and politically structured contexts shaping their everyday lives. While a full account of the analysis is beyond the scope of this chapter, some of the more salient themes are identified and discussed below.

THE DESIRE TO HAVE CHILDREN

One theme expected to emerge during the interviews was a strong desire from both women to create a family. Given the social expectation that all women should want to have children – and, by extension, the pathologisation of any decision not to (Knoesen, 2003; Lubbe, 2007b; Rose, 1990) – it was assumed that both partners in this relationship would express such sentiments. Interestingly, the couple had mixed feelings about starting a family, with J initially expressing some hesitation over having a child. The phrase 'never really featured in my plan' in the following quote may suggest that earlier in J's life (which, it must be noted, was before key legislative changes made ART more accessible for lesbian couples) she may have unconsciously absorbed dominant notions of homosexuality being inconsistent with family creation. J spoke openly about her early reluctance to start a family:

> If I could talk about my own desire, or it pretty much was a lack of desire, to have children. It never really featured in my plan, possibly

because I wasn't sure how I would 'get it together' as it were... Also, as I mentioned, when I had finished studying I went to work in a children's home, and I worked there for five years. And you know, working with a group of ten quite troubled kids is not quite the same as bringing up one or even more of your own children, but I think that I had far less a romanticised view of what it meant to be responsible for children. So yeah, I was probably quite concerned about what it meant to be taking on that responsibility, knowing that it was actually going to be 100 per cent of responsibility, 100 per cent of the time.

J's reference to her professional experience adds an interesting further layer to this statement. Having worked with children within a very particular context, one that destabilised and exposed the romanticised myth of motherhood, J was aware that 'families' are not always content spaces and that the responsibilities of parenthood are many. In contrast, B spoke of an overwhelming desire to have children, stressing that 'this was going to happen no matter what'.

Despite J's early reluctance, the couple's desires and attitudes eventually came together to create a context in which they mutually decided to start a family. J knew that B was determined to have children and, after much reflection, she felt that she had also reached a stage in her life in which she could make such a commitment. Discussing her motivations for having children, B identified similar reasons to those mentioned by participants in Touroni and Coyle (2002), including a love for children, a strong belief in her ability to be a good parent and, most notably, being at 'an appropriate stage of life'. As Touroni and Coyle note, the reasons for having children expressed by homosexual parents generally overlap with their heterosexual counterparts.

FEARS AND ANXIETIES
Three main sub-themes of anxiety emerged during the interviews.

The first was a fear of children being exposed to discrimination because of their parents' sexual orientation or 'alternative' family formation. The second related to the children wanting to know who their father was or being angry about the lack of a biological father in their life. The third anxiety was particularly interesting and related to the future influence of heterosexism on the children and the potential for this to lead to discrimination (or related stressful events) from their own offspring.

The anxieties identified by the participants in this case study support earlier research in the field. Touroni and Coyle (2002) and Navarro (2006) have identified a number of common concerns held by lesbian couples who have started, or who are thinking of starting, a planned lesbian-parented family. These concerns relate mostly to possible negative effects of raising children in a non-traditional family and the potential impact of discrimination. These fears are also often coupled with a lack of concrete informal support, which is often more readily available to heterosexual parents.

Touroni and Coyle's and Navarro's research shows that discrimination against children of same-sex parents should be seen as multi-layered, as these children may face stigmatisation for being conceived in an 'abnormal' way (i.e. a 'test-tube' baby) and/or for belonging to a same-sex family. There is also a potential for discrimination around the lack of a 'father' figure, a role that is positioned as essential and 'natural' within patriarchal family structures. Such discrimination may filter into the family unit itself, with the children over time displaying negative behaviours or attitudes towards their parents as a result of external social interactions.

The quote below demonstrates the way in which J experienced such anxieties:

> Ja, I suppose my one [fear] relates to that there would come a point where they would be embarrassed or maybe even ashamed that they have two mothers. That it would be, that it would be so… it would

be so atypical that they would actually, they would want to somehow hide it, and that they would therefore… that kind of… we would be excluded from their lives, and that they would… not quite have a double life, not quite that dramatic, but that they wouldn't feel comfortable to be completely who they are.

J's anxiety around this issue is also consistent with work conducted by Ferfolja and Skattebol (2007), who found that lesbian parents often fear that their children will experience discrimination due to their parents' sexual orientation. The significance of such anxieties cannot be overstated. As Touroni and Coyle (2002) correctly point out, although such fears may not always materialise, these emotions must not be invalidated, particularly given the dominance of heterosexuality within society and the pervasive othering and invalidation of same-sex families.

Hegemonic discourses relating to sexuality force individuals to unconsciously identify themselves in relation to the strict binary of 'normal' heterosexuality and 'abnormal'/perverted sexuality – essentially any sexual expression or identity outside of this rigid notion of heterosexuality. Hepburn (2003) among others has argued that this sexual dichotomy is both discursively constructed and value infused, with heterosexuality viewed as natural and morally right and, consequently, homosexuality viewed as unnatural and morally wrong. In Foucauldian theory, discourse is understood as organisations of knowledge or systems of thought that determine what is appropriate for people to think and do. For Foucault (1980), these organisations of knowledge are controlled by those in power to enforce and maintain social order – and, as a result, to consolidate and exert their own hegemony – through resources such as the media, public policy and the legal and health systems as well as through dominant religious and social institutions. As a result, certain understandings become so repeated and normalised in everyday experiences that they become customary, taken for granted and considered common sense.

Heteronormative understandings of gender and sexuality provide a telling example of the way in which certain dominant notions are privileged and eventually positioned as natural. Western religious and patriarchal discourses promote monogamous, procreative heterosexual relationships as morally right and the only 'correct' form of family creation. Such discourses become taken for granted by the heterosexual majority and simultaneously act as oppressive forces against homosexuals and other sexual minorities. Miriam (2007:2) speaks of heterosexism as 'the ensemble of social, political and cultural forces that naturalise and uphold heterosexuality as an entitlement and privilege, while threatening the social and existential survival of anyone who deviates from the heterosexual norm'. Dominant heteronormative ideals are then absorbed into understandings of what constitutes a 'normal' family unit – even at times by members of same-sex families themselves.

The negative effects of heteronormative discourses on same-sex parents, particularly in terms of their fears and anxieties, must not be downplayed. Gartrell et al. (1996) and Donovan (2000) both identify common anxieties among same-sex parents around how their children will respond to and be affected by not knowing the identity of, or having a relationship with, their biological father. Similar sentiments were expressed by B, who noted that:

> My fears are probably more around X in the sense that I don't know what it is like to be a young man and the kind of physiology... I mean I don't... I remember X, every time he used the toilet there would be wee all over the place, and it seems... I mean he starts weeing and it goes that way and... and he [a male family friend] was like 'it's completely natural'.

Later in the interview, she goes on to say:

> And it's kind of easy enough to ask about the little four-year-olds,

but when he's fifteen or so and I don't know what happens to boys' bodies really, and I guess… it's knowing that I have someone to be able to ask those questions… Is it normal for him to have these kind of mood swings?… So that's just really it. But it's got nothing to do with being gay… I suppose it does because otherwise you could have a father there to potentially answer these kinds of questions. Those are my… so that's my only fear. And also that… that they [the children] will go through a phase wishing they did have a dad… or want to find the sperm donor, um… which is their right to. If they want to, at the age of eighteen or something, they have the right to start a legal proceeding around that.

The reference to B's male friend in the quote above is particularly interesting. Her statement denotes awareness that, in the absence of a biological father, other close males can answer such questions and provide reassurance. Situations such as this challenge the notion that it is only the biological father who can play the role of 'father'. Of course, such an arrangement does not mean that B and J do not continue to have concerns about the lack of a primary male figure, but it shows that B has found alternative sources of support.

B's pondering as to whether such experiences may be exclusive to homosexual parents is also significant. Indeed, her affirmative conclusion indicates the absorption, on some level, of patriarchal discourses relating to the 'need' for a father figure. J also expressed similar feelings:

Who knows what will happen when they are slightly older, ja, because it might not be seen to be cool when you are twelve, you know, when boys might in particular say, 'Oh, yeah, I did this with my dad'. And I suppose part of me as well feels almost a little sad about that… that X would never be able to do that.

Almack (2006) suggests that concerns such as those expressed above should be understood in terms of broader discourses around the perceived needs of children raised in family structures outside of a heterosexual nuclear family. Almack argues that these 'needs', with their roots in psychology, are considered to be universal truths rather than recognised for what they are: social constructs shaped by specific historical and cultural contexts. Lesbians contemplating ART are faced with a variety of 'needs statements' revolving around what a child requires in order to develop 'normally'. Almack highlights two interlinking 'needs' in relation to lesbians using ART: the right (need) of a child to know his/her genetic origins and the need to have a father. By extension, this last point also suggests that families lacking a male figure will face myriad difficulties. Similar concerns were raised during the interviews for this case study, with both participants indicating anxieties around the absence of a father, particularly in relation to their son. Such anxieties illustrate the way that dominant patriarchal assumptions filter through society, even in situations when the heteronormative standard is resisted (such as in the family-creation process). In this case, the participants themselves, despite not believing that children need a father, were acutely aware that such structures, expectations and discourses may be imposed on their children.

Clarke and Kitzinger's (2005) work on constructions of male role models within lesbian-parented families sheds further light on B's statements. Their research focuses on the way in which lesbian mothers respond to arguments about the assumed need for male role models and the strategies these women employ to combat claims that their children are 'missing' something. Clarke and Kitzinger identify two primary responses to such arguments: first, 'highlighting the presence of men in the (extended) family' and second, 'emphasising that "we're not living on planet lesbian"' (140). This first strategy can be seen in B's statement that her male friend acts as a role model of sorts to her children. Such a response facilitates an amendment to the assumed insufficiency in a same-sex family structure. Interestingly,

Clarke and Kitzinger identify an inherent contradiction within this retort: 'in the very act of demonstrating that anti-lesbian fears about fatherless lesbian families are groundless, they reinforce the legitimacy of these fears' (143). This apparent contradiction highlights the way in which prevalent social understandings of 'healthy' families are simultaneously resisted and (re)produced by same-sex families. Moreover, it illustrates the complex ways in which such understandings and meanings are negotiated through the process of everyday experiences. The women in such studies are not activists in the traditional sense, but rather mothers who are attempting to make sense of their experiences against a backdrop of pervasive heteronormative ideals. This struggle highlights the active way in which people 'are constantly producing' themselves 'aided and abetted by others in our social world' (Burr, 2002:149).

BIOLOGICAL IMPORTANCE
In Western cultures, the 'traditional' family is deemed to be both heterosexual and biogenetically related. The creation of same-sex families through ART challenges this understanding at two significant, interacting and overlapping levels: the parents are, of course, homosexual and the children have been conceived independently of sexual intercourse. Despite this intrinsic destabilisation of ideas of 'normal' procreation, same-sex families often seek to integrate some degree of biological relatedness into the family-creation process. Jones' (2005:225) research, for instance, suggests that 'those seeking treatment are expected not to be treated with gametes provided by a donor of different physical characteristics unless there are compelling reasons for doing so'. This finding highlights the desirability of physical similarities, particularly in terms of helping a newly created homosexual family to pass as a genetic family. Jones contends that the 'practice of physical matching can also be interpreted as a means of establishing a figurative bio-genetic tie between a co-mother and

a donor-conceived child' (225). In B and J's case, the couple chose in-vitro fertilisation as opposed to adoption in order to have a genetic link to their progeny, though B did note that 'adoption was also an option – if this did not work out'. To further strengthen this genetic link, the couple opted for B to carry J's fertilised eggs, as opposed to those of an anonymous donor.

This case study supports the findings of Jones (2005), who disagrees with Sawicki's (1991) assertion that ART inherently creates moments of resistance to the family norm. Sawicki's work fails to consider how such technologies may (re)produce or leave unchallenged dominant norms of family construction, especially in relation to the desire for biogenetic relatedness. Indeed, the findings from this case study suggest that, despite challenging certain heteronormative family standards, lesbian couples do not necessarily challenge discourses of genetic relatedness. Most significantly, the findings highlight the complex ways in which same-sex families simultaneously challenge, reinterpret and reinforce dominant norms of family construction.

The desire for strong biological ties also relates to discourses around stability and what is perceived to be the optimal environment for raising children. Almack's (2006) research into societal pressures relating to 'ideal' family structures in the UK reveals that notions of stability in this context (as in many others) are often conceptually linked to the idea that children are best raised within the context of marriage and in the presence of *both* biological parents. These beliefs are perhaps partly responsible for the strong desire of many lesbian parents for their children to look as much like them as possible, thus ensuring the family does not deviate too much from heteronormative expectations. Interestingly, through the focus on biological motherhood and the need for genetic resemblance, lesbian mothers are (re)producing the idea that a 'real' family has to have biological and genetic connections, thus indirectly problematising other forms of family construction such as adoption.

EXPERIENCES WITH FAMILY MEMBERS

According to McVannel-Erwin (2007), the non-acceptance, and sometimes even overt rejection, of lesbians by their own families can be one of the biggest sources of stress and anxiety for same-gendered mothers. The participants of this case study described similar conflict-ridden encounters with family members, but noted that some relatives had become quite accepting over time. J explained that:

> My parents – and I [also] have a sister and a brother, and I don't know if I had been telling them a lot about it – but at the point where I started telling my parents about it, I think the way that I kind of communicated it was that it was B's thing that she was doing... I remember a couple of times my mum was kind of commiserating when there was the disappointment, and it was only when [B] actually was pregnant – and it was with my eggs – and my mother was like 'woohoo', and I said there was another surprise because they were my eggs.

Three important points surface in this quote. Firstly, when looking back at her experience, J noted that she downplayed the situation to her parents, perhaps due to a perceived lack of support or a desire to mitigate potential conflicts. This may also be viewed as a form of covering in that the issue was raised in a particular manner to ensure support and acceptance, and to accommodate the needs and emotions of others, namely heterosexual relatives. As Griffin (1991) argues, covering can be more about the desire to maintain self-integrity than about preventing exposure. Secondly, J acknowledged a lack of conversation around the topic, admitting that she did not speak extensively to her siblings. However, it is important to note that J specified she does not *remember* talking to them, which may not mean a total absence of conversation but rather that it was her mother who required the strategic approach mentioned above. Thirdly – and what is most interesting – is the crucial role that biology played in mediating

J's mother's reaction, which was quite positive once she learned that the eggs were her daughter's and that she would, therefore, be a genetic grandmother. The influence of socially enforced ideas of 'motherhood' on J's mother's reaction is significant. Her response is consistent with Rose's (1990) contention that women are socially programmed into the role of mother and nurturer, and that this role is positioned as 'natural' within broader heteronormative and patriarchal discourses. It is against these standards that women have to define and measure themselves. If considered in such terms, J's mother's excitement can be understood to be not only about the birth of a new child, but also about her daughter becoming a mother – and thus a 'successful' woman – and herself a grandmother.

Although B received support from some close relatives, she also experienced a breakdown of family relationships as a result of her decision to start a family. B shared the following account of her family's reaction to her sexuality and pregnancy:

> When I came out I was about 30. I then had a relationship with a woman from the age of 30, and probably came out fully at about 32 or something to my mum and dad. Mum flipped her lid and probably didn't talk to me for two more years, and then eventually kind of came around to it... It's not so much about us being gay, but it's about them coming out to their peer group... Yeah, but that [having a child] just pushed him [B's brother] over the edge completely... and when we were going through our court case he phoned our advocate to say that he was representing all the Y's [surname] in the world and he had contacted all the Y's in the world and my children weren't allowed to have the Y surname. And the attorney was kind of saying this case isn't about the children's surnames, and if you don't want your sister, [or] the children to have the Y surname, then you need to go and get your own advocate and go and start your own case. Ja, so now it's been eight years and I still don't have a relationship with my brother at all... it seemed the children were the edge.

B experienced an extremely hostile response from her brother, who completely rejected her because of her decision to start a family. Significantly, B describes a shift in her brother from being not so severely homophobic to being 'pushed… over the edge'. His behaviour demonstrates the multi-layered nature of heterosexism: while society may slowly be 'tolerating' homosexual people and their relationships, the idea of homosexual couples starting a family is often considered to have gone too far. Such a discourse continues to pathologise homosexuality and, in certain situations, to even consider it contagious. B's brother's response is not overly surprising given that relatively recent research (Clarke, 2002) has identified that lesbian parenting is frequently constructed as 'dangerous' for children who might be 'exposed' to it. B's brother's reaction is also consistent with the work of Mitchell, as cited in Laird and Green (1996), that reveals how previously supportive or tolerant family members often become overtly hostile towards lesbians who start families.

INSTITUTIONAL RELATIONSHIPS WITH THE MEDICAL FIELD

Both participants reported mixed experiences with the medical profession during the ART process. Their initial fertility doctor, a prominent specialist in the Cape Town area, was overtly homophobic to the point of initially (indirectly) refusing to assist them. The fertility doctor requested special supporting documentation including letters from a bank manager stating they had sufficient funds to have a child and a psychologist that they would be adequate as parents, as well as proof that the couple's parents supported their decision to have a child in this manner. At the time of the interviews, the participants felt that such demands were not standard procedure and that supporting documentation might not be commonly requested from heterosexual clients. J and B described the experience as follows:

B: We at that stage found the doctor extremely stressful.

J: He was a bit of a cold fish... and he didn't really seem to be terribly concerned or caring... and he started off the process by asking us both to go and see a psychologist to see that we were stable enough to have children. So we rushed off to a psychologist to get a report that we were stable enough to have children. He [the fertility specialist] then insisted that we go to our bank to get a letter from a bank manager that we could afford children. And so we got letters from our bank managers to say that we could afford children – whatever that means – which started getting me a bit uptight. I was like: 'Do you do this for your heterosexual couples?' And he was quite patronising.

B: I do remember my bank manager being absolutely 'Well, what do you want me to write?' [*laugh*] ... Ja, that is what's happening out there... It was just so patronising, you know? I mean, have you got enough money to have a child – what does that mean? God, can we go and like sterilise all the poor people in the country?

The participants then heard about a Johannesburg-based clinic which B wrote to and directly asked: 'I am a gay person – is this a problem for you?' The participants spoke favourably of their involvement with this clinic, explaining that that the staff was 'very welcoming to gays, and also had a very holistic view to the whole process in that they didn't just look at your ovaries'.

THE HETERONORMATIVE STANDARD AND RESULTING EXPERIENCES

While the couple in this case study did not report much overt discrimination, their ART and parenthood experiences have been, and continue to be, shaped by heteronormative standards and pressures. B noted that:

> There are times when you feel that you almost overcompensate, or over-parent, and I don't think one has to do that when you are a heterosexual parent. It's almost as if you have to keep proving that you are good enough parents, and there does not seem be this added pressure on heterosexual parents. I mean, for example, there have been times when I am really very busy at work and maybe can't go to watch X's cricket match, but no matter how busy I am I somehow manage to change things around and go. And when I compare it to heterosexual families I know, often if the main breadwinner can't make the match because of work issues, then it just seems to be accepted. But I feel that I almost don't have that option. Maybe it's a real thing that others may judge, or maybe even just my perception… so ja… or maybe even I would feel too bad for X.

This quote speaks to the deeply entrenched nature of the heterosexual 'norm', particularly the way in which this ideal regulates and impacts upon dominant notions of family. Being aware of the 'otherness' of a lesbian-parented family can force a degree of overcompensation, or at least a form of self-governance, that may not be as prevalent within heterosexual family units. In this case, B feels that 'no matter what' she *has* to go to this cricket match or else risk (self-)judgement.

This pressure to overcompensate supports Navarro's (2006) finding that lesbian parents often feel a need to justify to others their decision to have children. Navarro identifies what he labels the 'rhetoric of children's needs' (6) and explains how such discourses position the traditional heterosexual family unit as the most stable and optimal site for the development of children. Given that lesbian couples' decisions to create a family are similar to those of heterosexuals, feelings of guilt such as those expressed by B demonstrate the powerful effect of heterosexist discourses in (re)enforcing the heterosexual family as the ideal. It is important to note here that recent scholarship indicates that children from lesbian homes are equally as well-adjusted and developed as those from heterosexual homes and that, ultimately, it is the quality of parenting that is most important (Lubbe, 2007a). The lesbian participants in Almack's (2006) study were adamant that their children's psychological needs for security and stability could be met with the family units they were setting up that included one biological parent and one social parent of the same gender.

According to Dempsey et al. (2002), lesbians planning to start a same-sex family generally expect more challenges than their heterosexual counterparts. Their research identifies a number of specific challenges commonly mentioned by lesbian mothers, including fears and actual experiences of discrimination by their communities, prejudice and stigma at schools, rejection by family members, a lack of legal recognition and poor social support in general. Moreover, this research captures an alarming belief among lesbian parents that they often feel under investigation and that they are required to prove themselves more so than heterosexual parents. This latter aspect can be seen in the quote above in which B describes the pressure she feels to attend every one of her son's cricket matches.

The interviews indicate that B and J have experienced and negotiated a number of concerns and fears in relation to their same-sex family and role as parents, as well as suffering painful rejection by significant family members. While the couple appears to have had fewer direct experiences of discrimination than the subjects in Dempsey et al. (2002) and Navarro (2006), they have experienced the constraints and pressures of parenting within a heteronormative social environment. For example, in the following quote B talks about avoiding church out of fear of judgement. For B, the oppressive heteronormative beliefs of the institution close off the space from her and her children, who she fears will be unfairly influenced if they attend.

> I think probably one of the only areas that I found a bit difficult to introduce is perhaps the whole religious aspect or spirituality, where most of your kind of churches out there would obviously have issues around homosexuality. So I don't really want to take the kids

to a church with me where they are going to learn that their parents are wrong or… so it's… the children have never had any spiritual development, well not from us, none.

J responded to the above statement by noting that 'one can be spiritual without going to church', to which B replied:

Sure, but any formalised religion, they… certainly it seems at our school that – they just go to a public school in the area – and it seems to be very Christian-based and it's something that I have an issue with. Even last night X was asking me kind of lessons about, you know, did God make everyone good, and then did the devil make some of those bad, or did the devil make some good ones in the beginning and the devil made some bad ones in the beginning? And I was kind of saying there's Mohammed and Allah and… 'who [are] they?', 'there's only God and Jesus', 'no there ain't, you know'. So they obviously get a very Christian drumming at that school because we're not teaching them that.

The above dialogue shows how the couple, although they may not have experienced overt religious discrimination, have avoided certain spaces, most notably church services, out of fear the children may be taught their parents are wrong or immoral.

J has a slightly religious background in that she was part of a Christian charismatic church for about three years in her twenties, but now she feels alienated (as described by her later in the interviews) from the church. During the interview J expressed a desire to share some aspects of her spirituality, but noted that 'I don't know where to go'. While providing feedback after the formal interviews, J clarified that she is interested in introducing spirituality into the everyday lives of the children as opposed to formalised religion.

Many religious leaders and authorities continue to publicly disapprove of homosexuality, and it is because of such discriminatory doctrines that J and B are unwilling to engage with formalised religion. The couple's comments also illustrate a concern about the role and influence of Christianity on their children's schooling. J, in particular, is concerned that the children are being taught only one religious perspective and that her son is using this framework to understand the concepts of good and evil. It appears that her primary concern is the possible problematisation of her sexuality and relationship because of religious doctrine. Whether this risk is realised or not, the couple's concern powerfully demonstrates the way in which all people live within 'prevailing institutions and frameworks handed down to us by previous generations' (Burr, 2002:147). This is not to imply that people are passively determined by these institutions and frameworks, but rather that people 'struggle to negotiate what we can be and how we can conduct ourselves in the context of the social expectations, roles, narratives or discourses in which we find ourselves enmeshed' (Burr, 2002:147). For J, religion is one institution or framework that produces a particular struggle.

Both participants indicated feeling very accepted by their children's friends' parents, but they did recount one disturbing incident. While homophobic encounters were not prevalent in the couple's narrative, the following experience illustrates the kinds of unique challenges often faced by gay parents:

> I think there is one schoolchild of X and Y's now where I suspect there was a bit of homophobia, where the woman... her daughter wanted to come and play here with Y. She did, and then the mother came to fetch her later. We happened to have friends from Sweden here... There was this husband of my friend, and this woman assumed that this man was my husband. And I said no, no that's not my husband – I am a gay woman... and there's been no contact since. This child has not come here since, and they've made no contact, so I am assuming only that there was homophobia, you know, but apart from that... I mean from our Muslim friends to our Hindu friends

to our lesbian, black friends – everything – there has been absolutely complete acceptance.

This woman's reaction may suggest that she was not comfortable with her child being under the supervision of a lesbian parent. As Blake (2005) notes, such negative reactions often stem from the absurd idea that lesbian parents will provide an immoral parenting environment, pass on their homosexual identity and may even abuse children.

CONCLUSION
The themes discussed above shed some light on the way in which the two lesbian women understand and experience motherhood and the process of starting a family through ART. The analysis reveals the ways in which interpersonal and wider social relationships influence how these individuals negotiate what it is to be parents and an 'alternative' family within a broader heteronormative context. Ultimately, all of their experiences were mediated through a culture of heterosexism.

The family unit must be considered to be a socially created and experienced entity, one that needs to be expanded in definition to include existing and evolving formations that extend beyond traditional heteronormative ideals. The responses captured in this case study demonstrate how the participants are 'being' a new form of family, one that is set within a broader framework of pervasive heterosexist discourses. Such a process should be considered ongoing and continuous, with individuals actively producing new ways of being and demonstrating a sense of agency that allows for gradual change. However, such agency is always constrained by broader discourses, which explains why, although some discourses are challenged and destabilised by same-sex family units, others (such as the importance of biogenetics in a family and the discourse of women as needing to be mothers) are not.

REFERENCES

Almack, K. (2006). Seeking sperm: Accounts of lesbian couples' reproductive decision-making and understanding of the needs of the child. *International Journal of Law, Policy and the Family, 20*, 1–22.

Blake, P. (2005). *Correlates of lesbian-parented families.* (Unpublished doctoral thesis). Adelphi University, Adelphi.

Burr, V. (2002). *The person in social psychology.* East Sussex: Psychology Press Ltd.

Clarke, V. (2002). Sameness and difference in research on lesbian parenting. *Journal of Community Applied Social Psychology, 12*, 210–222.

Clarke, V. & Kitzinger, C. (2005). 'We're not living on planet lesbian': Constructions of male role models in debates about lesbian families. *Sexualities, 8*, 137–152.

Croucher, S. (2002). South Africa's democratisation and the politics of gay liberation. *Journal of Southern African Studies, 2*, 315–330.

Dempsey, D., McNair, R., Perlesz, A. & Wise, S. (2002). Lesbian issues, strengths, family matters. *Sexualities, 63*, 40–49.

Donovan, C. (2000). Who needs a father? Negotiating biological fatherhood in British lesbian families using self-insemination. *Sexualities, 3*(2), 149–194.

Ferfolja, T. & Skattebol, J. (2007). Voices from an enclave: Lesbian mothers' experiences of child care. *Australian Journal of Early Childhood, 32*(1), 10–18.

Foucault, M. (1980). Two lectures. In C. Gordon (Ed.), *Power/Knowledge: Selected interviews and other writings 1972–1977* (pp. 78–108). London: Harvester Wheatsheaf.

Gartrell, N., Hamilton, J., Banks, A., Mosbacher, D., Reed, N., Sparks, C. H. & Bishop, H. (1996). The national lesbian family study: Interviews with prospective mothers. *American Journal of Orthopsychiatry, 66*, 272–281.

Griffin, P. (1991). Identity management strategies among lesbian and gay educators. *Qualitative Studies in Education, 4*(3), 189–202.

Hepburn, A. (2003). *An Introduction to Critical Social Psychology.* London: Sage.

Jones, C. (2005). Looking like a family: Negotiating bio-genetic continuity in British lesbian families using licensed donor insemination. *Sexualities, 8,* 221–237.

Kitzinger, C. (1987). *The social constructionism of lesbianism.* London: Sage.

Knoesen, E. (2003). Speech to OUT AGM 2003. [Online]. Available at http://www.equality.org.za/archive/2–3/outagm.php

Laird, J. & Green, R.J. (1996). *Lesbians and gays in couples and families: A handbook for therapists.* San Francisco: Jossey-Bass.

Lubbe, C. (2007a). To tell or not to tell: How children of same gender parents negotiate their lives at school. *Education as Change, 11*(2), 45–65.

Lubbe, C. (2007b). Mothers, fathers, or parents: Same-gendered families in South Africa. *South African Journal of Psychology, 37*(2), 260–283.

Mauthner, N. & Doucet, A. (1998). Reflections on a voice-centred relational method: Analysing maternal and domestic violence. In J. Ribbens & R. Edwards (Eds), *Feminist dilemmas in qualitative research* (pp. 145–148). California: Sage.

McVannel-Erwin, T. (2007). Two moms and a baby: Counselling lesbian couples choosing motherhood. *Women and Therapy, 30*(1), 99–105.

Miriam, K. (2007). Toward a phenomenology of sex-right: Reviving radical feminist theory of compulsory heterosexuality. *Hypatia, 22*(1), 210–228.

Navarro, J. (2006). *Exploration of parenting amongst lesbians.* (Unpublished master's thesis). University of California, Los Angeles.

Parker, I. (1989) Discourse and power. In J. Shotter & K. Gergen (Eds), *Texts of identity.* London: Sage.

Rose, N. (1990). *Governing the soul: The shaping of the private self*. New York: Routledge.

Sawicki, J. (1991). *Disciplining Foucault: Feminism, power and the body*. New York: Routledge.

Touroni, E. & Coyle, A. (2002). Decision-making in planned lesbian parenting: An interpretative phenomenological analysis. *Journal of Community & Applied Social Psychology, 12*(3), 194–209.

Am I That Name? Middle-Class Lesbian Motherhood in Post-Apartheid South Africa[37]

Natasha Distiller

I BELONG TO A SO-CALLED ALTERNATIVE family, one which is comprised of two women, two children, and a dog and a cat. I am increasingly struck by how we are no different to what, in relation to our label, must be called ordinary families. Both those who are for us and those who are against us tend to invest in our difference. Homophobic interest groups insist we are not a family at all. The African Christian Democratic Party (ACDP), which opposed the South African Civil Union Bill of 2006 with its call for the extension of marriage rights to gays and lesbians, states on its website that, 'Not a single person making or supporting such a call is a product of such an unnatural and sinful relationship. We are all products of heterosexual relationships and not homosexuality. As a result, we reject the notion of the so-called homosexual marriages based on our biblical and cultural beliefs as African Christians.' The party also has a policy on 'The Family Institution', which begins, 'The family is an institution worthy of nurturing and protecting'. Clearly, my family is not a family at all in the eyes of the ACDP and my children, the products of homosexuality, fall outside of the realm of the intelligibly human. Historically, lesbians have been considered detrimental to the wellbeing of children, as the many custody battles lost by women who came out after having children attest (Lewin, 1993; Gottman, 1990; Tasker & Golombok, 1997). In addition, many people still believe that homosexuality is something a child can catch, like a virus, or be damaged into, like a wound, so homosexuals raising children is seen to be (problematically) increasing the likelihood of producing more homosexuals. From the other side, much pro-lesbian writing produced mostly in Anglo-America celebrates our intrinsic difference from and threat to the patriarchal order of Western culture (for example, Laird & Green, 1996:360; Mitchell, 1996; Muzio, 1993; Muzio, 1996; Sullivan 2004, ch. 3). Most of this literature explicitly or implicitly depends on what Muriel Dimen (1995) calls 'difference feminism' (306), that is, a way of thinking about sexual difference which assumes that women and men are fundamentally and essentially different, and which understands lesbian difference as the ultimate space for the development of a qualitatively different kind of femaleness.

As much as I would like to believe that we are intrinsically revolutionary (no need to recycle, then, since our credentials for a better world are already ensured), the daily routines associated with raising children feel very, very ordinary, if no less challenging for being shared by most people on the planet. Of course, in terms of the dynamics of our relationship, there are some differences, most notably the lack of established gender roles. I do think, though, that there is increased complexity between theory and practice. The ambiguities and ambivalences of daily life and people's interactions are not always captured by grand theoretical narratives, however much they strive to name real dynamics accurately. Not all heterosexual relationships are exclusively structured by and for male subjectivity. Certainly the examples of the relationships of friends and siblings suggest that heterosexuals can be in equitable and happy relationships as much as homosexuals can be in inequitable and unhappy ones.

With the birth of our first child, conceived through alternative insemination, it seemed to me that we become even more like any other family, on both an affective and a practical level. I felt part of the world in a way I never have before.[38] The one significant difference is we have to engage with other people's assumptions about our difference, their definitions of who we are and are not, and what we should and should not be doing. This is congruent with the literature, which suggests that the world's homophobia is the only harmful or difficult aspect of being the child of a gay or lesbian parent (for example Bos, Van Balen & Van den Boom, 2005). The single article I was able to locate at the time of writing which examines lesbian family functioning in South Africa emphasises the difficulties caused for the children of the participating families by the ignorance and prejudice of the world around them (Lubbe, 2008). Notably, there is no existing social recognition of the relationship of the non-biological mother of our child, reflected in the lack of a vocabulary to describe her (Sullivan, 2004). As a result, in South Africa we almost daily had to explain and describe who we three are to one another, in response to questions like, 'Which one is his mother?' or 'Are you his auntie?'

Our family's intrinsic sameness to most other families is denied by the assertions of our difference made both in our favour and in order to deny us our existence. At the same time, my declaration of sameness is not itself uncomplicated. For a lesbian to claim to be *the same as* in the context of a heteronormative patriarchal society is to allege an impossible relation, and so to participate in an act of social and self denial. It is also a claim that can only be made by lesbians with the power to pass, whether that power is class-based or comes from maternity or the performance of a recognisable and approved femininity. Despite what I have written above, I am profoundly ambivalent about being *the same as* heteronormativity, whether that sameness is skin-deep or not.[39] This paper will think about the politics of definitions in the context of the debate about the problems of mimicking heteronormativity. What does it mean to be different or to be the same in the context of post-apartheid South Africa's constitutional imperative to allow for difference? Can our post-apartheid language of rights accommodate the surprisingly complex relation between sameness and difference?[40]

I: EQUALLY HUMAN IN SOUTH AFRICA

The liberal humanist terms of a language of constitutional rights have long vexed many queer activists. Eng, Halberstam and Munoz (2005) place normative, monogamous gay and lesbian families alongside the worst political evils of the turn of the century, including Bush's war on terror, international xenophobia, and the collapse of the welfare state. They object to what they call 'queer liberalism', a term that for Eng et al. (2005) indicates an oxymoronic state of affairs, since a queer position should be the antithesis of liberal respectability. The inclusion of the rights of sexual minorities in the South African Constitution (found in Article 9 (3), the 'Equality clause') in its liberal humanist terms has not been without its critics from within the gay rights movement itself (if one can even speak of 'a' movement in South Africa – another definitional dilemma). The work of inclusion was done by the erstwhile National Coalition for Gay and Lesbian Equality, which was largely white, male, and middle class: the homosexuals with social and economic power. They strategically deployed a more conservative language of human rights, and did not focus on identity politics (Cameron, 2005; Massoud, 2003; Oswin, 2007). Furthermore, the Coalition itself, South African as it was, was not without its internal politics of exclusion, revolving around race, class and gender (Gunkel, 2010; Swarr & Nagar, 2003). The successful 'respectability' of the rallying cry for human rights is thus intertwined with the middle-class, white 'respectability' of a then-largely-Anglo-American oriented movement.

A human rights discourse, the deployment of the figure of the good citizen entitled to his or her place in the civic sun, can function to mask the lack of extension of these rights to less 'respectable' or socially empowered citizens, or other national Others: 'the idea of equal political rights attached to the concept of a "universal citizen" as the bearer of rights masks the material social, economic and political inequalities of subjects' (Van Zyl, 2009:365; Stacey & Meadow; 2009). Additionally, rights-based activism is limited in its ability to create opportunities for minorities (Stychin, 1996), not least because it tends to assert a coercive normativity. Local queer theorists have pointed out how, internationally, the extension of human rights to (certain) homosexuals has been used as evidence of their civility by governments implicated in other kinds of human rights abuses (Gunkel, 2010; Hoad, 2005).

The implications of the political compromises made by homosexual activists have been well-documented in the international LGBTI movement. For example, Nancy Polikoff (1993), in an article entitled, 'We will get what we ask for: Why legalizing gay and lesbian marriage will not "dismantle the legal Structure of gender in every marriage"', discusses the strategies available to American queers to achieve social and political rights. Reviewing the debates about how the American community has approached marriage rights, the right to serve in the military, and drawing a parallel with the struggle for abortion rights, she argues that the strategic approach, such as that advocated for by Edwin Cameron (1993) in the context of the inclusion of the rights of sexual minorities in the Equality Clause, ultimately entrenches a gender hierarchy, and can never 'dismantle' it (Sandell, 1994). Claiming access to the system requires operating under the terms of the system.

On one level, then, the fact of the South African Constitution's protection of same-sex rights is virtually guaranteed to assert the pressure of sameness on the citizens it aims both to protect and to construct. But South Africa also makes it clear why succumbing to this imperative to be seen as *the same as* may be a whole lot more radical than it looks to people like Eng and his co-authors. South Africa, like other parts of Africa, is currently knee-deep in state-sanctioned homophobia of the worst kind. The dominant discourse is that homosexuality is 'un-African', a 'Western' import or disease. Zimbabwe's president, Robert Mugabe, has called homosexuals 'worse than pigs and dogs' (Croucher, 2002:316; Gunkel 2010:25-6; Leatt & Hendricks, 2005; Oswin, 2007:101) [it is quoted in all of them]. This straightforward denial of the shared humanity of homosexually-oriented people finds confirmation in attitudes of the leadership of Uganda, Namibia, and Malawi, to name a few. The current ANC leadership is also clearly not supportive of gay rights. In 2006, then-deputy president Jacob Zuma told the *Sowetan* newspaper that same-sex marriages were 'a disgrace to the nation and to God' ('Zuma invokes gay wrath', 2006) and advocated violence against gays. He subsequently apologised, but in 2010, Minister of Arts and Culture in his government Lulu Xingwana called photographs by lesbian photographer Zanele Muholi, 'immoral, offensive and going against nation building' ('Minister slams "porn" exhibition', 2010). South Africa also appointed openly homophobic journalist Jon Qwelane Ambassador to Uganda in the middle of that country's labelling of a law which would have prescribed the death penalty for homosexuality. At the time of his appointment, Qwelane was facing charges of hate speech at the Human Rights Commission for an article he had written about homosexuals. And homophobia is not limited to those in political power. Jacklyn Cock (2005) notes the South African 'paradox' of a constitutional world-first entrenchment of gay rights together with the lack of support for these rights from the majority of the South African population. She also points out that the gay rights movement in this country has never had mass participation of its own.

One form homophobia is taking in South Africa, one expression of the belief that homosexuals are not equally human and so not entitled to the citizenship rights of other South Africans, is the so-called corrective rape of black lesbians, sometimes deliberately by HIV-positive men. Of course, this particular form of discipline intersects with the huge levels of violence against all women in the country. As with most forms of oppression, it is mostly women who are working-class and black who bear the brunt.[41] In this context, violence against lesbians is not reported, not taken seriously by community authority figures, and not given national attention or priority (Potgieter, 2006).[42]

Asserting the right to be *the same as* might be a way to accommodate difference by insisting on the shared humanity promised by a human rights discourse. This may not only be a capitulation to the status quo. It is literally a matter of life and death, not a theoretical squabble. It may also be the only way to force the heteronormative to change. Oswin (2007) has read the successful campaign for the inclusion of sexual orientation in the list of South African constitutional protections as the realisation of the queer potential of the 1955 Freedom Charter on which the Constitution is based. Sameness might be strategically used, in other ways, in a genuinely progressive manner.

The meaning of post-apartheid South Africa should by definition include re-conceiving, re-making, re-conceptualising. The country was born out of the construction and assertion of differences between people, in its colonial genesis (Distiller & Samuelson, 2005; Elphick & Gilliomee, 1979; Ward & Worden, 1998) and went on to make a hierarchical system out of difference which reached into, and helped to structure, every level of state and psyche under apartheid. We have recently been given a chance to rework who 'we', as members of an imagined community, can be. The last fifteen years have demonstrated that a clean break, a difference, from the past, is much more complicated to achieve than many of us realised. If we assert this break, we ignore the structural and psychological inheritances which then can continue to shape any future possible definitions unchecked and disavowed. But if we cannot find new ways to conceptualise ourselves and our relations to each other, new definitions, we remain bonded to a system we have struggled to overcome.

Post the arms deal corruption scandal; post the HIV/AIDS debacle; post worsening poverty, graft, and unemployment; post Jacob Zuma's rape trial and his 'traditional' attitudes to women and homosexuals; post Polokwane, it is clear by now that post-apartheid South Africa is not somewhere over any rainbow, or indeed, over its past. Instead our society is firmly ensconced in the same class and gender dynamics, even if its racial aspects have shifted to some degree for some people. It is in this context, of promise and possibility as well as of despair and denial and disappointment, that the experience of being both different and the same acquires particular resonances and ironies.

I write this article fully aware that for most lesbians in South Africa, or more accurately, since this paper is about definitions (and their difficulties), for most African women who desire other women,[43] the issues of sameness and difference are not at all theoretical. For most South African women-desiring women, the meaning of their identities, the meaning other people assert over their identities, is violent to a literal degree that finds no place in my experience of myself and my family. I acknowledge these women, and my difference from them. The choice to be a mother, the use of fertility treatment technology, the concept of the alternative family, all these originate with an experience and an identity which is foreign to many, if not most, South African women who are not heterosexually inclined. Some of these women have begun to tell their stories (Morgan and Wieringa [2005] provide narratives, as well as examples of the work of photographer Zanele Muholi; Brundrit [n.d.] also features the work of Muholi). The story told here is a different one. It is a story of privilege and of the South African class elite. The comparatively minor discomforts with which I live, in the face of heterosexism more than homophobia, do bear some relation to the rapes and murders of working-class black lesbians. We all face the results of our society's construction of homosexuals as different, albeit in very different ways. A hospital's refusal to facilitate the birth of my son, despite the existence of our Constitutional right not be discriminated against on the basis of our sexuality,[44] is related to the denial of the humanity of the women who suffer far more brutally, and often in silence.[45] Both experiences suggest that the Constitution's definition of citizenship, its implicit recognition of our shared humanity, is no guarantee that our fellow citizens will concede the same. Indeed, it is no guarantee even that the state which considers the Constitution its founding document will take the rights of working-class or elite lesbians seriously: The Joint Working Group, a coalition of organisations working on LGBTI issues, launched the 07-07-07 Campaign Against Hate Crimes, to try and achieve systemic justice for women and men brutalised and murdered in South Africa because of their sexualities (Joint Working Group, n.d.). And despite a Constitutional Court ruling that enforces their obligation to do so (handed down in 2004 and known as the J&B case to protect the privacy of the children concerned), it has taken almost four years (beginning in 2007), and countless engagements with a confused system, to get the Department of Home Affairs to put my partner's name on our children's birth certificates (Bamford, 2009).

II: WHAT THE LITERATURE SAYS (AND DOESN'T SAY)

The (heteronormative, patriarchal) status quo asserts itself by the power of the myth of sameness as safety, of repetition as healthy, and of deviation as sinister (Dollimore, 1991). The experience of being a white, middle-class lesbian mother in post-apartheid South Africa has been an object lesson in the affective power of sameness. What, exactly, is a lesbian mother? Is she somehow by definition different from a heterosexual mother? Is her relation to her child different? Is this difference, if it exists, fixed, so that all lesbian mothers will experience the same kind of difference, to whatever degree? Is it her relation to the world that makes her a different kind of mother? Is the difference intrinsic to her child's experience of the world, such that her label is in fact a marker of his positioning? Until recently, the phrase 'lesbian mother' was considered by many a contradiction in terms. Invoking the psychoanalytic vocabulary so useful to this topic, Cheryl Muzio (1993) describes the fundamental otherness of lesbian mothers. For lesbians to choose to become mothers, she says, is to choose 'to inhabit a kind of psychoanalytic netherworld where neither their passionate nor maternal relationships are deemed to have substance'; as lesbians their desires are denied or masculinised; as women their identities are inconceivable to a patriarchal order which understands women in relation to men, and as mothers in a genealogy which must be patriarchal (Muzio, 1993:219): with the increase in lesbians having children, 'We have witnessed the birth of the invisible (M)other'. On the other hand, in terms other than the psychoanalytic, in the daily performance of identity, being a mother makes one recognisable to society, allows for the expectations in terms of roles and behaviour that were absent from the lesbian relationship before the arrival of children. In becoming mothers, lesbians join heterosexual women in a particular organisation of identity which partakes of mainstream gender ideology... motherhood indirectly enables women (whether lesbian or heterosexual) to claim a specific location in the gender system (Lewin, 1993). (For a detailed discussion on the meanings of lesbian motherhood, see Schwartz, 1998:121–154).

The literature that has emerged in the late 1990s and early 2000s seems to agree that there has been a lesbian baby boom in Anglo-America. The first 'wave' of this process comprised those women who came out after marriage and childbearing, and the second comprised children born to lesbian couples. Despite the revolutionary wishes of the more activist feminist writing on the subject, much of the social scientific literature has tended to focus on how lesbian families are not really different to heterosexual families, in order to secure respectable visibility and socio-political rights for these families. Studies of these families, examinations of the definition of the lesbian mother and the consequences of this definition, with an emphasis on the effects of this creature on her children, have overwhelmingly asserted that she is, in fact, the same as most other mothers in the effects of her mothering. From within the field of social work, family studies, psychiatry, psychology, nursing, and law, researchers have found that the children of lesbian mothers are the same as other children: their gender identities are mainstream, their gender roles and behaviours are standard and 'correct', their sexual orientation will tend to be hetero-, their development is 'normal' (Golombok, Spencer & Rutter, 1983; Patterson, 1994; Schwartz and Gottman, 1990; Steckel, 1987, [all of which overview the literature to their respective dates]. See also Bos et al., 2005; Brewaeys & Van Hall, 1997; Hoeffer, 1981; Tasker & Golombok, 1997 [which traces the development of children from 1976–1991]). Recently, the political imperative of this literature has begun to receive attention. Jacqui Gabb (2004) was one of the first to make the point that the politics of the researcher will shape the findings, such that the coherent picture presented by the literature might conceal 'critical differentials'.[46] Engaging with essentially the same limitation from a different point of view, Stacey and Biblarz (2001) critique the defensive starting points of most of the research, which by necessity has to 'prove' that gays and lesbians can parent and form recognisable families. They suggest this defensiveness, while politically understandable, has implications for the research methodologies and findings.[47] They re-examine the studies which claim there is no difference between children of lesbian parents and others, in order to suggest that the political imperative to assert the 'normality' of our families has skewed findings which suggest that there are small but significant differences (see also Kirkpatrick, 2004).

And there are differences which have been charted so far, even as their implications have been minimised. One of the first studies to take the other mother seriously as a parent and to work with children who were born into lesbian partnerships, found that having two mothers results in a 'qualitatively different separation experience'

(Steckel, 1985:81). Children with a lesbian other mother instead of a father tended to be less aggressive, saw themselves as more lovable, and were more engaged with younger children, according to Steckel. The fact of a more involved co-parent, and a less dyadic relationship with the mother were factors that were theorised to influence the development of the children of lesbians (Steckel, 1987).

However, while it in some ways endorses and in other ways interestingly complicates Nancy Chodorow's thesis (1978) that absent fathers create difficulties for boys' gender identification, imbuing masculinity with a fundamental anxiety which is an important source of the perpetuation of unequal gender relations, Steckel's (1985) study has not proven to be conclusive. Patterson's study of children born to out lesbians – what Patterson designates '"new" lesbian mother families' in order to differentiate them from the 'old' way children found themselves with lesbian mothers, following the divorce of their parents (Patterson, 1994:156), found that Steckel's conclusion could not be confirmed. She did find that lesbians' children 'reported greater stress reactions than did children of heterosexual mothers (possibly a result of a homophobic world, possibly because they were more eloquent in their emotional vocabularies), but they also reported a greater overall sense of wellbeing' (Patterson, 1994:168).

Perhaps the most controversial findings have been that adolescents and young adults raised by lesbians might be more likely to be sexually explorative, before settling on their heterosexuality (Steckel, 1985), and that daughters of lesbian mothers are more likely to consider engaging in a lesbian relationship, even though they are not more likely to identify as lesbian or bisexual (Tasker & Golombok, 1997).[48] More than this, Stacey and Biblarz (2001:163) find it 'implausible' that children of gays and lesbians would not have a sexual identity that was different to a heteronormative one. We could reasonably expect that children raised by homosexuals would more easily access and display homosexual desire, they suggest. This is an explicit challenge to the discourse of 'normalcy', designed to put the concerns of the courts at ease by assuring them that lesbians can be counted on to produce straight children.

None of this literature deals with the specificities of lesbian-parent functioning in South Africa, or the differences that our particularly complicated history of the class/race nexus will bring. Carien Lubbe's (2008) pioneering study into the experiences of children of lesbian parents in South Africa offers an in-depth account of the methodological complexities of the research process, but does not engage with race and class in any detail. I suspect that this is because, as I have suggested above, these concerns are the province of a minority in the country, protected by both class and race privilege (Lubbe's sample contains some coloured families, which share in the protections that middle-class status provides). The problems of definitions I am exploring here insert these privileged few South Africans into an international LGBT discourse, where they partially belong. At the same time, the issues of access to South African citizenship are relevant to all South Africans, and perhaps even more so to those same-sex-identified African women who are most marginalised in everyday practice. Much more work remains to be done on what aspects of the Anglo-American literature relate to the broader South African context, and what lenses need to be developed to explore lesbian family functioning here more fully. In the meantime, since to be South African is also to be in the larger world, and to be a middle-class South African is to participate in the global LGBT discourse to some extent, I use this international literature as a point of reference here, even if it is a partial point of reference.

For all our asserted differences, then, overall the literature that exists suggests that we are spectacularly ordinary parents. Most important is the political implication of this sameness and the power of belonging it confers. For the sake of the children we want to raise as happy and self-confident, it is imperative that we are recognised as part of the society they will have to navigate. Regardless of whether or not the definition of parenting needs to change such that the raising of children who are different is not seen as pernicious or unfortunate (a change which practitioners of Disability Studies no doubt would also welcome), the daily reality of lesbian parenting in the mostly middle-class and mostly white families the international literature has mapped seems to be that it is not, in fact, substantially different from heterosexual parenting, with all the implications for the construction of an acceptable homonormativity objected to by critics like Riggs (n.d.) who, as a gay parent himself, dislikes the defensive attitude of the current psychological literature.[49]

The normativity mapped in the majority of the literature on (overwhelmingly white, middle-class, lesbian) homosexual family functioning may well be because most of the lesbian relationships to which children are born or into which they are adopted in these Anglo-American studies are structurally similar to the monogamous heterosexual unit so important to the proponents of so-called family values (the realities for most South African lesbian parents are very different; see Morgan & Wieringa, 2005:320–1). The really alternative family structures, in an Anglo-American sense, enabled by queer lives (Ainslie & Feltey, 1989; Sandell, 1994), and not only the lives of those who are sexually queer, are even further away from mainstream acceptance than the idea that two women who desire each other can and should raise children.

Because of the association of femaleness with maternity, middle-class lesbian parents have somewhat of an easier path than their gay, trans, or otherwise queer counterparts, especially of family units that are not comprised of a pair, and/or are not monogamous. So, as the birth mother in a monogamous lesbian relationship, legally protected and theoretically socially legitimised by the Civil Union Act of 2006, I am able to feel, and to assert, a sameness of intention and experience that enables my family to claim access to the right to be recognised and respected. Our social positioning as privileged whites also has everything to do with this feeling of entitlement. What I have been amazed by is how important it has been to me to be able to claim this right. While for most South Africans, the equality written into the Constitution remains purely theoretical, it has had a real effect on our lives in enabling us to be a family in the first place. In this privileged context of access to the rights of the Constitution, which seeks not only to protect but respect difference, and so enables its freedom of movement, why do I need for us to be seen as the same as? In the context of my own politics, why do I want to feel *the same* as a system I did not think I respected? Having a child has meant entering into the social Symbolic in new and unexpected ways, and has made me aware of normativity's reproductive power. This has come as a shock to me, especially in a country where normativity was so perniciously perpetuated for so long.

This paper's concern with definitions is therefore in part an attempt to articulate an embodied realisation of a theoretical moment: the implication of the self in the social has become inescapably apparent. Utopian dreams of living a privileged queer difference have been grounded in the adult reality of motherhood. The ironies and contradictions of achieving meaning, subjectivity, definition, are implicit in the Lacanian idea that we have to move through the shared, enter the always-already-social linguistic Symbolic, in order to be a person. I cannot be a mother, even, or especially, a lesbian mother, without implicating myself and my family in what other people say my motherhood means. The independence of difference my lesbianism conferred, its promise of self-definition in the disruption of gender and intimate gender roles it forced, has been replaced by the vulnerability of needing to be the same, for my child's sake.

While the experience raises the implicated complicities of the sameness/difference binary as I have described,[50] it simultaneously deconstructs them. It does so by re-entering individual emotion into community, by emphasising how experiences of care (motherhood, parenting, families, desire, partnership) insert us all in the shared realm of the human. This is to say, what the experience of being a 'lesbian mother' has left me with is the realisation, on a cellular level which is difficult to articulate without entering into the limitations of cliché, of the meaning of humanness, which means of my sons' reliance on me and my, and our, reliance on you. At the same time, our status and definition as an 'alternative family', reminds me once more of the impossibility of being *the same as* in the context of a structure whose function it is to define, which means also to exclude.

III: DIFFERENTLY HUMAN?

In *Undoing gender* Judith Butler (2004:2) writes:

> The terms by which we are recognized as human are socially articulated... And sometimes the very terms that confer 'humanness' on some individuals are those which deprive certain other individuals of the possibility of achieving that status... These norms have far-reaching consequences for how we understand the model of the human entitled to rights or included in the participating space of political deliberation.

Butler's 'we' here is generic, its referent the human in general. She goes on to make a more specific statement:

> One of the central tasks of lesbian and gay... rights is to assert in clear and public terms the reality of homosexuality, not as an inner truth, not as a sexual practice, but as one of the defining features of the social world in its very intelligibility. In other words, it is one thing to assert the reality of lesbian and gay lives as a reality, and to insist that these lives are worthy of protection... but it is quite another to insist that the very public assertion of gayness calls into question what counts as reality and what counts as a human life. Indeed, the task of international lesbian and gay politics is no less than a remaking of reality, a reconstituting of the human... (Butler, 2004:29–30)

Butler (2004) points out the significance of the individual's reliance on the social for recognition. This need for recognition has private implications, as I have been discussing. It is also central to the polis, to the public forum, and indeed, the argument here (both mine and Butler's) is that in the end the private cannot be removed from the public; they are co-constitutive. The importance of ensuring a safe family space for one's children involves not wanting them to carry the burden of a difference that actually has very little to do with them, and everything to do with their society's definitions of who is fully human. Central to the practical enactment of this recognition is the importance of public rights, which is why the theoretical citizenship conferred on gays, lesbians, and more recently, thanks to the work of Sally Grosz and the Intersex Society of South Africa, intersexuals,[51] by the South African Constitution is so important. Lesbians who have no substantive rights in countries which actively discriminate against them clearly cannot be citizens.

Ruth Morgan and Saskia Wieringa (2005), in their work with same-sex-loving African women, stress that one effect of discrimination against these women is to deny them access to full citizenship of their countries, and thus by implication to participation in the polis on the levels of both identity and action. South Africans are immensely fortunate to be in a better legal position, which makes an enormous difference to the lives of some gays and lesbians, and at least carries the hope of something better for the rest.

The inclusion of lesbians into the realm of the fully human, and from there the recognition of the sameness of lesbian mothers to other mothers, is an ontological problem. The assertion of sameness invariably entails buying into a system which by definition struggles to see lesbians as either citizens or humans. Entry into the concept of the authentic citizen of democracy means entry in a patriarchal system, structured by sexual difference and so by a particular use of a gender hierarchy.

How then do we begin to engage with the reality of the need for the rights of our 'alternative' families when gender norms continue to structure full humanity so as to exclude same-sex-loving women, and especially, in the power relations of South Africa, poor, black, same-sex-loving women? How do we navigate the irony that motherhood conveys social recognition only through its relegation to a definition of womanhood that is reliant on its subordination to masculinity in a heterosexist binary?

We must occupy the space of what Tim Trengove-Jones (2005) has described as 'inbetweenness', the desire to both have a queer history and identity acknowledged, and to claim ordinary citizenship rights, which registers 'a not always unawkward blend of sameness and difference' (Trengove-Jones, 2005:136). This is to see, finally, over and above the ontological difference we represent, the mundane human sameness which also structures our desires as products of the system. To be *the same as* is all that most alternatively-identified people want. In Potgieter's (2005) study of black lesbians' discourses, she noted the 'women's quest to be constructed as "everyday", "regular" women who are located within their communities' (Potgieter, 2005:178). This desire to be *the same as* – that is, the reality that most homosexuals are not revolutionaries (so we do need to recycle) – raises an important question. Why do homophobia and its sibling misogyny continue to deny sexual minorities (and especially same-sex-loving women) their religious, civic and *human* rights when in by far the majority of cases granting these rights would reinforce the current patriarchal and capitalist system?

Damien Riggs (n.d.) has pointed out how the logic of sameness, asserting gay and lesbian parents' fitness as parents in the terms of the current system, reproduces not only heteronormativity but negative stereotypes about gays and lesbians. The constant desire to counter them only gives them life by conceding to them, he says. I read his article, with its critique of the reification of a certain kind of psychological knowledge, with agreement and with respect. And I find myself saying, 'yes but', 'yes but'. Isn't the embracing of the marginal position, the assertion of the right to remain outside of the dominant signifying economy of humanness, something only the elite can afford?

Perhaps it is that my feelings fall short of my politics, a sign of my age or my inescapable bourgeois location. But I think we should start to reconsider the charge that to assert our sameness is only to collude with the system that excludes us and oppressed homosexuals and many others. We have to engage, especially those of us with privilege, in order to begin to effect some kind of real, sustainable, systemic (not theoretical or revolutionary) change. Butler (2004) theorises a new relationship to otherness and difference, one which would enable a 'process of remaking the human' (Butler, 2004:4). In this new relationship, relational humanity is recognised. This means that for those who are recognised as humans and are able to live what she calls viable lives, the call is to open the self to the difference of the other without understanding it. It is to submit to change, not knowing how one will be changed. It is to agree to go in the direction of the unknown. On the other hand, Butler also insists that the misrecognised Other does have the capacity to critique the system which denies her her humanity. In other words, despite the system's refusal to recognise her language, her protestations and resistance are meaningful, not because they 'celebrate difference as such' but because they can 'establish more inclusive conditions for sheltering and maintaining life that resist[…] models of assimilation' (2004:4). The human 'exceed[s]… its categorical definition' and there is always the possibility of 'opening up the category to a different future' (2004:13).

So are some lesbian mothers, in South Africa and elsewhere, reworking human potential, fundamentally challenging patriarchal economic and psychological relations, and so laying the groundwork for the only genuine feminist revolution possible? Or are we entering the mainstream, trading radical alterity for respectability and co-optation? The emphasis on sameness comes at the cost of disabling change to the system which generates homophobia in the first place. On the other hand, the insistence on difference acquires more than a theoretical inflection when it is embodied in time, in place, and in lived experience. So, in post-apartheid South Africa, where as middle-class citizens we have some kind of access to the constitutional protection of our right to exist even as, as lesbian women, we are problems for the terms of a liberal humanist framework, what are we? Can we enable one way for South Africans, as members of that powerful construct, a nation, to learn to do difference differently?

REFERENCES

Ainslie, J. & Feltey, K. M. (1991). Definitions and dynamics of motherhood and family in lesbian communities. *Marriage and Family Review*, 17, 63–85.

Bamford, H. (2007). City hospital turns away gay would-be mom. *The Weekend Argus*, 18 August, p. 3.

Bamford, H. (2009). Certificate red tape stymied gay parents. *The Sunday Independent*, 15 March, p. 2.

Benjamin, J. (1988). *The bonds of love: Psychoanalysis, feminism, and the problem of domination*. New York: Pantheon.

Benjamin, J. (1991). Father and daughter: Identification with a difference – A contribution to gender heterodoxy. *Psychoanalytic Dialogues*, 1(3), 277–300.

Bos, H. M. W., Van Balen, F. & Van den Boom, D. C. (2005). Lesbian families and family functioning: An overview. *Patient Education and Counselling*, 59, 263–275.

Brewaeys, A. & Van Hall, E. V. (1997). Lesbian motherhood: The impact on child development and family functioning. *Journal of Psychosomatic Obstetrics and Gynecology*, 18, 1–16.

Brundrit, J. (n.d.). A lesbian story: An exhibition project by Jean Brundrit. Catalogue.

Butler, J. (2004). *Undoing gender*. London and New York: Routledge.

Cameron, E. (2005). Presentation to the GLOW Action Committee and SHOC Workshop. In N. Hoad, K. Martin & G. Reid (Eds), *Sex & politics in South Africa* (pp. 178–187). Cape Town: Double Storey.

Chodorow, N. J. (1978). *The reproduction of mothering: Psychoanalysis and the sociology of gender*. Berkeley: University of California Press.

Chodorow, N. J. (1989). *Feminism and psychoanalytic theory*. New Haven and London: Yale University Press.

Clarke, V. (2008). From outsiders to motherhood to reinventing the family: Constructions of lesbian parenting in the psychological literature 1886–2006. *Women's Studies International Forum, 31*, 118–128.

Cock, J. (2005). Engendering gay and lesbian rights: The equality clause in the South African Constitution. In N. Hoad, K. Martin & G. Reid (Eds), *Sex & politics in South Africa* (pp. 188–209). Cape Town: Double Storey.

Connell, R. W. (1987). *Gender and power*. California: Stanford University Press.

Coyle, A. & Kitzinger, C. (Eds) (2002). *Lesbian and gay psychology: New perspectives*. Oxford: Blackwell.

Croucher, S. (2002). South Africa's democratisation and the politics of gay liberation. *Journal of Southern African Studies, 28*(2), 315–330.

Dimen, M. (1982). Seven notes for the reconstruction of sexuality. *Social Text, 6*, 22–30.

Dimen, M. (1995). On 'our nature': Prolegomenon to a relational theory of sexuality. In T. Domenici & R. C. Lesser (Eds), *Disorienting sexuality: Psychoanalytic reappraisals of sexual identities* (pp. 129–152). London and New York: Routledge.

Dimen, M. (2003). *Sexuality, intimacy, power*. London: The Analytic Press.

Distiller, N. (2008). *Desire and gender in the sonnet tradition*. Oxford: Palgrave.

Distiller, N. & Samuelson, M. (2005). 'Denying the coloured mother': Gender and race in South Africa. *L'Homme, 16*(2), 28–46.

Dollimore, J. (1991). *Sexual dissidence: Augustine to Wilde, Freud to Foucault.* Oxford: Clarendon Press.

Elphick, R. & Gilliomee, H. (Eds). (1979). *The shaping of South African society 1652–1820.* Cape Town: Longman.

Eng, D., Halberstam, J. & Munoz, J. E. (2005). What's queer about queer studies now? *Social Text, 84–85*(23), 1–17.

Fester, G. (2006). Some preliminary thoughts on sexuality, citizenship and constitutions: Are rights enough? *Agenda, 67*, 100–111.

Folgerø, T. (2008). Queer nuclear families? Reproducing and transgressing heteronormativity. *Journal of Homosexuality, 54*(1/2), 124–149.

Gabb, J. (2004). Critical differentials: Querying the incongruities within research on lesbian parent families. *Sexualities, 7*(2), 167–182.

Goldner, V. (1991). Towards a critical relational theory of gender. *Psychoanalytical Dialogues, 1*(3), 249–272.

Golombok, S., Spencer, A. & Rutter, M. (1983). Children in lesbian and single-parent households: Psychosexual and psychiatric appraisal. *Journal of Child Psychology and Psychiatry, 24*(4), 551–572.

Gottman, J. (1990). Children of gay and lesbian parents. In F. Bozett & M. Sussman (Eds), *Homosexuality and family relations* (pp. 177–196). New York: Harrington Park Press.

Gunkel, H. (2010). *The cultural politics of female sexuality in South Africa.* New York: Routledge.

Hoad, N. (2005). Introduction. In N. Hoad, K. Martin & G. Reid (Eds), *Sex & politics in South Africa* (pp. 14–25). Cape Town: Double Storey.

Hoeffer, B. (1981). Children's acquisition of sex-role behaviour in lesbian-mother families. *American Journal of Orthopsychiatry, 51*(3), 536–544.

Johnston, N., Tshabalala, T., Ndlovu, N. & Dibetle, M. (2009). Comment & analysis. *Mail & Guardian*, 30 January – 5 February, p. 19.

Joint Working Group (n.d). Retrieved 19 August 2009, from http://www.jwg.org.za/content/blogcategory/17/74

Judge, M., Manion, A. & De Waal, S. (2008). *To have and to hold: The making of same-sex marriage in South Africa*. Auckland Park: Fanele.

Kirkpatrick, M. (2004). Comments on Dr Walter R. Schumm's paper, What was really learned from Tasker and Golombok's (1995) study of lesbian and single-parent mothers? *Psychological Reports*, *94*, 1185–1186.

Lacan, J. (2004). *Écrits*, trans. Alan Sheridan. London and New York: Routledge.

Laird, J. & Green, R. (Eds). (1996). *Lesbians and gays in couples and families: A handbook for therapists*. San Francisco: Jossey-Bass.

Leatt, A. & Hendricks, G. (2005). Beyond identity politics: Homosexuality and gayness in South Africa. In M. van Zyl & M. Steyn (Eds), *Performing queer: Shaping sexualities 1994–2004, Volume I* (pp. 303–322). Roggebaai: Kwela.

Lewin, E. (1993). *Lesbian mothers: Accounts of gender in American culture*. Ithaca and London: Cornell University Press.

Lubbe, C. (2008). The experience of children growing up in lesbian-headed families in South Africa. *Journal of GLBT Family Studies*, *4*(3), 325–359.

Massoud, M. F. (2003). The evolution of gay rights in South Africa. *Peace Review*, *15*(3), 301–7.

Minister slams 'porn' exhibition (2010). *Times Live*, 2 March. Retrieved April 2010, from http://www.timeslive.co.za/local/article332784.ece

Mitchell, V. (1996). Two moms: Contributions of the planned lesbian family to the deconstruction of gendered parenting. In J. Laird & R. Green (Eds), *Lesbians and gays in couples and families: A handbook for therapists* (pp. 343–357). San Francisco: Jossey-Bass.

Morgan, R. & Wieringa, S. (2005). *Tommy boys, lesbian men and ancestral wives: Female same-sex practices in Africa.* Johannesburg: Jacana.

Muzio, C. (1993). Lesbian co-parenting: On being/being with the invisible (m)other. *Studies in Social Work, 63,* 215–229.

Muzio, C. (1996). Lesbians choosing children: Creating families, creating narratives. In J. Laird & R. Green (Eds), *Lesbians and gays in couples and families: A handbook for therapists* (pp. 358–369). San Francisco: Jossey-Bass.

Oswin, N. (2007). The end of queer (as we knew it): Globalization and the making of a gay-friendly South Africa. *Gender, Place & Culture, 14*(1), 93–110.

Patterson, C. J. (1992). Children of lesbian and gay parents. *Child Development, 63*(5), 1025–1042.

Patterson, C. J. (1994). Children of the lesbian baby boom: Behavioural adjustments, self-concepts, and sex-role identity. In B. Greene & G. M. Herek (Eds), *Lesbian and gay psychology: Theory, research and clinical applications* (pp. 156–175). London: Sage.

Polikoff, N. D. (1993). We will get what we ask for: Why legalizing gay and lesbian marriage will not 'dismantle the legal structure of gender in every marriage'. *Virginia Law Review, 79,* 1535–1550.

Potgieter, C. (2005). Sexualities? Hey, this is what black, South African lesbians have to say about relationships with men, the family, heterosexual women and culture. In M. van Zyl & M. Steyn (Eds), *Performing queer: Shaping sexualities 1994–2004, Volume I* (pp. 177–192). Roggebaai: Kwela.

Potgieter, C. (2006). The imagined future for gays and lesbians in South Africa: Is this it? *Agenda, 67,* 4–8.

Riggs, D. W. (n.d.). I'm not gay, but my four mums are: Psychological knowledge and lesbian-headed families. *Radical Psychology, 9*(2). Retrieved May 2011, from http://www.radicalpsychology.org/vol9-2/riggs.html

Sandell, J. (1994). The cultural necessity of queer families. *Bad Subjects*, 12. Retrieved 4 April 2008, from http://bad.eserver.org/issues/1994/12/sandell.html

Sanders, M. (2002). *Complicities: The intellectual and apartheid*. Pietermaritzburg: University of Natal Press.

Schumm, W. R. (2004). What was really learned from Tasker and Golombok's (1995) study of lesbian and single-parent mothers? *Psychological Reports, 94*, 422–424.

Schumm, W. R. (2008). Re-evaluation of the 'no differences' hypothesis concerning gay and lesbian parenting as assessed in eight early (1979–1986) and four later (1997–1998) dissertations. *Psychological Reports, 103*, 275–304.

Schwartz, A. E. (1998). *Sexual subjects: Lesbians, gender, and psychoanalysis*. London and New York: Routledge.

Stacey, J. & Biblarz, T. J. (2001). (How) Does the sexual orientation of parents matter? *American Sociological Review, 66*, 159–183.

Stacey, J. & Meadow, T. (2009). New slants on the slippery slope: The politics of polygamy and gay family rights in South Africa and the United States. *Politics & Society, 37*(2), 167–202.

Steckel, A. (1985). *Separation-individuation in children of lesbian and heterosexual couples* (Unpublished doctoral dissertation). The Wright Institute Graduate School: Berkeley. Retrieved from http://www.apa.org/pi/lgbc/publications/lgpstspec.html

Steckel, A. (1987). Psychosocial development of children of lesbian mothers. In F. Bozett (Ed.), *Gay and lesbian parents* (pp. 75–85). New York: Praeger.

Stychin, C. F. (1996). Constituting sexuality: The struggle for sexual orientation in the South African Bill of Rights. *Journal of Law and Society, 23*(4), 455–483.

Sullivan, M. (2004). *The family of woman: Lesbian mothers, their children, and the undoing of gender*. Berkeley and Los Angeles: University of California Press.

Swarr, A. & Nagar, R. (2003). Dismantling assumptions: Interrogating 'lesbian' struggles for identity and survival in India and South Africa. *Signs, 29*(2), 491–516.

Tasker, F. L. & Golombok, S. (1997). *Growing up in a lesbian family: Effects on child development.* London and New York: Guilford Press.

Trengrove-Jones, T. (2005). Mystifying history: The thing that goes bump in the night. In N. Hoad, K. Martin & G. Reid (Eds), *Sex & Politics in South Africa* (pp. 136–139). Cape Town: Double Storey.

Van Zyl, M. (2009). Beyond the Constitution: From sexual rights to belonging. In M. Steyn & M. van Zyl (Eds), *The prize and the price: Shaping sexualities in South Africa* (pp. 364–387). Cape Town: HSRC Press.

Ward, K. & Worden, N. (1998). Commemorating, suppressing, and invoking Cape slavery. In S. Nuttall & C. Coetzee (Eds), *Negotiating the past: The making of nemory in South Africa* (pp. 201–220). Cape Town: Oxford University Press.

Zuma invokes gay wrath (2006). *News24.com*, 26 September. Retrieved April 2010, from http://www.news24.com/SouthAfrica/News/Zumainvokes-gay-wrath-20060926#

SECTION 4

Relationships Up Close: Real Lives, Real Issues

Breaking the Silence: A Discussion on Intimate Partner Violence in Gay-Male Relationships

Gabriel Khan and Yolan Moodley

INTIMATE PARTNER VIOLENCE (IPV) within LGBTI relationships continues to receive scant scholarly attention and, in many ways, is a problem still yet to be acknowledged by activists, researchers and service providers. Despite prevalence rates being the same for homosexual and heterosexual relationships, IPV as an issue is often side-lined within the LGBTI sector in favour of more evident or accepted issues such as bullying or coming out. In the South African context, where brutal hate crimes against LGBTI individuals are a regular occurrence, violence is often conceptualised solely in terms of homophobia enacted by heterosexuals as a way to exert power and to punish sexual 'deviance'. Such a limited understanding of violence and its impact on LGBTI lives is, of course, highly problematic. Indeed, the lack of discussion around IPV not only makes it difficult for people to access support and services, it also plays a key role in perpetuating stigma, shame and, in many situations, denial.

Here, Gabriel Hoosain Khan of Gay and Lesbian Memory in

Action (GALA) speaks with Yolan Moodley about his recent research into IPV within gay-male relationships. Conducted as part of a Master in Psychology at the University of the Witwatersrand, this qualitative study investigated the meanings and constructions of violence within gay-male relationships, and how these understandings compare with the way that people think about violence more generally.

This study's sample was multiracial and comprised six gay men, five from the Gauteng region and one from Cape Town, all of whom live in highly urbanised areas. Participants ranged in age from twenty-five to fifty-two years. To participate in the study, individuals had to meet four criteria: they had to be over the age of eighteen; had to self-identify as gay; had to have experienced violence in any past intimate relationship with another man (thus allowing for the inclusion of victims and perpetrators as well as people who had experienced IPV in non-monogamous relationships); and had to have ended the relationship in which IPV was involved at least six months prior to the interview. Gay men who were currently in or who had very recently left abusive relationships were expected to be under stress related to their daily living conditions, and thus may require greater levels of support than could be provided as part of the research.

Gabriel Hoosain Khan: In terms of your research, what do you mean by violence? Is it just physical violence? Or are you talking about other forms of violence as well?
Yolan Moodley: For this study, I'm looking at violence across the board. The way that people tend to think about violence is, in a way, different in different settings – you have the public health way of conceptualising it (for example, the definitions used by the United Nations), you have more critical feminist understandings, you have readings focused on hegemonic masculinities, you have the actual

type of violence and so on. What I found in the literature on IPV is that it is predominantly produced in heterosexist terms. By that I mean violence is usually constructed as something that only happens between a man and a woman. So I've decided to look at how gay men in South Africa construct violence in relation to these heterosexist notions and how they draw on these understandings when they talk about IPV. I am analysing the data using a critical discourse analysis perspective because it is a very useful tool to interrogate the power relationships inherent in particular constructions of violence.

Do you want to list some of the forms of violence, or maybe categories is a better way to put it, that you have come across in your research?
I've come across everything, the whole range of violent behaviours: from the extreme physical stuff – such as hitting, punching, objects being thrown at people – to threats of violence and emotional intimidation. An extremely popular form was control: controlling one partner's access to other people, to support, to their friends and so on. There was also verbal abuse, usually in the form of belittling the partner in some way. In terms of economic power and control, there was only one person in the study who was financially dependent on the abusive partner. This person's parents were paying some of his board, but he never had spare money to do anything else, so he was dependent on the abusive partner. This was interesting for me because it contradicted the stereotypical picture – with my participants, the abused person was the one often footing the bill.

Those were the main forms of violence. But when people were asked or talked about 'violence' or 'abuse', the first things that came to mind were the physical things. You had to prompt them by enquiring if their partner had ever put them down and things like that. Participants would often respond to this question with a statement such as 'oh yeah, all the time', but for them, when they are talking about their abusive partner, it is the physical violence that first comes to mind.

Was sexual violence something that came up as well?
Actually, no, it didn't come up at all. Participants said they were not sexually coerced. However, sex did come up in other ways. People did talk about the violence *being* sexual, in that a few people mentioned that after a physical fight they would be highly aroused and have great sex. Here violence was produced as 'sexy'. In these situations, the violence was associated with a certain roughness and a kind of masculinity that was connected to desire. These interviewees suggested that if it weren't for this association with masculinity and desire, then maybe they would have seen that the relationship was very self-destructive much earlier. In this sense, violence was constructed at the intersection of intimacy and masculinity.

In terms of direct sexual violence, that was something that didn't come up in the interviews. This doesn't mean that sexual violence against partners isn't something that occurs in other gay-male relationships, but it wasn't something that was identified by any of the participants in this research.

When people talk about violence in relation to gay-male or LGBT experiences in South Africa it is usually homophobic violence that is being referred to. As far as I'm aware, there are very few – if any – discussions locally around IPV among queer or LGBT people. From a research perspective, has there been much critical engagement, specifically in South Africa, with this topic?
There has been some, but very little. There was a study done on prevalence that tried to establish the local rate of IPV and to compare this to what is known internationally (Stephenson et al., 2011). That study was actually conducted over the internet by researchers in the US, who got a South African sample through social networking websites. There were also a couple of good articles on violence and abuse in gay-male relationships that focused on power differentials (Henderson & Shefer, 2008; Henderson, 2012). Off the top of my head, they are the only three studies that I can think of.

Why do you think this topic is something that hasn't been discussed academically or in other spaces?
I would say that there is a whole range of reasons. This is actually a question that has been asked many times and people have differing opinions. Some of the reasons centre on an idea of a gay utopia of sorts, on the belief that lesbian and gay people want to focus on the positive. According to this argument, LGBT people just want to celebrate and be happy. They don't want to acknowledge when things are not all rosy, because they think doing so will tarnish the way that they, and the LGBT community broadly, are perceived. Basically, this explanation is based on the assumption that there is already so much stigma against gay people so we should try to avoid showing society this side of things because it will just bring down our good image.

I would argue, based on my research, that the way IPV is constructed precludes the possibility of it occurring in non-heterosexual contexts – that is, if it isn't between a man and a woman, then it doesn't actually exist. It is almost as if there is a blind spot in the discourse of violence: the way we speak of and understand IPV means that there has to be a perpetrator and a victim and that one of those, the perpetrator, has to be a man and the other person, the victim, has to be a woman. So intimate violence between gay men may not be seen as violence in light of these discourses, similar to the way that corporal punishment wasn't seen as violence until relatively recently, until societal views changed. This is what discourse analysts mean by social phenomena, such as violence, being socially constructed. In different times and in different spaces, what does and does not count as violence changes. This may make it hard to consider something as abuse. For instance, you might have friends who are in an abusive relationship and they don't actually tell you about it. You might think 'well, two guys can't possibly' or 'oh, he will be able to defend himself' or 'that is just a couple of guys messing around' or something else along those lines. You don't really take what is happening seriously and thus it's easy for the abuse or violence to go unnoticed. So what people expect violence to look like can affect and limit how it is talked about in the context of gay-male relationships. The whole idea of abuse in gay relationships kind of shatters many expectations of IPV, such as the dominant gendered notion of the female victim and male perpetrator, and so unless you're really looking for it, it's easy for IPV in non-heterosexual relationships to go unnoticed or unacknowledged.

Some people in my research also mentioned being embarrassed. They reasoned that they should be able to deal with the situation: 'I'm a guy, I should be able to defend myself; this is really embarrassing.' Some people noted that they and their partner had come out together and they thought that their parents accepted them because they were adhering to a heteronormative standard of a long-term monogamous relationship. These participants felt that they couldn't now go and tell their parents that there is trouble in paradise because the parents had accepted their sexuality on the grounds that the relationship echoed heterosexual monogamous ideals.

Overseas there has been more research on IPV within lesbian relationships, and some people have suggested that there might be more lesbian or feminist academics who are motivated to study this issue than academics who are focusing on gay relationships.

Finally, homophobia in general may mean that people do not have as many support networks and so in some circumstances it becomes harder to tell someone or to talk about IPV. That could be another factor in why it just doesn't get talked about.

Something that you seem to be saying is that when it comes to IPV, and maybe even gender-based violence more broadly, it tends to be looked at and understood in rather heteronormative terms. Why do you think that is?
As I mentioned, IPV is, in terms of social discourses, constructed in a certain way. And at present the 'rules', if you like, for how we are supposed to understand and make sense of IPV say that there has to be a male perpetrator and a female victim. Why that is? Well there is a long history of factors that contributed to our present notions. I'll

focus on just a couple here. A lot of research on IPV comes out of the medical or public health sector. These studies often employ what is called a black box epidemiology that looks at risk factors and outputs – that is, you have various risk factors going into the 'box' and then you have violence coming out. And no one really knows – well I guess it's more that researchers don't really interrogate *how* – being gay results in violence.

In terms of the public health approach, the emphasis is always on risk factors themselves, so researchers will go and focus on risk factors associated with being gay or a woman or on risks related to stigma. The research will focus on all of these things, on trying to identify these risks, but the interrogation of the processes, of *how* risk factor A actually leads to behaviour B, is not really looked at. So if this risk-factor approach is the way that researchers are looking at IPV then they are never *really* going to interrogate what it is about being a man or what it is about being a woman or being gay or being lesbian that intersects with other underlying factors to produce violence. If they are only getting certain inputs going in and you just look at the problem in that way, you're not really going to think about the exceptions to the rule.

There are, of course, more critical conceptualisations of violence that have been very influential such as those emerging from feminism, particularly the way that the feminist movement politicised violence, which was crucial for highlighting abuse that until then was simply unacknowledged. Statistically, the majority of intimate violence *is* conducted by men against women. In the 1970s, feminist activists had to work really hard to challenge dominant views that it was okay for a man to beat up his wife. Perhaps people feel that to acknowledge that some women are violent and that some men are victims would detract from a view that imbeds violence within patriarchy. This conceptualisation may have led to other forms of IPV not really being looked at, so maybe that is why this issue has historically been framed in heteronormative terms. In my research I found that patriarchal discourses do find their way into gay men's constructions of violence, so these lines of thought need not be adversarial. So the task I would say for the present generation of activists and researchers is to politicise IPV beyond heterosexist constructions in the same way that feminism politicised domestic violence beyond patriarchal ones.

To follow on from some of the points that you have raised, perhaps we should look at three things: (1) what are the factors that have been linked to IPV when it comes to gay men; (2) what is actually happening – how do these factors link to the manifestations of violence in the relationship; and (3) how do people deal with the violence – for instance, do they disclose it to people?

To begin, what are the factors that you've come across that have been linked to IPV?
Gender was quite significant. Some participants adopted hetero-patriarchal gender roles such that the abuser was constructed as the 'masculine' partner and the abused as the 'feminine' partner, which seemed to replicate gendered power relations. For example, a participant said that in his society [Mamelodi Township] he had to be gay and his partner had to be 'the man', and with this understanding came a whole lot of assumptions about allowing the 'man' to dominate and not talking back or resisting control.

There were elements of shame where a participant communicated embarrassment that he wasn't able to fight back, but he believed that this was expected of him, that he should be able to defend himself.

Money was often an issue. My findings actually seem to challenge notions of masculinity, because in many situations the abuser was financially dependent on the victim. Here violence was constructed as a way for abusers to assert their authority in the relationship, as a way to override the financially disempowered position they found themselves in. The reasoning was along the lines of 'yes, you are earning a lot more money and yes, it's your car, but *I* can still put you in your place if I want to'.

There were some class-related issues that intersected with sexuality. The person I spoke to who lived in Mamelodi said that he would never consider bringing up the issue of violence within a relationship. He noted that his social environment – I think his words were 'our people', referring to LGBT people living in that township – has changed in that now if you are gay you are kind of tolerated but don't you dare have the audacity to ask for services or come with issues – just be happy that you are tolerated. So this person would never go to the police. There were also no services he could easily access: he would go to an NGO and wouldn't be able to get a referral to any local support services or providers. He felt that his partner knew that no matter what happens, he would not get caught, he would not have to go to jail for his crime. The person I interviewed thought that this lack of access to services kind of gave his partner, and other people in a similar situation, carte blanche. I probed him more on this idea by asking whether he thought he would be taken seriously if he reported the situation at, say, Hatfield police station [a reasonably affluent suburb of Pretoria]. He was very adamant in his response, which was along the lines of 'yes, definitely, because there you've got white people and Indian people, and they have a different mentality, they are more accepting and they will take you seriously. But with our people, it's very hard'. So issues of race and class intersected in this participant's account.

The intersection between gender and sexuality is also important. Sometimes there are homophobic attitudes against the subordinate 'feminised' person, who would often be belittled for being feminine. This person is expected, or maybe they choose to adopt, that role, but then they are put down for taking on a feminine role. So the abuser demands that this feminised person pays for everything because he believes the feminised partner should be so lucky to be with him, and he also expects the feminised partner to always be there, on demand. This person is also expected to play a nurturing role, but although the abusive partner might appreciate this at the time, later when he needs to assert his dominance he will criticise the feminised partner for being caring, for being pathetic and unmanly. In a way, it's like the abused person is being bombarded from all sides and never knows what to do.

Another factor that seemed to precipitate IPV in these relationships was perceived threats. A lot of times when I asked my interview subjects what they were talking about before a fight, it would inadvertently come down to something that the abuser felt threatened by. Usually this related to something the partner had done – or was perceived to have done – such as they went out, or they had a new friend or something like that, and the partner saw this as 'I'm going to be rejected, I'm going to lose this person, I'm going to be abandoned' and so on. So here intrapsychic factors were used to explain IPV.

You mentioned earlier – and correct me if I'm wrong – that you don't like the 'black box' way of looking at the problem. In terms of your analysis, what would you say seems to be happening in this black box? How does violence manifest in these relationships? Does anything come to mind from the interviews?

Well for my study, given the perspective I was looking at IPV from, discourses were operating within the black box. These discourses helped to construct IPV in many ways: there were discourses of IPV as having a natural or biological base, such as through a 'natural' male aggressive drive, IPV as a form of control and IPV as intolerable. There were also discourses of IPV as not serious, IPV as acceptable between men, IPV as an equal exchange. Then there were discourses that seemed to intersect with gender and these seemed to destabilise the category of the male victim. Some interesting constructions of IPV drew on discourses of love and intimacy. IPV was produced as part and parcel of a monogamous relationship, as part of the 'battle' that one is expected to wage for love and as a conduit to intimacy.

Some of these understandings in a way harked back to gladiatorial discourses of male bonding through violence.

The primary underlying discourse is always power, and where there is power there will likely be resistance. Thus while there were hetero-patriarchal gendered power relations being enacted through violence, there were also many resistances to these, such as participants expressing agency within their oppressive situation.

Did you find there was a link between IPV and drug or alcohol abuse?
For some people, yes; some people, not so much. Where there was a link, it would be either alcohol constructed as a pathology to explain why the abuser got violent or alcohol as a catalyst – that is, there was already some tension, then the abusive partner might come home drunk and blow up. There were also people who were being abused who would drink a lot. They said it was to cope, but when they would drink a lot, they would sort of be less submissive. So, say the abused person felt their partner was spending all their money or something like that, they would pick on it more if they were under the influence of alcohol. Other times they would think, 'I should leave it, I shouldn't say anything' and just avoid a fight. But after a few drinks they would be more likely to bring it up. The alcohol would, in a way, give them a bit of agency, but afterwards they would end up being beaten.

Would you say that there is anything unique about the ways that IPV manifests in gay relationships as compared to heterosexual or other relationships? Is it somehow different?
In some ways there were similarities, particularly when hetero-patriarchal power relations were re-inscribed in the context of two men. These have been mentioned earlier. In other instances there were resistances to this formation, situations where abused men sought to highlight their agency through resisting victimhood. Some straight research on IPV has also found resistance to victimhood in women's accounts of IPV.

I suppose the 'unique' elements in the present study – and I say unique in inverted commas because it could be that researchers weren't looking for this stuff much before – were some of the more novel ways gay men resisted the victim position. For example, violence being constructed as erotic, which sort of attracted some people to the abusive partner in the first case. One person I interviewed said, 'yeah, I like bad boys' and this statement seemed to draw on many constructions of masculinity, particularly in the way that it played into the notion of gay men desiring 'real' or manly men. There is a certain sense of agency too in this comment. A sense that 'I chose to have this type of guy'. Of course, this is not suggesting that the person chose to get beaten up, but they chose this kind of wildness, so it's quite different to the 'he did this to me and I am just a victim' way in which relationships are sometimes understood. You don't hear much about this link between aggression and desire in the straight literature. I think it would be very problematic for feminism to think about that, but that doesn't mean it doesn't exist in heterosexual relationships.

There was also IPV as a conduit to love, in the sense that violence was seen as something that needed to be endured in order to achieve a monogamous heteronormative ideal relationship. A distaste for what some reported as a polygamous, 'fickle' gay scene was constructed as rationale to endure IPV – that is, the person believed that despite the violence, this couple was different from 'all' the other gay men out there by sticking with the relationship. Then there was violence as the fulcrum on which intimacy and gay sexuality is hinged. Here a 'natural' aggression between men as a way to bond characterised constructions of IPV.

In terms of this form of agency, do you think that it is linked to the fact that being a man, at least within hetero-patriarchal understandings of masculinity, gives you more power in a way? Do you think that male privilege plays a role in how violence manifests in these relationships?
I think so. I would say that the people, at least in my research, are

coming from less disempowered positions. At the time they met their partner they may have been very vulnerable and they may not have had support because of homophobia and things like that, but they managed to pull themselves out of the situation and were only in the relationship for a year or two. And I don't think they had the kind of structural inequality that a woman can have, such as you aren't financially independent or you're socialised into thinking that it is okay to be beaten up or other things like that. So yes, I think that is quite possibly a factor.

Which links to another question about other social factors such as poverty, access to education, race and class, et cetera. How did those factors play a role?
In the case I mentioned earlier about the person living in the township, in Mamelodi, the abusive person had quite an impoverished life. And there was also a lot less access to services and support than there would be in some other places. That person talked about heterosexist ideas in his community and how there has been a shift in that homosexuality is, on the surface, now accepted, but that it has an almost unreal quality. This person was saying that homosexuality is kind of rubber stamped but not really accepted, in the sense that people think 'we won't be mean to you, but we're not going to really look under the surface, and don't bother bringing your problems to us because that's just a burden'. So he was saying that in some ways homosexuals in this township context are better off than they were before, but in terms of class, in that neighbourhood, being of a lower class meant that you did not get the kind of acceptance that the Constitution would insist that every South African has. Interestingly, this person never said 'black' but rather 'my people'. And he said that a lot of his people came from rural areas where they have a certain mind-set, and so he linked race to class in that way, saying that people from rural areas with this mind-set will never really get *it*, whereas people in more resourced areas will make time for you as they understand

more. So that was the main thing in terms of how this person spoke about his experiences.

Some people also spoke about access to information. I asked participants about how people in the LGBT community think about violence in relationships and one person said that there are two schools of thought. One relates to LGBT organisations, which tend to have a fair bit of information on this issue. This guy said that his friend was involved with one of these organisations and through his friend he had some access to brochures and so on, and so he knew violence was bad and wrong. The other way that abuse is thought about relates to the more informal, conversational way that people speak about violence. This guy said that people would joke that your boyfriend beats you up because he really loves you and that otherwise he would just go off with some other person, and other things like that. So again, it's harking back to this romanticised construction of violence.

I would like to explore further this idea of sexual pleasure coming from violence within these relationships. You mentioned earlier that this is maybe something unique to gay-male relationships and I was wondering why this is the case – why do you think it plays out in this way?
There is a body of research that looks at this reification of masculinity. I forget the name of the researcher, but he was saying that after gay liberation you had the hyper-masculine othering of femininity within gay-male circles. So perhaps this reification of hyper-masculinity – this desire to *be* real men, to *have* real men, to *sleep* with real men – has an impact. This feeds into all the ideals and stereotypes of 'real' men – all the construction workers, the body builders, all the visions of men are strong, powerful, virile, aggressive and so forth – and maybe there is this thing of aggression being very masculine and therefore attractive. As such, a guy who has these qualities is very desirable. I certainly don't think, however, that people desire or seek to be beaten up. If they did this would cross into sadomasochism, which some

researchers argue shares a blurry line with IPV.

One person shared that his boyfriend's brothers would call him to be a mediator when he got angry, as he knew what to say and how to calm the boyfriend down. For the first year, this played out like a 'beauty and the beast' kind of thing: 'he's my monster, but I understand him'. But then it started to change and the violence was directed against him, and the erotic quality faded. I think relationships such as this are connected to desiring masculinity. But I also think that it's a general society thing that gay men have really picked up on. I'm sure straight women do that too. Critical theorists would argue that this is a feature of systems of power: these systems act upon people in insidious ways such that the person feels their own practices come from within.

Do men tend to stay in relationships where they are being abused or where the partner is violent?
Yes. I think the shortest relationship in the study was a year and the longest was about five years.

Why do you think they stay in the relationship?
It may partly be because of the things that we've been talking about already: it fulfils a function of 'I enjoy having a guy who's in control' or 'I enjoy these kinds of things' but only to a point. Once it starts getting serious, people begin to think that it isn't right, that it isn't healthy. And then it will be things like fear making them stay in the relationship. By that point you might already have it drummed into you that you won't make it without the abusive partner. I mentioned earlier one participant who was concerned about how his family would think of him because he believed that his sexuality was accepted on the condition of being in a long-term monogamous relationship. He had always told his family how wonderful his partner was as a way of getting them to accept his coming out. So then he felt like it was too late to say 'by the way, he's actually a monster'. The only reason that

this person told anyone about the abusive nature of the relationship was when a family member witnessed a violent episode; it was only because of this that he confronted the violence.

A lot of people said that they were in love and that they always had this hope that their partner was going to change. As we know from the cycle of violence theory, after a violent episode there will be a period of the abuser trying very hard to make reparations and promising the world, and that really works in terms of convincing the other person.

I also spoke with young people who said they didn't know any better. For some it was their first relationship. Others also noted that there was an age difference in the relationship. These people shared how at the time they thought their partner was completely wonderful, but really the partner was talking circles around them and they just didn't really get it at the time. In that situation, a lack of support was a vital part of the problem.

There are also the things we've been talking about like social construction and accepted understandings of violence – for instance, people may ask themselves if what they are experiencing really is IPV. Similarly, when a guy retaliates to defend himself, the abuser often responds with 'well, you hit me too'. And it might take a long time for that person to realise – and you must remember that at the point in an abusive relationship it is very hard to fully comprehend the situation – that actually it's *always* the other person starting the conflict and then twisting it around so that in the end it is the abused person who feels guilty. There is a lot of messing with people's minds, a lot of twisting things around. Abusers often say thing like 'I'm not violent; it's because you do these things that I become aggressive' followed by 'look, you are also violent'. This sort of reasoning leaves the abused very confused and often a lot of time passes without this person having an outside source of reason, such as a friend, to help them recognise what is going on. A lot of times it's very hard for a person to do this on their own. And then on top of this there is often a romanticisation of the relationship: 'somehow I will make it last, I will survive, I shouldn't give up on "us".'

What do you think are some of the challenges faced by individuals in a relationship where there is IPV? In particular, challenges related to navigating a space that is potentially violent, including finding support or help, or working out how to leave the relationship.

One of the biggest challenges is isolation. So yes, there is not enough information out there about this issue and yes, it is very hidden, but it is also often about people not having adequate support structures. Often there is information available, but people just don't see it at the time or they don't take advantage of it. So it is almost like the information has to be more active in terms of reaching people who need it.

People outside of the relationship also need to be more active. Often people think that they shouldn't get involved because it's a private thing or that they need to wait for the 'right time' or some other excuse. And then there are situations in which people have been told by friends that what is happening is wrong, but the person is still convinced that escaping the relationship is something they have to go through themselves. So I think one big challenge is the people around the abused person – either they're not being there, or not *really* being there, or not *really* making it clear that they are there. People also tend to become frustrated or angry about their friend staying in the relationship or going back to the abusive partner. It's often hard for people outside of the relationship to understand all the mind-games that are going on below the surface and all of the other things that make it hard for the person to just leave. And so either these friends or relatives are not available or they are only available to a point, and so the issue becomes a very individual problem for the abused person. As a result, a lot of people in these relationships adopt the stance that it's their problem and they are the ones that have to sort it out. If people were more supportive, more reassuring,

253

it might have a substantial impact. People can't expect people in these relationships to just leave, to magically fix things.

What services do you think would be useful to people in abusive or violent relationships?
I think there needs to be shelters in every city in the country, a place that the person can escape to. These do not have to be separate for gay men exclusively; lesbian victims of IPV could share the space, if managers deemed this appropriate. These services need to be well advertised as well. There is one in Cape Town only.

More generally, the issue of IPV needs to be put on the agenda more. Even within the LGBTI sector, within NGOs and other service providers, IPV needs to be considered part and parcel with all the other issues that organisations deal with. It needs to be seen as a central issue alongside things like bullying, homophobia, coming out, HIV, *et cetera*. Normalising the issue will help people not to feel so scared or embarrassed. It will also contribute to the discourses on IPV so that people can begin to challenge heterosexist ways of seeing violence and the potential for silencing that accompanies these. This will help to change these understandings in a similar way that straight domestic violence and corporal punishment evolved from acceptable to unacceptable. Prevalence rates are the same as with straight people, so this is something that really does need to be addressed.

I also think that there needs to be something like Brothers for Life, but a programme that works with abusive partners. One of my participants who was abusive was young and had a lot of anger inside him at the time. He was happy to come forward and tell his story because he felt it would help other people, and I think it's important to access people like this as a way to tackle the issue from the other side, to work with the people who are being abusive. It makes sense to me to approach the issue from that direction as well. Some of the perpetrators I spoke with had serious issues that may be hard to resolve, but not all of them. So I think that would be a good angle to break some of the behaviour, reaching out to people who have perpetrated violence. Perhaps a support group of sorts.

You mentioned earlier that the individual you spoke to from Mamelodi didn't feel comfortable reporting the violence because of the attitude of people in his area and the lack of services. What about the other participants – did they tend to report violence?
All of the participants said no. One didn't think that he would be believed. In this relationship, the abuser was powerful and had all these people around him who would do whatever he said. For the partner, it was like talking into the wind: no one actually listened to him. Other people said that they didn't expect it to be taken seriously. One person had a fear of police because some officers had once beaten him up after pulling him off the road for something. This person thought there was no point going to the police because they would just beat him up.

One person mentioned that when his abusive partner threw a brick through their car, he reported the incident. But this person felt comfortable reporting it because it involved damage to his property and he felt that it was something the police would understand. When the police came to arrest the guy, the couple were in bed and the police were laughing about the suspect and the complainant – two men – being in bed together. But the police still arrested the guy. So that was the only instance where something was reported and taken seriously, even though the grounds of the report was not the actual beating. So for IPV to be taken seriously it had to involve something the police could see, like property damage. More discreet forms of IPV in gay-male relationships seem to be invisible or laughable to them.

Overall, people didn't think that they would be taken seriously by the authorities; they believed that they would be ridiculed for reporting the incident. Others were afraid of the police or just embarrassed about what was going on. Embarrassment is an important point. The person from Mamelodi said that he had a friend who went to report being abused and it was just a humiliating experience. Here the police found it impossible to conceptualise IPV in non-heterosexual terms and they began mockingly referring to the gay-male complainant as a lady. Furthermore they made a public spectacle of the complainant so that the event became a thoroughly dehumanising one.

On a different note, did you find any intersection between IPV and HIV?
I didn't actually. It's not something that anybody talked about in the interviews. I have come across it in research, mainly in terms of HIV being used as another tool of control, but nothing relating to this issue emerged during the interviews I conducted.

What about other health issues? Did you find that IPV affected the health, either physically or emotionally, of people within the relationship?
Yes, there were definitely physical injuries. People reported going to hospital and having to constantly come up with ways to explain or hide their injuries. And this just made people even more afraid to take the initiative and do anything ending the relationship. One abused gay man reported that he began to abuse alcohol as a coping strategy.

You have already somewhat answered this question so I want to phrase it a bit differently. Are there any mental health or mental illness issues other than the ones you've mentioned that contribute to the development of IPV in a relationship?
Abuse in a person's family of origin, both in terms of receiving and witnessing abuse, seemed related to perpetrating IPV. Two abused participants reported witnessing abuse of their mothers as well. Psychological theories would argue that people re-enact ways of relating in childhood in later life, but often it is more complex than that.

In terms of mental health, I would say that certain personality disorder traits seem to feature such as chronic paranoia, fear of abandonment, extreme jealousy, a feeling of being undermined all the time, a fear of being ridiculed or laughed at. Well, that is the way people often described their abusive partners. There was one participant whose partner suffered from what he thought was bipolar disorder.

And what about mental health impacts, so to speak? Are there any mental health issues that culminated during or after the relationship?
Yes, people took a long time to get over the violence and the betrayal and the loss and all those things. A lot of people were still fearful and not so ready to trust people. So it took out a really big chunk of their life, even beyond the time in the relationship. I'm not quite sure what the impact on the abusers would be. From what people have said, it seems like they have new boyfriends and they are the same. The abusive participant said he spent much of his life racked with guilt. Some people were stalked for a while, slightly. The abused partner has also always had the abuser at the back of his mind. All of the people I spoke with were kind of over it, but if they were to see their partner again, it would be quite traumatic.

I think we've covered most of the major themes and issues relating to IPV in gay-male relationships. Is there anything else that comes to mind that you would like to discuss? I have to say, I have found what you've been saying about the influence of heteronormativity in the way that violence plays out quite fascinating.
I definitely think that heteronormativity is creeping in; the stereotyped ways that people think about violence definitely influences gay relationships. But it's not always an exact mirror and that, I think, is because people have variable levels of power; power in these relationships is not as circumscribed as it might be in a heterosexual relationship. On the flipside, gay men don't have resources and the support of society in general. If a woman were to report that her boyfriend is beating her, the police are likely to be there straight away

and arrest him. There is likely to be more of an aghast reaction from others than perhaps with a gay man. Well, I guess that depends where one lives. But in terms of gay relationships, the violence is something the victims often have to bear in silence.

What message would you want to send to the victims of IPV in LGBT relationships?
Just tell someone. Find someone who you can trust and tell them. And there *are* resources, not many, but there are resources like anonymous telephone lines that you can make use of. Also, you are not going crazy. Finally, if you were to try and talk about some of these things then you might find ways to deal with the situation – in whatever way is best for you. But most importantly, don't hold it in.

People who are experiencing intimate partner violence can contact LifeLine on 0861 322 322. They are available twenty-four hours a day. In Cape Town one can contact the Pride Shelter Trust on 021 423 2871.

REFERENCES

Henderson, N. & Shefer, T. (2008) Practices of Power and Abuse in Gay Male Relationships: An Exploratory Case Study of a Young, IsiXhosa-Speaking Man in the Western Cape, South Africa. *South African Journal of Psychology*, *38*(1), 1–20.

Henderson, N. (2012) Narratives of Power and Abuse in Gay Relationships in the Cape Metropole. *South African Journal of Psychology*, *42*(3), 323–332.

Stephenson, R., De Vous, A. & Sullivan, P. S. (2011). Intimate partner violence and sexual risk taking among men who have sex with men in South Africa. *Western Journal of Emergency Medicine*, *12*, 343–347.

Coming Out to Families: Adolescent Disclosure Practices in the Western Cape

Veronica Robertson and Charmaine Louw

'All people are equal; it is not birth but virtue alone that makes the difference'

– Voltaire

AT NO OTHER TIME IN HISTORY HAVE sexual minorities received so much scrutiny and attention, nor enjoyed such widespread acceptance within mainstream society. But, despite these considerable advances in visibility, inclusion and recognition, many lesbian, gay and bisexual (LGB) individuals, particularly youth, remain fearful of disclosing their sexuality. Indeed, the prospect of revealing one's sexual orientation to family and friends has been identified as one of the most stressful sexuality-related life events for homosexual youths (D'Augelli, 2006). A desire to escape the threat and stress of stigmatisation leads many LGB youth to conceal their sexual orientation or to disclose it to a select few only. This is a deeply worrying trend, as hiding one's sexuality means that relationships are based on deceit and a fear of discovery, which in turn can lead to insecurity, social withdrawal and demoralisation (Davis, Saltzburg & Locke, 2009). Given the significant negative impacts that often accompany the transitional 'coming out' stage, it is important for psychologists and other service providers to understand how LGB youths respond to and cope with feelings of shame and guilt, and the process leading up to disclosing one's sexuality to family members.

Few issues have as profound an impact on family life as an adolescent's disclosure of his/her homosexuality. Recent research suggests that since the removal of homosexuality from the *Diagnostic and Statistical Manual of Mental Disorders* in 1973, increasing numbers of adolescents are coming out to their parents at earlier ages, but that LGB youth – because of negative social attitudes and discrimination – are at greater risk of depression, suicide, victimisation and substance abuse (D'Augelli, 2006; Meyer, 2003). Despite a growing body of international scholarship on LGB youth as an at-risk group, there has been scant research conducted in South Africa, particularly around disclosure and related issues. This lack of critical attention has led not only to a limited understanding of the experiences of local LGB adolescents but also to inadequate service provision. This research gap has, in part, provided the impetus for this research, which aims to identify and analyse the experiences and meanings of adolescent disclosures.

THE SOUTH AFRICAN CONTEXT

To appreciate fully the critical need for research of this kind, it is necessary to understand the South African political and social context as it relates to LGB individuals. The influences of colonisation, apartheid and the human rights movement mean that South Africa has a complex history when it comes to the legal and social status of sexual minorities. Homosexuality was illegal under the apartheid regime, which enacted several laws denying lesbians and gays recourse for victimisation, thus leading to an invisibility of crime against same-sex attracted people. With the adoption of the new constitution in May 1996, South Africa became the world's first jurisdiction to constitutionally prohibit discrimination based on sexual orientation. Although the legal system theoretically guarantees equality, there remains limited social acceptance of homosexuality, particularly in non-urban areas. Conservative and/or traditional attitudes persist across South African society, with the vast majority of the population having grown up within a strongly heterosexist social environment. Lesbian and gay studies continue to be side-lined in academia and research, a trend that Hames (2003) views as indicative of South African society's heterosexual bias.

In the 'new' post-apartheid South Africa, sexual minorities continue to face a disproportionate amount of oppression, marginalisation, discrimination and victimisation because of their sexual orientation and/or gender presentation. 'Corrective rape', a term first used in the early 2000s by human rights organisations to describe sexual violence targeting lesbians, remains rife and is rarely – if ever – adequately investigated and prosecuted. This shocking practice involves the rape (sometimes under the supervision of family members or communities) of lesbians, particularly those living in black townships, as a means of 'curing' their 'deviant' sexuality (Hames, 2003).

Despite South Africa's progressive Constitution and increasingly visible LGB sector, homophobic prejudices continue to assert influence over individuals' public and private lives. Heteronormative discourses permeate all aspects of society, including politics, organised religion and education. Of course, LGB persons cannot be considered a homogeneous group, and experiences of oppression and discrimination are always moderated through an individual's race, gender and socio-economic status. South Africa remains a deeply patriarchal society, despite some gains being made in recent years by the women's movement, with clear gender divisions across all aspects of life. As a result, black lesbians frequently encounter intersecting oppressions due to their race, gender and sexual identity (Cock, 2003).

Although only a cursory overview of the South African context, the above account provides some sense of the complex political and social environment negotiated daily by LGB individuals. Indeed, with its legacy of apartheid, strong patriarchal traditions and significant socio-economic disparities, South Africa – despite its celebrated constitutional protections – must be considered a somewhat hostile environment, particularly for young people coming to terms with and disclosing their sexual orientation. This study attempts to address some of the gaps in local research by investigating how LGB adolescents navigate the disclosure process within this complex and in many ways contradictory social context.

TRENDS IN PROFESSIONAL PSYCHOLOGY

The 1970s heralded a major shift in the way that professional psychology understands and deals with LGB individuals. In 1973, as a result of political activism and undeniable empirical evidence, the American Psychiatric Association removed homosexuality from its list of mental disorders. In 1975, the American Psychological Association followed suit by adopting a resolution urging its members to lead the charge against the long-held association between homosexuality and mental illness. An affirmative perspective model subsequently emerged within psychology practice and research that focuses on helping individuals cope adaptively with the impact of stigma, their minority status, and differences with the heterosexual mainstream (Matthews, 2007). Despite these advances, mental health professionals continue to vary widely in their adherence to unbiased practice standards.

Research indicates that non-heterosexual youth continue to be at increased risk of mental distress due to negative social attitudes and behaviours. While openness about sexual orientation is seen by most mental health professionals as beneficial for psychological wellness, disclosure is often an extremely stressful process for adolescents, many of whom hold realistic fears of discrimination and rejection (Pachankis & Goldfried, 2004). It is because of this context of prejudice, victimisation and social exclusion that psychologists must be aware of, and pay close attention to, the unique needs of LGB youth.

RESEARCH DESIGN AND METHODOLOGY

This research used a qualitative research methodology within an interpretive/constructivist paradigm. The population of interest was lesbian and gay youth who had disclosed their sexual orientation to a family member during their adolescence. Participants were selected through a society providing support to LGB youth at a university in South Africa's Western Cape province.[52] Participants had to be between eighteen and twenty-six years of age and must have disclosed their sexual orientation to at least one family member while he/she was between thirteen and eighteen years of age. No discrimination was made in terms of race, religion, socio-economic status or culture. Youths were sought as participants (as opposed to current adolescents) because it was felt that they, as older and more mature individuals, would be able to clearly express and reflect upon their experiences. Given the often traumatic nature of coming out, it was thought that older interview subjects would be more comfortable reflecting on their experiences rather than those currently in the process of disclosing their sexuality. The biographical details of the participants can be viewed in the following table.

Table 1: Biographical details of research participants

Participant	Age	Gender	Sexual identification	First language	Community size
P1	22	Male	Gay	Afrikaans	Small city/suburbs
P2	24	Male	Gay	English/Afrikaans	Farm/small town
P3	26	Female	Lesbian	English	Large city/urban
P4	21	Female	Lesbian	English	Small city/suburbs
P5	25	Female	Lesbian	Afrikaans	Small city/suburbs
P6	23	Female	Lesbian	Afrikaans	Small city/suburbs
P7	26	Female	Lesbian	Afrikaans	Farm/small town
P8	20	Male	Gay	English	Small city/suburbs
P9	26	Male	Gay	English	Large city/urban
P10	26	Male	Gay	Sotho/English	Large city/urban

Semi-structured individual interviews were used as the primary method of data collection. Reflective notes were used to supplement the interview material, as these are useful for reflecting on specific events (Denzin & Lincoln, 2011). The ten participants were interviewed in the privacy of their homes and were invited to reflect on the interview process as a form of debriefing (this material constituted the reflective notes). Participants were asked to answer questions regarding their thoughts and attitudes about the focus of the study, as well as their experience of participating in the research. Qualitative content analysis was then applied to the interview data, revealing a number of themes and sub-themes.

ETHICAL CONSIDERATIONS

Research clearance was obtained from the Ethics Review Committee at the University of Stellenbosch. Permission was also granted by the Director of Institutional Research and Planning, the Dean of Students, and the chairperson of the society through which the participants were sourced for the study. Informed consent was obtained from all the participants, and care was taken to protect identities by allocating each interviewee a numbered code.

The researchers were aware that the experiences being discussed may have been emotionally sensitive for participants in ways that could not be anticipated. Care was taken to monitor participants' emotional state for any signs of discomfort or for any negative reactions that might require referral for individual counselling.

RESULTS AND DISCUSSION

The following section discusses the key themes that emerged during this study and analyses the ways in which participants constructed meanings within these broader narratives. Quotations from the individual interviews and reflective notes are used throughout this chapter to illustrate and support key findings.

The Process of Coming Out

Early LGB identity development models, such as those proposed by Cass (1979) and Troiden (1989), identified a fairly standard sequence of events beginning with a lack of awareness of sexual orientation that then develops into a dawning awareness (often accompanied by

265

negative feelings), followed by self-affirmation, immersion in the lesbian or gay community and finally a disclosure of sexual orientation. Rosario, Hunter, Maguen, Gwadz and Smith (2001) suggest that identity development is actually a multidimensional process that encompasses sexual identity; attitudes toward homosexuality; comfort with homosexuality; self-disclosure; and involvement in lesbian and gay communities. For the individuals in this study, coming out was understood to be a process, somewhat similar to the models suggested by Cass and Troiden, but at the same time it is considered a continuous and emergent life process that is context dependent. This reading of disclosure as an ongoing process was mentioned by participants time and time again. P3 described coming out as 'the first step: there are lots of processes that happen before and after [coming out] with regard to finding your own identity and being okay with yourself in this new space.' She also mentioned that the coming out process is repeated in different ways throughout life: 'I have to "come out" at some point during the process of getting to know anyone I wish to know as more than a mere acquaintance.' Another participant said that 'coming out is a process and there are different challenges as you go along' (P10). Interestingly, P4 distinguished between the process of coming out and the continuous process of living a homosexual life: 'coming out is filled with steps, it's the easy part; continuing to be gay, living your life as a gay woman, that is the difficult part... to be gay is actually much more difficult.'

As mentioned above, there is some evidence to suggest that the average age of homosexual self-awareness and coming out has lowered in recent years (Savin-Williams & Ream, 2007; D'Augelli, 2006). According to Savin-Williams (2005), the age at which individuals become aware of same-sex feelings and first identify as homosexual is considerably younger among contemporary adolescents than in previous studies. For instance, studies published during the 1990s identified the average age of participants disclosing their sexuality to be nineteen years of age (Sears, 1991; D'Augelli & Hershberger,

1993; Herdt & Boxer, 1993; Savin-Williams, 1998), which is three years older than some contemporary studies.

D'Augelli's 2006 study of 542 youths between the ages of fourteen and twenty-one, (62 per cent male and 38 per cent female) found that the average age for participants becoming aware of same-sex feelings was ten, with this reported as occurring slightly earlier for males. Self-labelling as homosexual occurred around five years after the initial awareness, with males again reaching the milestone slightly earlier. First disclosure of sexual orientation for both male and female youths occurred at the age of about seventeen. Savin-Williams' 2005 study of 317 youths between the ages of fourteen and twenty-three found that participants reported an awareness of same-sex desires around the age of ten, with the average age of homosexual self-labelling being sixteen years for females and fifteen and a half years for males. First disclosures of sexual orientation were reported at seventeen years for both females and males, though some participants indicated this happening as young as ten and as old as twenty-three years. A study by Maguen, Floyd, Bakeman and Armistead (2002) reported similar findings. This study looked at sixty-three males and fifty-four females from south-eastern United States between fourteen and twenty-seven. The mean ages for first awareness of same-sex attraction was eleven years, for first same-sex sexual contact sixteen years and for first disclosure of sexual identity seventeen years.

In this study, awareness of same-sex attraction was reported as occurring between the ages of six and ten, with the majority of participants (eight out of ten) indicating that they could vividly remember this realisation. First disclosures tended to be near the end of participants' high school years and were prompted primarily by the urge to share the person's sexual orientation with a close and trusted confidant. In many cases, disclosure took place only after the participant had entered into a same-sex relationship or had become sexually active. Participants identified a number of specific reasons motivating them to reveal their sexual orientation, including a desire to share their confusion, to seek advice and to share their true selves with others.

There has been considerable research into the developmental process of moving from early awareness of difference to self-identifying as lesbian or gay. Over time, individuals tentatively begin to identify sexuality as the source of a perceived difference and this eventually leads to an acknowledgement by the individual of their sexual orientation/identity (Cass, 1996; Fassinger & Miller, 1996; McCarn & Fassinger, 1996; Troiden, 1989; Sophie, 1986). Participant responses in this study support this model, as can be seen in the following quote from P3: 'Looking back I can remember – as far back as eight years old – an attraction to girls. It was not a sexual attraction, but I guess, looking back on it now, maybe [it was] the beginning of my "gaydom"'. Thinking back on their process of self-awareness, many participants in this study described their joy upon finally discovering the term 'homosexual': 'I was excited by the fact that I had discovered who I really was and [had] made peace with it. I was filled with this overwhelming sense of joy' (P1). P4 mentioned that this realisation was accompanied by a sense of clarity: 'It was like "oh my gosh" now I realise why I thought I was a guy, why I pretended I was a guy. Things started to make sense. It was like an epiphany – I am not really a guy, now I don't need to go for sex surgery; I am a woman, a woman, and being lesbian is perfectly okay.'

For eight of the ten participants, disclosure to their parent(s) only occurred after they had come out to supportive friends, had integrated their sexual identity and had established a sexual or romantic relationship. Of those participants who had a relationship with both parents, most were likely to disclose their sexuality to the mother rather than the father, and most did so in a face-to-face encounter. This largely occurred because the mothers had asked about the participant's sexuality and because the participant had a closer or more invested maternal relationship. Among those participants whose parents were divorced, many did not tell their fathers because they did not have a close relationship and it mattered less to them whether their fathers knew. Participants cared more about the reactions of parents with whom they were close, and indicated that they were able to share personal issues more easily with parents if there was already a strong relationship. Overall, the more positive the existing relationship between the participant and their parents, the more positive the parental reaction to the disclosure. It must be noted that disclosure of sexual orientation may in some circumstances actually increase the closeness between the adolescent and their parents.

Meanings of Sexual Identity

All of the participants felt strongly that their sexual orientation is not a choice, and many were able to offer convincing arguments supporting this assertion. A common explanation was that homosexuality is not the 'norm' and that no child would thus choose to be gay or lesbian. P3 believed strongly that LGB individuals who are out should talk about their experiences to help dispel the myth that homosexuality is a choice: 'there are misconceptions about being gay that need to be cleared up, and this can only happen if gay people are out and if there is more information available to help people understand that being gay is not a choice.' Similarly, P5 stated that 'a lot of people think that it is a choice that you make, that one day you just decide that you are going to be gay, that it is a switch. But it isn't – it is not like that. I believe that you are born gay. What ten-year-old do you know who would make that choice?'

A theme that emerged strongly in the interviews was that participants do not consider their sexual orientation to be the defining part of their identity. This view was evident in statements such as 'I do not want to be defined by my sexuality' (P2) and 'It is a huge part of me, but not all of me' (P4). Furthermore, participants indicated that the nature and meaning of their gay or lesbian identity changes at different points of their life. This finding resonates with earlier studies that describe a shift in the importance ascribed to sexual identity and labels. Research has found that as adolescents with same-sex attractions become increasingly more visible to themselves and others, their desire to name their sexual orientation often decreases. Savin-Williams notes that adolescents might use 'the gay word' as a shorthand form for describing their attractions, but 'implicit in this usage is a rejection of gay as an identity' (2005:16). Similar sentiments were expressed during the interviews for this study, with participants articulating a dislike of terms such as 'lesbian', 'gay' and 'homosexual'.

Several participants did indicate, however, that they have since come to embrace these terms. P3, for instance, noted: 'I don't mind the term lesbian anymore. I actually embrace it. I used to hate the term. This was a process that happened after I came out. There was a time just after I came out when I believed that people must think "Oh that's [name] the lesbian" and I felt strange about that. That feeling has faded, though. Our society categorises interactions on a daily basis: you're either single or seeing someone, married or not married, or divorced. Relationships define us. I have to "come out" at some point during the process of getting to know anyone I wish to know as more than a mere acquaintance. Once you come out, it categorises you. I don't think being a lesbian defines me, but being a lesbian defines how I am placed in society.' Statements such as this highlight the importance – especially for clinicians – of acknowledging that issues faced by LGB individuals may not be intrinsically linked to their sexual orientation. Rather, an LGB individual's difficulties may arise from society's negative reactions to alternative sexual orientations (Pachankis & Goldfried, 2004) or indeed myriad other causes.

STRATEGIES FOR PRESERVING AN OUTWARD APPEARANCE OF HETEROSEXUALITY

Denial was used as a strategy by several participants to preserve the appearance of heterosexuality, even when confronted by family members about their orientation. P1 and P9 also reported telling their parents that their sexuality was just a phase even after incriminating evidence had been found in their bedrooms.

Many participants spoke of feeling a need to conceal their sexual identity by hiding and monitoring their behaviour. P2 described in detail constant self-monitoring: 'I think that a lot of gay boys are watchful of other boys and girls from a young age; they are busy watching everybody else so as to be aware of what traits they need to hide in themselves. I remember doing voice control – you know, you train your voice to sound deeper – because naturally I have a nasal twang in my voice... There was a way to stand; I remember watching the way straight boys stood. In retrospect, I have been doing this for years: I have been watching people... The thought process I had all the time was "quickly, you need to make this change" when you realise something is amiss – quickly change or quickly do this.'

Dating opposite-sex individuals was also cited as a common strategy. Interestingly, this practice was used not only to prove participants' heterosexuality and thus please their parents, but also to 'make sure' (P2) of their same-sex attractions. P10 recalled trying to get a girlfriend under 'the premise that now I need to get a girlfriend so that nobody will suspect that I am gay'. P6 mentioned that she 'tried to be the daughter that [my mother] wanted me to be. I tried to date guys but I found that I couldn't because I was constantly thinking about this one girl... I could not force myself to like a guy.'

Strategies for Coping with Same-sex Attractions

Many non-heterosexual youths experience psychological and behavioural difficulties, such as feelings of isolation and a lack of acceptance by peers, as a result of strict heterosexual socialisation (Ritter & Terndrup, 2002). P3 explained that to cope with her same-sex attraction she 'actively created a twin brother... Whenever I liked a girl or admired a girl, I would think to myself "if I had a twin brother, he would like her"'. This provided a way for her to 'accept' her thoughts and feelings: 'I was so aware that I shouldn't have these feelings, because *those* people do that, people who come from bad homes do that, it doesn't happen in my neighbourhood.' It was evident from the interviews that many participants suffered some degree of internalised homophobia.

The interviews also revealed a general struggle for self-acceptance, with several participants recalling turning to prayer in the hope of changing their sexuality. P3, who described herself as religious in high school, explained that before she disclosed her sexuality to her parents, she 'often challenged God on [her same-sex attraction] in prayer, because if this is it, please can You change it. So when people tell me it is a choice I really get upset because I feel as if I have explored all avenues regarding trying to change it.'

The participants in this study also said that they often attempted to minimise, mask or banish sexual thoughts about same-gendered individuals. P3 stated: 'I was analysing why I thought about this girl so much and for a flash I thought, maybe I am a lesbian and then I argued it away.' P2 mentioned that in order 'to fool myself when masturbating I would always include a woman in my fantasies… she didn't have any role to play in [the fantasy], but just to make it okay.' P7 explained that 'when I admired a woman and realised [it], immediately I would banish it [the thought]'. P8 mentioned that he 'tried to push those feelings aside and they started bubbling up again at the age of 13'.

Reasons For and Against Coming Out
Studies have identified a number of common motivations behind disclosing one's sexuality, including a desire to share one's life, to end concealment, to gain more freedom, to increase intimacy with parents and to stand up as a person. Research undertaken by Ben-Ari in 1995 identified the most common reasons as 'being honest, not to hide, not to live a lie'. The findings in this study are consistent with those in Butler and Astbury (2005) and Pachankis and Goldfried (2004), with

participants most often citing a desire to share their lives, to be honest with themselves and others, to share their happiness, or because of a catalyst event. For six of the ten participants, the decision to come out was made after a confrontation by a family member.

According to international research, common reasons for not coming out include fear of being rejected, of provoking parental guilt, of worsening the relationship with parents, of being blamed and of hurting or disappointing parents (D'Augelli, Grossman & Starks, 2005). Similarly, participants in this study cited a fear of rejection, of financial loss and of public ridicule/scorn as well as a desire not to hurt or disappoint their parents. P9 explained how she 'was ashamed of telling her [mother]. I was scared she would look at me and be disgusted with me and hate me, so I told her that I was bisexual; I didn't tell her I was gay.' Many participants also mentioned religious values as a factor in delaying their disclosure, as they feared rejection on the grounds of their family's belief system. The homophobic attitude of immediate family members was also identified as a significant factor in participants deciding to hide their sexuality.

A fear of rejection was overwhelmingly the main reason identified by participants for not disclosing their homosexuality. P1 recalled that his 'concerns were that I would be disowned and told to never come back'. Likewise, P3 described a long period of anxiety before coming out to her family: 'It took a long time; I was terrified to tell them. It took me about a year to tell them. I decided to start with my mum, as I was even more terrified of telling my dad. Rejection is the main fear, and wondering if they will literally chuck you out the house, which unfortunately does seem to happen.' P2 mentioned that while he was fearful of rejection from his family, he was also 'scared of the social consequences' for them: 'being in a small town where you have to be friends with all those people who are homophobic and who are not forgiving for that type of thing.'

For many participants in this study, the feelings of estrangement and a fear of discovery, the loss of financial support, the possibility of violence and expulsion, as well as actual encounters with homophobia, led them to start planning for their survival. P2 shared the thought process he went through in the lead up to his disclosure: 'I am going to wait until I have a degree behind my back and I know that I can survive' but noted that he 'ended up doing it earlier'. P3 mentioned similar fears: 'you are worried that you will be thrown out of your house, which they [parents] seem to think is so ridiculous when you tell them afterwards… I literally started saving up money in case they did chuck me out… you start to plan. I thought: "What must I do? Must I move out first? Then they can't chuck me out. Must I have this much money? Must I go study?" But then it didn't work out that way.'

Parental Reactions
An adolescent's disclosure about his/her homosexuality is often followed by emotional responses such as panic, shock, disappointment, anger and sadness (Davis et al., 2009; Saltzburg, 2004). Earlier research conducted by Savin-Williams in 1998 suggests that parental reactions are more likely to be negative than positive, and he notes that common reactions range from extreme disruption to expulsion from the family home. However, more recent studies indicate that while LGB youth may still experience rejection and/or verbal and physical abuse after coming out, most families are able to work through the initial turmoil and find ways to retain, or even strengthen, familial bonds (Davis et al., 2009; D'Augelli et al., 2005; Saltzburg, 2004). Parental reactions strongly impact on adolescents' mental health; D'Augelli (2002) observes that those adolescents who meet with rejection from both parents report significantly more issues relating to suicide ideation, feelings of worthlessness, stress and shame than those participants whose parent(s) are accepting.

The participants in this study all expected negative reactions from their parents, thus the thought of disclosing their sexuality caused considerable distress. While they were most fearful of parental rejection, participants also listed a number of other reasons for not coming out: fear of ejection from the family home; possible loss of financial support; fear of verbal and/or physical abuse; and a desire not to disappointment their parents. Another significant factor was exposure to their parents' negative comments about homosexuality, as well as frequent verbal abuse from peers and teachers. Similar justifications are recorded in earlier research (Butler & Astbury, 2005; D'Augelli, Pilkington & Herschberger, 2002). Participants in this study also talked about witnessing verbal and/or physical victimisation of other (either openly or perceived homosexual) youth and noted that exposure to such hostile behaviours increased their desire to conceal their sexuality.

Parental reactions in this study ranged from extreme outrage and expulsion to support and acceptance. The majority of participants experienced, in varying degrees, a negative reaction from their parents, with many reporting emotional outbursts (usually in the form of crying) that were often followed by a state of denial. P1, for instance, experienced a violent and emotional reaction to his disclosure: 'My mum freaked out: that night she threw rocks [small pebbles] at me – she literally tried to attack me. She kicked me out of the house; she screamed and shouted.' P1 described staying at his uncle's house for a few days after this episode while the family received counselling from a priest. He remembers that his mother increasingly denied his sexual orientation while simultaneously attempting to persuade him to change. He described his mother's argument to the family priest as follows: 'Well, why didn't he just decide to keep this to himself, get married and have children, and move on with his life?' P1 was particularly upset by this reaction and hurt by his mother's lack of understanding and support. Looking back on the situation, he felt that she behaved in this manner because 'that one dream that she had for her only son has gone completely haywire and she doesn't know what to do, and that is scary for her.'

Two participants reported physical violence, and many reported some form of verbal or emotional abuse. Two were also kicked out of their homes, and another chose to leave due to extreme conflict surrounding her sexual orientation. Other participants were made to suffer for their sexuality by having financial allowances withheld, by being denied access to lesbian and gay friends, and by being coerced to change. In P6's case, her mother forbade her from seeing lesbian friends or girlfriends.

The majority of parents also insisted that their child attempt to change or cure their homosexuality. P8 described how his father and stepmother decided that he must visit a brothel despite only being seventeen years of age: 'they were sort of listening at the beginning and then I just remember my stepmum saying "we are going to get a prostitute for you"… I didn't think she was being serious. Then I was grounded and had to work in the garden, and I wasn't allowed to see any of my friends and my phone was taken away.' At first he did not realise that his father and stepmother intended to follow through with their plan, but was then taken to a brothel under false pretences. Once there, the manager refused his father's request because P8 was a minor: 'I just sat there and pretended like I didn't know what was going on, and my dad came back and said, "We have to leave, you are not allowed to be here".' Reflecting on this experience, P8 described it as humiliating, shaming and hurtful. Similar painful experiences were echoed by seven of the ten participants.

While initial reactions were almost always negative, many parents were eventually able to accept their child's sexual orientation. Participants described this as a gradual development, and often framed the process as their parents slowly coming to terms with their disclosure. This finding resonates with those of similar studies (Davis et al., 2009; Saltzburg, 2004; D'Augelli, Grossman & Starks, 2006; Butler & Astbury, 2005). This gradual process of parents 'coming to terms' is comparable to the stages of grief identified by Kübler-Ross (1969) and often involves parents having to renegotiate their relationship with their child in light of his/her embodiment of negative perceptions of homosexuality (Mattison & McWhirter, 1995).

The participants' narratives discussed in this section illustrate the serious and often painful impact that parental homophobia has on the lives of LGB adolescents. Adolescents may experience a lack of emotional support from their family, which may cause further emotional distress during the coming-out process. Most of the participants in this study indicated that the emotional unavailability of their parents significantly hindered their ability to come to terms with their sexual orientation, a finding that echoes Butler and Astbury's 2005 study of South African LGB youth. This observation also draws attention to the crucial need for additional support for at-risk groups such as LGB youth. Because of the importance of family and the centrality of school in the lives of adolescents, chronic tensions at home and/or anxieties associated with school can have far-reaching consequences for an individual's developmental. With increasing numbers of adolescents disclosing their sexual orientation at earlier ages, it is essential that families and schools support LGB youth during their transition to adulthood. However, it must be noted that parents are often ill-prepared and initially unable to support their child during this often traumatic period.

Hoped-for Reactions from Parents
The majority of the participants reported that, at the time of their disclosure, they desired greater emotional support from their parents. P9 explained the complexities of the situation as follows: 'If your parents could understand, then they would be in a better position to support their children. They play such an important role in your life and have an effect and influence on how you feel about yourself. Parents can have so much power over their children: they can destroy them so easily, often without even realising that they are doing so.' He also recounted the pain he had experienced because of his parents'

negative reaction: 'It is so hard to be punished for something that you didn't choose; it is hard to hear [your parents] say you are going to hell or that [homosexuality] is where AIDS comes from, from two men kissing, it's hard.' As Butler and Astbury (2005) note, this lack of emotional support from parents may not be an intentionally homophobic act, but rather due to their inability to understand what it means for their child to be homosexual.

Additional Stressors

There is overwhelming evidence that sexual-minority youth are at greater risk than their heterosexual counterparts for stress-related mental health disorders such as depression, substance use and abuse, and suicide. This increased risk is primarily linked to the daily stigma and prejudice that LGB youth encounter during this critical developmental phase (D'Augelli, 2006; Meyer, 2003; Floyd & Stein, 2002). Over half of the participants in this study indicated having contemplated suicide, with three reporting actual suicide attempts directly related to their sexual orientation. These participants reported that, during this traumatic time in their lives, they believed it would be easier to die than continue living. P4 recalled thinking that suicide may be the best solution to her situation: 'I didn't care if I died, because if I did then I wouldn't be living with this pain.' She attributed this belief to the fact that the 'school community was not supportive, and I did come up against prejudice: teachers and other kids teasing me and talking about my being gay. They didn't throw condoms in my face like they did to another guy, but things like that – and other little things – can propel someone into becoming suicidal.' She, P3 and P9 all felt that having a lack of support or someone to talk to increases the risk of adolescent suicide.

Strategies of Support

Participants offered many support strategies for others coming out, many of which can be integrated into clinical practice. The majority mentioned that it is helpful to have a good support network; to identify a positive role model; to accept oneself before coming out; to be honest with oneself and others (if not in danger for doing so); to research homosexuality to help with answering questions; to thoroughly assess the situation before disclosing; to be aware that family members will need time to process a disclosure; to find a positive outlet for frustrations; and to reflect upon the journey.

Of particular importance is an appreciation of the psychological consequences of stigmatisation and victimisation (Rivers & Carragher, 2004). When discussing this issue, participants in this study suggested that visible societies within schools and/or communities would serve as a valuable and much-needed source of support for sexual-minority youth, especially for those facing family or peer rejection. It must be noted, though, that the participants in this study demonstrated strength and resilience despite the prejudice and inner turmoil that they suffered during the coming-out process. As D'Augelli (2006) notes, openness about sexual orientation may put adolescents at risk, but it also provides them with an opportunity to obtain the social resources required to integrate sexual orientation into other aspects of their lives.

LIMITATIONS AND STRENGTHS OF THE STUDY

Although limited in its scope, this study was able to capture detailed and valuable qualitative data. Furthermore, the small sample size was appropriate for the methodology used and allows for findings to be compared with similar research. Be that as it may, the researchers acknowledge that the small size of the sample prevents the generalisation of the data to encompass the experiences of all LGB youth in South Africa.

Although an equal gender distribution was obtained, the researchers would have preferred a more diverse distribution of language and/or cultural groups. Regrettably, interview subjects were not forthcoming from all of the South African cultural groups. It is likely that the experiences of youths from those language or cultural groups not represented in this study are quite different, and this is an issue that this study was unable to address.

One of the key strengths of this study is the openness of the participants during the interview process. All participants were able to freely express their opinions, and this helped to create an environment in which the subjects were comfortable discussing intimate and often distressing experiences. Several participants described their involvement as personally beneficial in that it provided an opportunity for them to reflect on their experiences and to identify shifts in their relationships and sense of self. Some participants likened the experience to that of a therapeutic conversation, noting that it was a valuable and pleasant experience that allowed them to grow.

RECOMMENDATIONS AND SUPPORT STRATEGIES

- There are several implications of these findings for mental health professionals working with LGB adolescents and youth. Most generally, professionals need to acknowledge the existence of LGB youth and to understand that the development of alternative sexual orientation accelerates around puberty (D'Augelli, 2006). Mental health practitioners should empower themselves with knowledge regarding the process of disclosure, as well as knowledge of the topic of adolescent disclosure with regard to family reactions and processes preceding disclosure; available community support services; and online support communities. Mental health practitioners should also be aware of their own biases against alternative sexual orientations and, if they cannot come to terms with these, it is vital that they refer.
- Mental health professionals (counsellors and psychologists)

need to realise that certain issues and life events are likely to be associated with increased distress for LGB individuals. Youths who disclose their sexual orientation during adolescence should be considered to be at considerable risk of stress, low self-esteem and depression. Support, constructive guidance and current research should be provided to both the adolescent and his/her parents during counselling sessions. Support from parents, peers and teachers may also mitigate the development of mental health problems.
- Parents should be informed of other sites of support. Research has indicated that connecting parents with specialist support groups is extremely helpful during the adjustment phase (D'Augelli, 2002).
- When discussing the possibility of disclosure with an adolescent, it is crucial that professionals carry out a careful assessment of the family environment, particularly the likely reactions of parents. Unless the mental health professional is assured of at least one parent's acceptance (preferably both), careful consideration should be given before advising the client to proceed with the disclosure, as this may put the adolescent at risk of harm – both physically and emotionally – for a number of years to come.
- School counsellors can help to support sexual-minority adolescents as they face some of the challenges associated with coming out. School counsellors can also play a critical role in developing school policies that adequately address harassment and discrimination based on sexual orientation.
- Increased visibility of positive lesbian and gay role models in the media may also aid in enhancing self-esteem and reducing internalised homophobia. Lesbian and gay activists and organisations could also implement strategies to increase self-esteem through the positive portrayal of lesbian and gay issues.

- Teachers should be educated to be tolerant of and respectful towards LGB youth.
- Mental health professionals, school counsellors and other support providers must create non-judgemental and welcoming spaces for LGB adolescents and those who are questioning their sexuality.

CONCLUSION

The process of disclosure is difficult at any age, but is especially challenging when combined with the normative stressors associated with adolescent development, negative societal attitudes, a lack of support, and guilt or internalised homophobia. These factors inevitably add an inordinate amount of psychological strain for a young person coming to terms with their sexual identity. Mental health professionals can generate knowledge and understanding around the unique challenges faced by sexual-minority youth.

We concur with Butler and Astbury (2006), who argue that as adolescents become aware of their sexual orientation and develop appropriate coping mechanisms, they become capable of responding to the demands of their culture and their society. Satisfaction with self can contribute to the development of respect for self and others, and eliminate the sense of isolation. We furthermore agree with Hames (2003) in that it is essential that homophobic attitudes and acts of violence are continually challenged so that non-heterosexual youth are not exposed to unnecessary risks during disclosure. As noted by the participants in this study, LGB youth need to understand that their sexuality is normal and acceptable, as this awareness will help them to overcome the fear, pain and guilt so often experienced during the coming-out process.

REFERENCES

Ben-Ari, A. (1995). The discovery that an offspring is gay: Parents', gay men's and lesbians' perspectives, *Journal of Homosexuality*, *30*, 89–112.

Butler, A. H. & Astbury, G. (2005). South African gay and lesbian youth coming out to their families: Analyzing various decision-making pathways and outcomes, *Journal of Child and Youth Care Work*, *20*, 22–42.

Butler, A. H. & Astbury, G. (2006). The use of defence mechanisms as a precursor to coming out: A South African gay and lesbian youth perspective. *Journal of Homosexuality*, *55*(2), 223–244.

Cass, V. C. (1979). Homosexual identity formation: A theoretical model. *Journal of Homosexuality*, *4*, 219–235.

Cass, V. C. (1996). Sexual orientation identity formation: A western phenomenon. In R. P. Cabaj & T. S. Stein (Eds), *Textbook of homosexuality and mental health* (pp. 227–251). Washington, DC: American Psychiatric Press.

Cock, J. (2003). Engendering gay and lesbian rights: The equality clause in the South African Constitution. *Women's Studies International Forum*, *26*(1), 35–45.

D'Augelli, A. R. (2002). Mental health problems among lesbian, gay and bisexual youth ages 14 to 21. *Clinical Child Psychology and Psychiatry*, *7*, 433–456.

D'Augelli, A. R. (2006). Developmental and contextual factors and mental health among lesbian, gay and bisexual youths'. In A. M. Omoto & H. S. Kurtzman (Eds), *Sexual orientation and mental health: Examining identity and development in lesbian, gay and bisexual people* (pp. 37–53). Washington, DC: American Psychological Association.

D'Augelli, A. R., Grossman, A. H. & Starks, M. T. (2005). Parents' awareness of lesbian, gay and bisexual youths sexual orientation. *Journal of Marriage and Family*, *67*(2), 474–482.

D'Augelli, A. R., Grossman, A. H. & Starks, M. T. (2006). Childhood gender atypicality, victimization and PTSD among lesbian, gay and bisexual youth. *Journal of Interpersonal Violence*, *21*(11), 1462–1482.

D' Augelli, A. R. & Hershberger, S. L. (1993). Lesbian, gay, and bisexual youth in community settings: Personal challenges and mental health problems. *American Journal of Community Psychology*, *21*, 421–448.

D'Augelli, A. R., Pilkington, N. W. & Hershberger, S. L. (2002). Incidence and mental health impact of sexual orientation victimization of lesbian, gay and bisexual youths in high school. *School Psychology Quarterly*, *17*(2), 148–167.

Davis, T. S., Saltzburg, S. & Locke, C. R. (2009). Supporting the emotional and psychological wellbeing of sexual minority youth: Youth ideas for action. *Children and Youth Services Review*, *31*, 1030–1041. doi:10.1016/j.childyouth.2009.05.003

Denzin, N. K. & Lincoln, Y. S. (Eds) (2011). *The SAGE handbook of qualitative research*. (4th Ed.). Thousand Oaks: Sage.

Fassinger, R. E. & Miller, B. A. (1996). Validation of an inclusive model of sexual minority identity formation on a sample of gay men. *Journal of Homosexuality*, *32*(2), 53–78.

Floyd, F. J. & Stein, T. S. (2002). Sexual orientation identity formation among gay, lesbian and bisexual youths: Multiple patterns of milestone. *Journal of Research on Adolescence*, *12*(2), 167–191.

Hames, M. (2003). The women's movement and lesbian and gay struggles in South Africa. *Feminist Africa: Changing Cultures*. Retrieved 10 February 2011, from http://www.feministafrica.org/index.php/the-women-s-movement-and-lesbian-and-gay-struggles-in-south-africa

Herdt, G. & Boxer, A. M. (1993). *Children of horizons: How gay and lesbian teens are leading a new way out of the closet*. Boston: Beacon Press.

Kübler-Ross, E. (1969). *On death and dying*. New York: MacMillan.

Maguen, S., Floyd, F. J., Bakeman, R. & Armistead, L. (2002).

Developmental milestones and disclosure of sexual orientation among gay, lesbian and bisexual youths. *Applied Developmental Psychology*, *23*, 219–233.

Matthews, C. R. (2007). Affirmative lesbian, gay and bisexual counselling with all clients. In K. J. Bieschke, R. M. Perez & K. A. DeBord (Eds), *Handbook of counselling and psychotherapy with lesbian, gay, bisexual and transgender clients* (pp. 201–219). Washington, DC: American Psychological Association.

Mattison, A. M. & McWhirter, D. P. (1995). Lesbians, gay men, and their families: Some therapeutic issues. *Psychiatric Clinics of North America*, *18*(1), 123–127.

McCarn, S. R. & Fassinger, R. E. (1996). Re-visioning sexual minority identity formation: A new model of lesbian identity and its implications for counselling research. *The Counselling Psychologist*, *24*(3), 508–534.

Meyer, I. H. (2003). Prejudice, social stress, and mental health in lesbian, gay and bisexual populations: Conceptual issues and research evidence. *Psychological Bulletin*, *129*(5), 674–690.

Pachankis, J. E. & Goldfried, M. R. (2004). Clinical issues in working with lesbian, gay and bisexual clients. *Psychotherapy: Theory, Research, Practice, Training*, *41*(3), 227–246.

Ritter, K. I. & Terndrup, A. I. (2002). *Handbook of affirmative psychotherapy with lesbians and gay men*. New York: Guilford Press.

Rivers, I. & Carragher, D. J. (2004). Social-developmental factors affecting lesbian and gay youth: A review of cross national research findings. *Children and Society*, *17*, 374–385.

Rosario, M., Hunter, J., Maguen, S., Gwadz, M. & Smith, R. (2001). The coming out process and its adaptational and health-related associations among gay, lesbian and bisexual youths: Stipulation and exploration of a model. *American Journal of Community Psychology*, *29*(1), 113–160.

Saltzburg, S. (2004). Learning that an adolescent child is gay or lesbian: The parent experience. *Social Work*, *49*(1), 109–118.

Savin-Williams, R. C. (1998). The disclosure to families of same-sex attractions by lesbian, gay and bisexual youths. *Journal of Research on Adolescence, 8*(1), 49–68.

Savin-Williams, R. C. (2005). *The new gay teenager*. Cambridge, MA: Harvard University Press.

Savin-Williams, R. C. & Ream, G. L. (2007). Prevalence and stability of sexual orientation components during adolescence and young adulthood. *Archives of Sexual Behaviour, 36*(3), 385–394.

Sears, J. T. (1991). *Growing up gay in the South: Race, gender, and journeys of the spirit*. New York: Harrington Press.

Sophie, J. (1986). A critical examination of stage theories of lesbian identity development. *Journal of Homosexuality, 12*(2), 39–51.

Troiden, R. R. (1989). The formation of homosexual identities. *Journal of Homosexuality, 26*, 41–56.

Western Cape Province (n.d.). In Wikipedia. Retrieved on 15 November 2012, from http://en.wikipedia.org/wiki/Western_Cape

List of Contributors

ABOUT THE EDITORS

Carien Lubbe-De Beer holds a PhD in Educational Psychology with a thesis titled 'The Experiences of Children Growing up in Same-Gendered Families'. She is an associate professor in the Department of Educational Psychology at the University of Pretoria. She is an NRF-rated researcher and her research interests focus on lesbian-parented families, specifically the experiences of parents and their children, as well as sandplay therapy in vulnerable communities. She serves as a representative of the Psychology Society of South Africa (PsySSA) on the International Network on Lesbian, Gay and Bisexual Concerns and Transgender Matters in Psychology (INET), which is hosted by the American Psychological Association. Prof. Lubbe-De Beer received the Emerging Researcher award in 2012 from the Educational Association of South Africa.

John Marnell is the Publishing and Communications Coordinator for

Gay and Lesbian Memory in Action (GALA). He holds a BA (Hons) in classical literature and an MA (editing and communications), both from the University of Melbourne. Since 2008, he has worked as an editor for a number of Australian academic journals, including *Overland*, *Metro* and *Screen Education*. He is also the coordinator of *Overland*'s Connections Project, an initiative that seeks to foster greater editorial diversity in Australian publishing by supporting emerging writers from marginalised communities and backgrounds.

ABOUT THE AUTHORS

Diana Breshears received her PhD from the University of Nebraska-Lincoln in the field of interpersonal and family communication. She is currently a postdoctoral fellow in the Department of Educational Psychology at the University of Pretoria. Diana's research interests include the communicative creation and maintenance of identity among individuals with non-traditional, stigmatised familial identities. To date, her work has included studies of adult children of alcoholics, and parents and children from lesbian/gay-parented families.

Jean Brundrit is a visual artist who works with photographic media. She has exhibited extensively in South Africa and contributed to a number of international exhibitions. She is a senior lecturer at the Michaelis School of Fine Art, University of Cape Town, where she teaches photography. She is an NRF-rated researcher. Her research interests are primarily concerned with exploring identity, specifically lesbian identity, and strategies of representation within a South African context.

Natasha Distiller holds a PhD in English literature and a PhD in Gender Studies. She was Associate Professor of English at the University of Cape Town, and Chief Research Officer at the Institute for the Humanities in Africa (HUMA). She is currently an honorary research associate of HUMA, and is completing a clinical psychology degree at John F. Kennedy University in Berkeley, California. She has published extensively, authoring monographs, editing collections of essays, and publishing in peer-reviewed journals. She has also been editor of *Social Dynamics*.

Natalie Donaldson is an emerging researcher in the field of sexualities in South Africa. She holds a Master of Social Science degree and is a lecturer in the Department of Psychology at Rhodes University. She is currently working on publications based on her Master's thesis (completed in 2011), which focused on how self-identified lesbian women interpret and talk about lesbian representations made available in South African media. She teaches in the field of gender, sexuality, queer theory, social psychology, developmental psychology, and qualitative research methodologies. Her research interests fall under the broad umbrella of critical gender psychology and sexualities studies. Specifically, her research interests involve investigating how various social institutions construct sexualities and sexual identities within a South African context.

Kerry Frizelle is a registered counselling psychologist who currently lectures in psychology at the University of KwaZulu-Natal, Howard College campus. Kerry lectures in the field of social/community psychology. Kerry is particularly interested in researching and teaching in areas relating to gender and sexuality.

Gabriel Hoosain Khan is the former archivist and current Youth and Education Coordinator at Gay and Lesbian Memory in Action (GALA). He holds a BA (Hons) in English literature and psychology from the University of the Witwatersrand. Gabriel has a keen interest in the history of LGBTIQA struggles and its intersection with other struggles for justice, especially within the South African context. He also has a keen interest in working with LGBTIQA youth, and has spent the last two years doing hands-on work with various LGBTIQA youth groups in South Africa. Gabriel's research interests include intersecting identities (sexuality, gender and ethnicity) and immigrant communities within the context of post-colonial Africa.

Aliza le Roux is an NRF-rated behavioural ecologist studying cognition and communication in wild animals at the University of the Free State's Qwaqwa campus. As a new senior lecturer, she has also become fascinated with the scholarship of teaching and learning, which is developing into an exciting research direction. In the United States, she was actively involved in the Association for Women in Science, advocating for young women in academia. She hopes to continue this advocacy work in South Africa, broadening her scope to encourage openness and diversity in academia on multiple levels.

Charmaine Louw is a lecturer at the Department of Educational Psychology at the University of Stellenbosch. She teaches in the areas of assessment and psychometry and is also involved in the training of counsellors and educational psychologists. She holds an M Ed (Psych) degree and is a registered educational psychologist. She has, among others, a keen research interest in LGBTI psychology.

Ingrid Lynch (PhD) is a lecturer in the Department of Psychology at the University of Pretoria. She has published in the field of critical gender, sexuality and health studies. Her current work focuses on how bisexual identities are enabled and constrained by different discourses. This includes an exploration of ways in which dominant discourses and binary orders can be challenged and expanded by South African women claiming a bisexual identity. Her other research interests include LGBTI psychology; critical interrogations of gendered identities; reproductive decision-making; and feminist theories.

Yolan Moodley was born in Durban, South Africa. He is completing a Master's in community-based counselling psychology at the University of the Witwatersrand. His research interests lie in community development, social action and prevention.

Tracy Morison is a research psychologist who currently holds a position as a postdoctoral fellow in the Human and Social Development Research Programme at the Human Sciences Research Council (Pretoria). She is an honorary research associate in the psychology department at her alma mater, Rhodes University, where she attained her PhD. Her main research interests lie in the area of sexualities and reproductive decisions (including pathways to parenthood and child-freedom). She also has an interest in families, households, discursive methodology and feminist theory.

Vasu Reddy is Deputy Executive Director of the Human and Social Development Research Programme at the Pretoria offices of the Human Sciences Research Council. He is an honorary associate professor and research fellow in gender studies at the University of KwaZulu-Natal, where he obtained his PhD. He sits on various boards and is also an editorial collective member of *Agenda* journal. Vasu has written extensively on the topics of gender and sexuality, HIV and AIDS, social cohesion, families, and households. He is also interested in critical theory, and humanities-focused research. He is the lead editor of *From social silence to social science. Same-sex sexuality, HIV & AIDS and gender in South Africa* (HSRC Press, 2009) and co-author of *The country we want to live in: Hate crimes and homophobia in the lives of black lesbian South Africans* (HSRC Press, 2010).

Veronica Robertson is a registered educational psychologist. Since her graduation she has worked in the field of special-needs education. She worked in the field of autism as part of an outreach team which helped to diagnose and develop programmes of learning as well as place learners in a school environment suitable to their needs. She is currently working as a special educational needs coordinator at a school. She has a special interest in childhood, adolescent development and LGBTI psychology.

Cherith Sanger holds an her LLB degree from the University of the Western Cape and an LLM *cum laude* with a specialisation in gender, health and human rights from the University of California, Los Angeles School of Law, through the UCLA Law/Sonke Gender Justice Fellowship. She was admitted as an attorney in the Cape High Court in 2007 and practised as an attorney in the private sector until mid-2008. From 2008 to 2011 she litigated women's rights gender cases and conducted legal advocacy in the non-profit sector. Currently, Cherith works as Policy Advocacy and Research Manager in Sonke's Policy Advocacy and Research Unit. Here, Cherith conducts policy advocacy for gender transformation and the integration of work with men and boys into law and policy.

Nadia Sanger is a research specialist in the Human and Social Development Research Programme at the Human Sciences Research Council in Cape Town. Her interests include post-colonial feminist theory, constructs of identities, and the multiple intersections between gender, race, sexuality, and species in fiction, non-fiction and popular culture. She holds a PhD in women's and gender studies from the University of the Western Cape, and a postdoctoral Fulbright scholarship in the Women's Studies Department at the University of Maryland in the United States. Nadia has published a number of journal articles on the links between race, gender, and sexuality.

Karl Swain is currently a clinical psychologist and lecturer at the UKZN Department of Behavioural Medicine. He originally obtained a BCom degree majoring in accounting in 2003 and thereafter pursued a career in psychology having completed his MSocSci *cum laude* in 2008. He is currently doing his PhD in the area of the neuropsychological effects of traumatic stress in adolescents. He also works in a private practice at Entabeni Hospital and is currently the chairperson of the Durban Practicing Psychologists Group (DPPG). His research interests are focused on neuropsychology; trauma; gender and sexuality; and critical psychology.

Lindy Wilbraham is a research psychologist who works within developmental and social psychology as well as health education fields. She has particular research interests in parenting, children and household arrangements in various circumstances of living, communication within families about sexualities and risk, and life-writing (memoir) of families struggling with poverty, disability and illness. She is a professor in the Psychology Department of Rhodes University, Grahamstown, and is currently Head of Department.

Notes

1 We follow Lubbe (2008a) in our usage of the term 'same-gendered family' to refer to families formed by gay parents. Such families are also commonly referred to as 'lesbian' or 'gay' families or 'same-sex' families, and these terms are also reflected in the text. Though these terms may be used interchangeably at times, our preference is for the term 'same-gendered'. This term captures the constitutive and regulatory effects of discourses that serve to fashion both sex and gender.
2 This term, coined by Desmond Tutu after South Africa's first democratic elections, draws on the biblical image of the rainbow which appeared after Noah's flood and describes the ethos of post-apartheid South Africa, which embraces diversity and multiculturalism.
3 Distiller uses this term in a discussion of the importance of social recognition for same-gendered families. Our meaning may differ somewhat from hers in that we wish to invoke the disparity between official legitimation of homosexuality and actual experiences of LGBTI people in relation to exercising the rights they have been accorded.
4 For an appraisal of this work in relation to the South African context, see Distiller (2011).
5 The term 'neo-colonial' in this chapter refers to the continuance of colonial history through new strategies of control and dominance.
6 For a nuanced discussion on this issue see Dlamini, 2006; Msibi, 2011; Reddy, 2006.

7 We use the term 'citizenship' in this context to refer to a sense of belonging that does not exclude foreign nationals, refugees and migrants to South Africa.
8 See, for example, Gqola, 2010; Lewis, 2011; Magubane, 2001; Osha, 2004; Ratele, 2006; Tamale, 2011.
9 Although there are various contested uses of the term in South Africa, in this chapter 'queer' will be used to refer to persons who identify/are identified as lesbian, gay, bisexual, transgendered, transsexual, or intersexed. It will be used in this chapter interchangeably with the term 'non-heterosexual', which is arguably also a contested term as it centralises 'heterosexuality' as the norm from which all other gender and sexual identities are understood.
10 For the purpose of this chapter, and in accordance with the Constitution and the Children's Act 38 of 2005, a child is defined as a person under the age of 18 years.
11 Section 7(2) of the Constitution.
12 Section 10 of the Constitution.
13 *National Coalition for Gay and Lesbian Equality* v *Minister of Justice* 1998 12 BCLR 1517 (CC).
14 See, for instance, Currah, 1997.
15 The Population Registration Act of 1950 classified South Africans as either white, African, coloured or Indian. Within these racial groups were further divisions based on ethnic and other perceived differences. According to these definitions, 'coloured' persons were neither 'black' or 'white', but were considered 'mixed' and, hence, inferior.
16 See Brady, 2011.
17 For an interesting discussion on this incident, see Ratele, 2006; Sanger, 2010.
18 *National Coalition for Gay and Lesbian Equality and Another* v *Minister of Justice and Others* 1998 (12) BCLR 1517 CC, 1593 at para. 37.
19 For example, *Greyling* v *Minister of Welfare and Population Development* Unreported 98/08197 (W); *National Coalition for Gay and Lesbian Equality* v *Minister of Justice* 1998 12 BLLR 1517 (CC); *National Coalition for Gay and Lesbian Equality* v *Minister of Home Affairs* 2000 1 BCLR 39 (CC); *Du Toit* v *Minister of Welfare and Population Development* 2002 10 BCLR 1006 (CC).
20 *Dawood and Another* v *Minister of Home Affairs and Another; Shalabi and Another* v *Minister of Home Affairs; Thomas and Another* v *Minister of Home Affairs and Others* 2000 (8) BCLR 837 (CC) 841.
21 *Du Toit and Another* v *Minister of Welfare and Population Development* 2002 (10) BCLR 1006 (CC), 1013.
22 *Minister for Welfare and Population Development* v *Fitzpatrick and Others* 2000 (7) BCLR 713 (CC).
23 For more discussion on the significance of this, see Sanger, Williams & Arnott, 2011
24 Section 9(2) of the Constitution holds that 'to promote the achievement of

equality, legislative and other measures designed to protect or advance persons, or categories of persons, disadvantaged by unfair discrimination may be taken'.
25 See, for example, Almack, 2006; Chabot & Ames, 2004; Donovan & Wilson, 2008; Leiblum, Palmer & Spector, 1995.
26 See, for example, Distiller, 2011; Lewin, 1994; Strah, 2003.
27 For an excellent up-to-date comparison of the details of these two locations with regard to lesbian and gay marriage rights, see Stacey & Meadow (2009).
28 From within the disciplines of social work, family studies, sociology, psychiatry, psychology, psychoanalysis, nursing and law, researchers have found that the children of lesbian mothers are the same as other children: their gender identities are normative, their gender roles and behaviours are standard, their sexual orientation will tend to be heterosexual – their development is, overall, 'normal'. For an overview of the literature to their respective dates, see Golombok, Spencer & Rutter, 1983; Steckel, 1987; Gottman, 1990; Patterson, 1994. See also Tasker & Golombok, 1997, which traces the development of children from 1976–1991; Bos, Van Balen & Van den Boom, 2005; Brewaeys & Van Hall, 1997; Hoeffer, 1981.
29 See Clarke, 2008. Gabb (2004) argues that the politics of the researcher will shape the findings, such that the coherent picture of 'normalcy' presented by the literature might conceal 'critical differentials'. Stacey & Biblarz (2001) critique most research's defensive starting points, which by necessity has to 'prove' that lesbians and gays can parent and form recognisable families. They suggest that the political imperative to assert the 'normality' of these families has skewed findings suggesting that there are small but significant differences. And there are (overwhelmingly positive) differences that have been charted so far, even as their implications have been minimised – see, for example, Steckel, 1985; Steckel, 1987; Tasker & Golombok, *Growing Up in a Lesbian Family*; Stacey & Biblarz, 2001; 'Child abuse rate at zero per cent in lesbian households', 2010; Park, 2010.
30 For a man's testimony about being part of a queer family under apartheid, see John, 1994.
31 In her review essay of queer theories, Marcus (2005:205–6) outlines the radical potential in asserting the normality of queer families: 'Only a decade or so ago queerness was understood as the antithesis of the normative nuclear biological family… For much of the twentieth century, Western Europe and the United States did indeed define queerness in opposition to the holy trinity of heterosexuality, biological reproduction, and the nuclear family. As Carolyn Dean has shown, French discourse between the world wars dismissed homosexuality as sterile (2000:12–13). Hollibaugh recalls the fight against the California Briggs initiative that defined homosexuals as the ultimate threat to families and children (2000:63). Newton writes in her book on Cherry Grove that gays are "outside the realm of kinship" and thus perpetually defined

as children (1993:290). Terry shows how popular social theories identified homosexuals as threats to the family and defined good parenting as the prevention of homosexuality in children (1999:24, 61, 215)... In the epilogue to her 1991 book, [Kath] Weston noted that a queer baby boom, then most notable among lesbians and now also visible among gay men, was beginning to break down the orthodoxy of nonprocreative homosexuality (193). The increasing profile of queer families and the quickening pace of debates about gay marriage are abrading what was once a stark distinction between straights ensconced in families and queers exiled from them. Reinventing the family rather than replacing it has become a prevalent way of theorizing queerness, a task that links lesbians and gays to straight men and women reinventing kinship.'

32 Recent examples include Dalton & Bielby, 2000; Dunne, 2000; Hequembourg, 2004.

33 See, for instance, De Vos, 2004; Lubbe, 2007; 2008.

34 The findings in this chapter are based on research undertaken as part of my Master's thesis, see Donaldson, 2011.

35 The few recent studies on this topic include Almack, 2005; 2006; Donovan & Wilson, 2008; Dunne, 2000; Jones, 2005; Kranz & Daniluk, 2006; Stevens et al., 2003; Touroni & Coyle, 2002

36 The responses of the participants are recorded verbatim, with only very light editing, in order to preserve their authenticity.

37 This article has previously appeared in the journal, *Studies in the Maternal*, and is now reprinted with permission from the editor and journal. Distiller, N. (2011). Am I that name? Middle-class lesbian motherhood in post-apartheid South Africa. *Studies in the Maternal*, 3(1), available at http://www.mamsie.bbk.ac.uk

38 One of Maureen Sullivan's respondents in a study of lesbian families said, 'There's something about having children that really links you to every other person who has children. I really feel much more a part of the world' (Sullivan, 2004:188). The sometimes verbatim similarity to my statement is coincidental, although I believe the shared experience is not.

39 See Judge, Manion and De Waal (2008) for more, and more detailed, narratives of queer ambivalence about inclusion in heteronormative family structures, specifically civil union.

40 On the topic of language: the terms used to denote non-heteronormative identities are even more vexed in a southern African context than in an Anglo-American one. This article has, with the help of the anonymous reviewers, moved away from 'queer' as an umbrella term to try and deal with this complexity, and has tried instead to use more or less specific terminology as the context determines. I want to acknowledge here the equally problematic umbrella quality of 'LGBTI', and to point out that it has the advantage over 'queer' for the purposes of this article of removing from the equation the ontological

problematisation of definitions. I am specifically working on making a case for the development of a queer vocabulary for South Africa, but that discussion is beyond the scope of this article.

41 Since the achievement of the Constitution, violence against women in general seems to be on the increase, with violence directed specifically against lesbians also seeming to escalate since 1994 (Cock, 2005; Fester, 2006). As I wrote the first draft of this paper, the president of the ANC youth league, Julius Malema, was making headlines with his vicious comments about a rape survivor who is also a lesbian, comments which were cheered by university students (Johnston, Tshabalala, Ndlovu & Dibetle, 2009).

42 I would like to acknowledge here Cheryl-Ann Potgieter's (2005) point that it is important not to replicate racist stereotypes by representing black communities as more homophobic than white communities; her study of the experience of black lesbians revealed that there was no generalisable family or community response to coming out.

43 For more information on the difficulties of naming same-sex desires and practices in the region, see Morgan and Wieringa (2005:310). They add, of their research project: 'At present there does not seem to be any word with a positive connotation in any of the indigenous languages used by the respondents in any of the countries represented in this project' (2005:322), that is, South Africa, Botswana, Kenya, Namibia, Swaziland, Tanzania and Uganda. In terms of the point I go on to make in section III below about the importance of citizenship enabled by the Constitution's non-discrimination clause, it is highly significant that they found that 'The South African women seem to be the only ones who do not have problems identifying as a lesbian [sic]. This is probably the result of the progressive Constitution that prevents discrimination on the basis of sexual orientation, although there is still a great deal of homophobia on the ground' (Morgan & Wieringa, 2005:322–323). The definition of 'lesbian' is not only an issue for African or other non-Western women. See Schwartz (1998:13–40)

44 I was told, 'We don't help people like you' (Bamford, 2007).

45 There is a growing weariness among black lesbians of being identified only with the figure of the silently suffering, raped woman. The outrage caused by corrective rape and by the state's lack of response and failure to prosecute easily fuels the presentation of the black lesbian only as a victim. Again, the difficulty is one of definitions: it is imperative to recognise the differences between the experiences of a protected middle-class white woman and many working-class black women in South Africa. At the same time, concentrating on the differences caused by race and class privilege risks overwriting the human sameness of the lives of poor black women.

46 Although it was twenty years ago that Sandra Pollack (1987, as cited by Clarke, 2008) protested that 'comparative psychological research' precisely because 'favourable' to lesbians in finding for their fitness as mothers (that they are not

different and do not produce children gendered differently) 'defines lesbian mothers out of existence' (Pollack, as cited by Clarke, 2008:124).
47 Unfortunately this has also been noticed by those who would deny rights to gay and lesbian families (detailed in Stacey and Biblarz, 2001). See also Schumm (2004), who assumes reproductive heterosexuality is a 'socially valuable outcome' and who entertains the idea that homosexuality might be 'cured'. He continues this critique in 2008, with concerns, among others, that no account was taken of 'social desirability' in the studies which assert there are no substantive differences in gay parenting, and that evidence has been ignored which relates to children's sexual orientation as adults, i.e. that a finding which shows children raised by gays and lesbians are more likely not to be heterosexual is implicitly a negative finding.
48 Schumm assumes that this finding means 'open homosexuality may encourage consideration of homosexual conduct even in the absence of homosexual attraction' (Schumm, 2004:423). His implication is that gay parenting promotes a mechanical kind of homosexual sexual behaviour, one which cannot even lay claim to the justifications made by 'real' homosexuality (he later considers the possibility of 'successful interventions aimed at sexual orientation changes'). Besides the obvious objections to his logic and the political implication of assuming that a society should and would prefer to discourage homosexuality, it is worth noting that he never considers how heterosexism and homophobia historically are far more adept at promoting heterosexual sexual behaviour regardless of the subject's desire.
49 See Gunkel (2010) for more on the problematics of homonormativity, particularly in a southern African context.
50 I use the term 'complicities' in the sense developed by Mark Sanders (2002).
51 See http://www.intersex.org.za.
52 Located in south-west South Africa, the Western Cape is one of the country's nine provinces. According to the 2011 census, the province has a population of almost six million. The Western Cape is the only province that is governed by an opposition party, the Democratic Alliance, and also has one of the fastest growing economies in the country.